The Economic Emergence
of a New Europe?

For Katrina, Michelle and Kristina

The Economic Emergence of a New Europe?

The Political Economy
of Cooperation and Competition
in the 1990s

Grahame F. Thompson

Senior Lecturer in Economics
The Open University, UK

Edward Elgar

Published by
Edward Elgar Publishing Limited
Gower House
Croft Road
Aldershot
Hants GU11 3HR
England

Edward Elgar Publishing Company
Old Post Road
Brookfield
Vermont 05036
USA

British Library Cataloguing in Publication Data
Thompson, Grahame
　Economic Emergence of a New Europe?:
　Political Economy of Cooperation and
　Competition in the 1990's
　I. Title
　337.1

Library of Congress Cataloguing in Publication Data
Thompson, Grahame
　　The economic emergence of a new Europe: the political economy of
　cooperation and competition in the 1990s/Grahame F. Thompson.
　　240 p. 23 cm.
　　Includes bibliographical references and index.
　　1. Europe—Economic integration.　I. Title.
　HC241.T48　1993
　337.1'4—dc20　　　　　　　　　　　　　　　　　　　93–1122
　　　　　　　　　　　　　　　　　　　　　　　　　　　　CIP

ISBN 1 85278 560 8

Printed in Great Britain at the University Press, Cambridge

Contents

Figures

Tables

Preface

Events in Europe are moving fast. This book reflects these changes, but it also tries to establish the nature of the longer-term evolutionary trends that have shaped the Europe of the 1990s. How Europe weathers the stormy passage of its integrationist moves in the post-Maastricht period remains to be seen. I hope this book will add to a critical understanding of this process, and in its own small way perhaps contribute to a successful resolution.

As is usual with a book written by a single author, this volume actually owes much to the collectivity of both scholarship and friendship. In particular I would like to thank Philip Arestis, Graham Dawson, Shaun Hargreaves Heap, Paul Hirst, Tony McGrew and Jim Tomlinson for their supportive comments on various parts of the book as it was being prepared. In addition, those who attended the seminars and conference sessions at which parts of the book were presented also contributed their comments, which were gratefully received. I extend my gratitude to them all.

Chapter 2 of this book is partly based upon my essay for the Open University course, 'Europe and the Global Economy', first appearing in 1993. Chapter 3 is a heavily reworked version of the article appearing under the same title in *Economy and Society*, vol. 21, no. 2, February 1992. Chapter 4 is partly based upon 'The Role of Economies of Scale in Justifying Free Trade: The US–Canada Free Trade Agreement and Europe 1992 Programme Compared', in the *International Review of Applied Economics*, vol. 5, no. 1, pp. 47–72; and J. Grahl and G. Thompson 'European Economic Union and Development Models', mimeographed, May 1992. An early version of Chapter 5 was given as 'Conceptions of Money, Inflation and European Monetary Union: Some Issues and Problems', delivered at the European Association of Evolutionary Political Economy Annual Conference, Florence, 15–17 November 1990. Chapter 6 is a heavily reworked version of the paper, 'What Europe can Learn from America (via Japan): The Case of Management', given at the Conference on Economic Regeneration in Urban Areas: US and European Comparisons, Sheffield, 1–2 October 1990.

1. Introduction

Issues of European political and economic integration have been placed firmly on the policy agenda as we enter the late 1990s, despite a difficult period in mid-1992. This book explores the arguments and forms of analysis deployed by those pressing for closer integration. It does this mainly for the period since the early 1980s, during which the latest round of political initiatives driving the aspiration for closer European union emerged. However, there is also some historical analysis of the process forging European cooperation in the post-war period.

Something of the character and tone of the approach adopted by this book can be seen from its title. An important point about the main title is the question mark after *The Economic Emergence of a New Europe?*. This is there to indicate a scepticism about whether a 'new Europe' is actually going to be created in the wake of the current integrationist moves, or whether there is actually an emergent innovative economics of this process. Clearly, one does not wish to be totally sceptical. Things are changing within Europe and it would be silly to deny this. But quite whether a 'new' Europe is being created, and if so in what form, is open to interpretation and doubt, particularly at the time of writing in mid-1992, as the aftermath of the Danish and French referenda throw the forward march of integration into further confusion. In addition, the economics of this process are open to considerable criticism and debate, both in terms of their intellectual structure and in terms of the actual processes of integrative cooperation under way or planned. Thus it is a sceptical tone in this sense that is indicated by the question mark. It is there to open up a space for a critical assessment of the arguments, both theoretical and practical, that have been deployed to justify the current integrationist initiatives.

As the sub-title suggests, the book does this from an overtly political economy perspective. But using the term 'political economy' is not meant to imply an exclusive Marxist or neo-Marxist focus for the analysis. Nor, at the other end of the spectrum, does it simply embrace the neoclassical political economy approach as it typically deals with the nature of institutions and the economic process though, as we shall see, the analysis below is crucially concerned with institutional developments. Again, nor is the analysis here singly guided by that political economy approach most closely associated

1

with the American 'new institutionalists'. These are mainly political scientists, who are strongly represented in the contemporary international relations literature.[1]

While these are the three main ways in which the term political economy has entered the traditional analytical framework in recent years, this book does not propose an exclusive focus on any of them. However, this does not mean that they are rejected out of hand. Far from it. Where it seems fit, these more traditional approaches are deployed, drawing upon their specific analytical strengths, but also pointing to their weaknesses. The argument in the main text is one sensitive to a plurality of theoretical positions. It is, however, an argument particularly concerned with institutional and evolutionary forms of analysis.

Thus the approach adopted here is to combine developments within both economics and politics in a pragmatic and contingent way that reinforces the insights gained from each. There is no single exclusive theoretical position driving the analytical approach of this book. Indeed, it speaks for a theoretical and policy pluralism. As far as is possible, political and economic considerations are developed in tandem, though within such a combination, political imperatives are seen to both motivate and constrain economic imperatives.

However, the economics of the processes investigated are not placed in a secondary role as a consequence of this emphasis. The intention is quite the reverse. Economic analysis is foregrounded in what follows. But this is foregrounded within a framework where economic programmes are seen as subject to the dictates of a political initiative that has as its objective a rapid advancement to a greater integration of the European states. One of the main issues explored in the chapters that follow are the reasons for this imperative – what have been the forces pushing for it, how has it been advanced, what are its likely impacts as manifest in their post-Maastricht form, and so on.

An influential way of situating the issue of political imperatives towards further European economic integration has been to pose it in terms of a grand intellectual vision on the one hand, compared to an *ad hoc* pragmatic response to particular and definite policy problems on the other (Wallace, 1990).

Thus we could view the recent moves emanating from the European Commission as just another chapter in that long road which has as its goal a unitary state for Europe, or a federal one, or even a con-federal one (these different possible forms of the European proto-state are raised again in the final chapter). This 'vision' for Europe is often traced back to the hopes of the 'founding fathers' of European integration – Monnet, Schuman, Auderhaur, and so on – who after the Second World War were instrumental in generating the first steps towards European economic and political unity with their plans and programmes for economic restructuring. In this tradition Jacques Delors is just the most recent of a long line of (predominantly) mainland continental European thinkers and political leaders who have had as their objective the political and economic union of Europe, whatever the cost or whatever the misgivings of a presumed more 'Eurosceptical' population or electorate.

In distinction to this 'visionary' scenario, the other major way of looking at the periodic re-emergence of a strong integrationist tendency within Europe is to see it as a reaction to particular events and problems without these having all the overtones of some grand intellectual or political schema. The problems confronting Europe after the Second World War were obvious, and the particular configuration of military, economic and political forces in that period inevitably shaped a common response that saw Europe as developing as a whole, at least initially in some restricted economic sense. The emergence of the European Economic Community (EEC) in 1957 was a consolidationist move to build on the success of the European Coal and Steel Community (ECSC – see Chapter 2). Subsequent developments such as the establishment of the European Monetary System (EMS) in 1979 were again dictated by a reaction to events; the collapse of the post-war Bretton Woods exchange rate regime and the desire to see some stability in European exchange rates *vis-à-vis* the US dollar. Finally, the renewed moves towards even closer economic and political union over the mid- to late 1980s again represented a simple and sensible response to the waning of American global economic and political power, along with the emergence of other centres of power such as Japan.

Although by now a rather tired debate, stating it in this bland manner serves to highlight a real contrast in approach to understanding the nature of European integration. Clearly, some of those involved in the early establishment of pan-European economic regulatory mechanisms did conceive of these as just the beginning of further, more ambitious, developments. In addition, those early economic management mechanisms were institutions with a definite political character as well as an economic one. As will be argued in more detail later, it is impossible to develop market integration without simultaneously developing a politically driven regulatory structure to govern it at the same time (see Chapters 2, 3 and 7 in particular). Thus it is only to be expected that political and economic integration would proceed in tandem. But this is not to say that either is necessarily driven by a single grand vision of eventual full economic and political union.

The point of this preliminary discussion of the dynamic of European integration is to stress that the choice between the visionary and the evolutionary approach, if one might put it like this, is not a very productive one. It is probably better to view these, not as alternatives, but as complements to one another. Furthermore, what is of interest about the various stages through which the dynamic of European integration has passed is the *forms* of the relationship between *ad hoc* evolutionary and pragmatic responses to events *combined with* the particular visionary impetus to which this has given rise.

A second introductory point raised by the sub-title of this book concerns the terms 'cooperation' and 'competition'. The characteristic way of thinking about activities of nation states in the international economic arena is to pose this in terms of cooperation *versus* competition. But again, perhaps a more productive way of posing this is to see these twin poles as being complementary to each other, rather than in opposition. To illustrate this we can first draw an analytical distinction between economic and political levels as these operate in international economic affairs. It is more usual to discuss the relationship between cooperation and competition in its economic sense, where the means of competition include cooperation as one of their forms. Thus cartelization or merger activity, as forms of 'cooperation' between economic agents, are as much the means of competition between them as are, for instance, price wars or competitive real investment strategies.

But what about the political level? Here we seem to be faced with sovereign and autonomous states that either cooperate or compete with one another. In fact they may also be competing *while* they are cooperating. In this case cooperation becomes one of the means of competition understood in similar terms to the discussion of economics above, where in this case that cooperation is organized via the process of diplomacy. Thus at the political level it is diplomatic activity that acts as the means of competition between nation states.[2]

As we shall see later, the present stage of European integration poses complex problems of competitive cooperation between the countries involved. An implication of this analysis is that cooperation – or even the weaker notion of coordination – is not necessarily 'neutral' in its effects on the parties involved. In game theoretic terms, solutions to these kinds of situations can be classified as zero-summed, positive-summed or negative-summed. In a zero-sum game, what one party gains the other loses, so there is no overall gain in benefit. With positive-sum games both parties at least gain something. In the case of negative-sum games, by contrast, both parties lose. The question is, which of these outcomes is the most likely in situations of the EC political and economic union type? The official ideology emanating from Brussels is that all parties gain, that is, that the process is positive-summed for the Community as a whole. Clearly, some countries may stand to gain more than others, and this we discuss in the chapters which follow. There may indeed be a zero-sum outcome, though this would be difficult to identify empirically. However, another possibility is that the game will become negative-summed, so that all parties lose something via economic and monetary union (EMU). This would be the case if the strategy failed and the EC was plunged into an overall recession as a result of the particular policy mix embarked upon. This we discuss more formally in Chapter 5 in particular.

Perhaps the most likely outcome is the mixed one of the powerful gaining, either at the expense of the less powerful or to a much greater degree. But the most powerful country also bears a high risk in leading the coordination/ cooperation and in policing it. A fine balance in gain and loss terms characterizes any country that either strives for hegemonic leadership or has it thrust upon it in the modern integration game (so-called 'leadership games').

One way of formalizing this discussion is to present it in terms of defensive positionalism *versus* common interest (Grieco, 1990). The usual way to set up a formal game theoretic situation is shown in terms of Figure 1.1. This takes a simple two-player, two-strategy illustration and asks how conditional cooperation can be forged under assumptions of individual pay-off maximization (Colman, 1982).

SADDAM

		Withdraw	Stay put
GEORGE	Blockade/ sanctions	3,3 (mutual compromise)	1,4 (Saddam's victory)
	Air strike	4,1 (George's victory)	0,0 (mutual destruction of forces)

Figure 1.1   Generating cooperation

Figure 1.1 represents the following scenario. There are two players, Saddam and George. Saddam has invaded a small and helpless state, while George has come to its rescue. George has decided upon two strategies in his attempt to persuade Saddam to leave the invaded state. The first involves the imposition of sanctions and a blockade of Saddam's country. The second is to threaten an all-out air-strike-led war against Saddam's country. In reaction to this, Saddam sees himself as faced with two options. He can either withdraw under these threats/actions, or he can stand firm against them. The pay-off matrix for this 'game' is sketched in Figure 1.1. The problem we are confronting here is one of the generation of trust and 'cooperation' between two players whose interests seem so totally opposed.

The figures in this matrix (ordinal measures) are designed to represent a simple 'chicken game' which meets the rank order $T > R > S > P$.[3] Both sides wish to avoid an outright and devastating 'mutually assured destruction' of their forces, which is the least desirable outcome $(0,0)$.

George would like to win a prestige victory on the account of his boldness in threatening and carrying out the air strike; on the other hand Saddam would lose face if he withdrew under this threat. Thus for this outcome, the pay-off values are $(4,1)$. But suppose that the blockade against Saddam was ineffective and he was able to maintain his position in the invaded country. Saddam would claim a stunning victory over George under these circumstances. George, on the other hand, would be left with the cost of the ineffective blockade, which he would consider a defeat. Thus the pay-off here is symmetrically the opposite of the previous case $(1,4)$. Finally, there is the possibility that George's blockade will be effective in forcing Saddam to withdraw. This 'compromise' outcome, while not as attractive to Saddam or George as an outright victory for either of them, is at least better than the mutually assured destruction of their respective forces. Thus, for this outcome, the pay-off value is $(3,3)$.

This kind of chicken game is one of a set of games of the 'prisoner dilemma'-type that do not have completely convincing rational (or equilibrium) solutions. For this they need a principle of choice based on collective interests. In its absence, the temptation to 'go it alone' remains strong (thereby scoring 4 in the pay-off matrix). Without trust, individual interests override collective ones. But the collective outcome, the 'cooperative compromise' of a withdrawal and no military victory for either, would give a higher pay-off overall $(6 > 5 > 0)$. What this illustrates is the difficulty of generating a cooperative outcome, which would remain even if both parties actually preferred the compromise anyway.

The assumptions that underlie this analysis are important and controversial. In the first place any conditional cooperation that was forged amongst the players emerged solely from a desire to maximize their individual long-term pay-offs. The players are akin to neoclassical economic actors who act as rational egotists, maximizing their expected individual utility functions. What is more, these utility functions are quite independent of one another. In this situation, player-states do not care whether other player-states achieve or do not achieve any gains from the cooperative relationship. Strictly speaking, therefore, it rules out the analysis of situations characterized by common but mixed interests. If V_A is the individual player-state A's absolute pay-off, the utility function U_A is $U_A = V_A$.

However, in situations such as with the EC and EMU, it is precisely the fact that utility functions might be interactive, that common and mixed interests prevail, so that the relative position of power gain becomes important. Here, the forging of cooperation might be more dependent upon the perceived changes in relative capabilities that the cooperation would bring about. If this were the case, the utility function would not just involve the term V_A, but also an additional term, W_B, designating the partner-state B's pay-off. One way of thinking about W_B would be to view it as 'negatively' contributing to the state-players' utility, so that if the capability 'gap' between any two players were to increase, the individual state-player, A, would feel threatened. In this case the utility function becomes:

$$U_A = V_A - k(W_B - V_A); \ 0 < k,$$

with k representing the state-player's coefficient of sensitivity to potential capability advantages or disadvantages perceived to arise as a result of cooperation. Note that with this formulation it is only gaps in gains favouring partners that reduces the utility a state enjoys from cooperation. Thus, this could lead the relatively disadvantaged state-player to avoid cooperation altogether, even though the joint action promised it some individual absolute gain. This would happen if the gain gap ($k(W_B - V_A)$) was sufficiently in its disfavour to outweigh the absolute individual gain (V_A).

Clearly, in this example state-player utility is at least partially interdependent so that one state-player's utility affects another's. Another formulation of this relationship might be a 'positive' one where $U_A = V_A + W_B$. In this case the utility function is joint; the state-players gain not only through their own absolute advantage but also when the other state-player gains as well. Indeed, it might be possible to discern a utility function of the form $U_A = W_B$, a clear case of pure altruism.

However, the most widespread form of the utility function is likely to remain the case of 'defensive positionalism', analysed through the gain gap mechanism just described. This captures a good deal about the suspicious manner in which governments go about approaching cooperative institution-building in the European context. It will be argued below that, particularly in the post-Maastricht era, states are increasingly looking to national interest in an interdependent framework as a working model for their approach to further economic and monetary integration. In the European case, of course, there are a number of countries involved, not just two. Thus the general form of any country's utility function will be more complicated than that set out above, but the simple form captures the essentials of the situation.

However, there is another important way to express the manner in which cooperation could come about; it may *evolve* (Axelrod, 1990). In this example, cooperation emerges gradually as a result of a number of conditions; random signals and their interpretations; the testing out of those interpretations to increase conviction and lessen misunderstandings; the gradual learning of the rules and norms; and the solidification of a mutual interest in cooperation as a result. The message of this analysis is that cooperation does not necessarily have to be either 'taught' or 'imposed' from outside. As this is a strategic analysis of evolution, not a genetic one, it is applicable to situations of economic and political interactions. The crucial issue at stake in this analysis is the need for a 'cooperative outlook' to be fostered. According to Axelrod this can come about if the game is played over and over again. If the expectation is that the players will have to deal with each other repeatedly and frequently, this can counter the temptation to defect or counter-defect. Thus from this perspective the foundation of cooperation is not necessarily trust, but rather the durability of the relationships involved. It develops spontaneously (and possibly tacitly) between reciprocating parties. The *reputation* of the parties for cooperation rather than for competition becomes *expected* and 'socially embedded' as a result.

One way this kind of evolved cooperation might be made manifest is through the notion of a 'regime'. A regime is the institutionalization of principles, norms, rules and decision-making procedures around specific policy areas where actor expectations converge. Such regimes can assist the development of cooperation by improving the quality and flow of information, reducing uncertainty and the incentive for opportunist defection, and promoting mechanisms for monitoring compliance (Keohane, 1984). Examples of such regimes in the case of European integration could be the early ECSC, the EMS and the ECOFIN (Council of Economic and Finance Ministers).

Another useful frameworking device for this kind of analysis can be discussed in relation to Figure 1.2 (Guerrieri and Padoan, 1989). This refers specifically to the role of diplomacy and domestic political realities in the determination of negotiating solutions. Supposing governments have the objective of maximizing their *reputations* (as suggested above), which are made up of their international power/standing and their skill at implementing domestic (non-inflationary) economic policies. Assume a single policy variable, X, which each government controls. If this is, for the sake of argument, a variable that increases as expansionary inflation-inducing policies are implemented, the government's reputation will be in an inverse relationship to X. This is shown by the curve R in Figure 1.2. As X increases, R decreases, since the government is assumed to be losing control of inflation under these circumstances. With any particular international 'regime' setting the rules as to what is acceptable domestic economic behaviour in respect to X and inflation, a unique reputation function, R, can be specified.

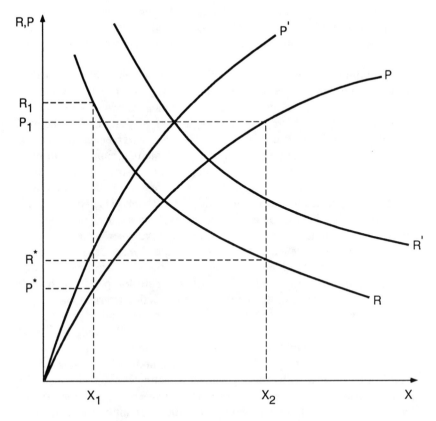

Figure 1.2   International and domestic policy interaction

If that international regime were to change, however, say by becoming more amenable to expansion by all the countries involved, the R function would move out to the left, to R'.

At the domestic level, the government will try to maximize its popularity and win elections. Here, we assume that its popularity, P, is an increasing function of X, the economic expansion-producing variable. The position and shape of this function depends upon the particular political and economic characteristics of a country. Any country with a 'lose' compromise between its constituent groups and interests might be expected to attempt to increase or maintain its popularity with 'generous' increases in X. This will produce a flatter P function. Alternatively, if there were a very strong corporatist compromise, with few separate groups efficiently organized via peak body bargaining, the function might be expected to be steeper, at P'. Similarly with ideological orientation of the government; the more conservative the government, the more it is likely to put the control of inflation at the forefront of its policies, and to restrict the expansionary variable out of choice and in the light of its ability to maintain popularity. Thus, in this case also, P' might be the likely position.

The optimum 'international' position is one in which the government maximizes its reputation subject to the popularity constraint. The optimum 'national' position is one in which the government maximizes its domestic popularity subject to the reputation constraint. If we designate R^* the minimum level of international reputation needed to get agreement on cooperative policies (the reputation constraint), and P^* the minimum level of popularity needed to secure re-election (the popularity constraint), the conditions sketched in Figure 1.2 will give a 'win set' of feasible policies between X_1 and X_2. This satisfies the condition $R > R^*$ and $P > P^*$. This win set can be understood as the interaction of the two levels of policy action in which the solution of one game is subject to the solution of the other game.

Obviously, the existence and the extent of the win set depends upon the relative position of the R and P functions. A no-win set can be quite easily constructed (see Guerrieri and Padoan, 1989, Figure 1.4, p. 25, and also the discussion in Chapter 8 of this book). A too restrictive international regime, or a too sensitive or loose domestic popularity profile requiring over-expansionary policies to secure re-election, can undermine the integration strategy. But this then directs attention towards what can be done to loosen each of these constraints. One possibility is to try and modify the existing international regime by increasing the expansionary sentiment and thereby pushing the R function out to the right. Alternative work could be done on the domestic front to modify the existing distributional coalition and push up the P function.

All manner of strategies are open to governments under these circumstances. In the first place, the international regime can be used as a lever on the home situation; weaker governments relying on the international reputation arguments to help force domestic change. Secondly, strong international players can use their power to alter the international regime in one way or another. This would be the case where a clear 'hegemon' exists (such as Germany possibly exercises in the European context), which in turn depends upon its domestic popularity surplus and its willingness to pursue expansionary policies. In situations of cooperative integration without a hegemon, attention shifts to the domestic environment with an attempt to alter the popularity function in the first instance. Clearly, in all these cases it is the interaction between the domestic and the international environment that is crucial; altering the position and shape of the functions alters the extent of the win set, the crucial variable for integrational cooperation.

These formulations will be returned to in the chapters that follow. But while they provide a framework for much of that analysis, they are also subject to a critique by it. All the analytical examples suggested so far in this introduction concern the generation of trust and/or cooperation, as a prelude to integration, in the context of the rational calculation of interests by sovereign governments. As mentioned before, the agents in this process are conceived of as being akin to rational egotists, even as modified by the incorporation of other countries' welfare within their utility functions or as seen as evolving towards cooperation. These models begin from a position of non-trust/non-cooperation/non-integration and ask how trust/cooperation/integration can be generated. They begin with a set of already known interests and ask how these can be maximized, how they interact or how they might be modified in the process of that interaction.

There are a number of criticisms that can be levelled at this kind of conception. These will be explored further in the following chapters, but are worth broaching in a preliminary way here.

First, why begin with a situation in which interests are already fully known before entering into any negotiation? It could be that the negotiation itself *establishes* those interests. Governments may not fully know their 'interests' before they enter into any negotiation. If there is to be a space in which genuine diplomacy operates, and in which diplomatic activity has effects, then this activity will at least in part determine what are conceived to be the interests at stake and how they are made manifest. Secondly, and in the same spirit, why should we begin by assuming a radical situation of non-trust/non-cooperation and ask how it can be generated from this absence? As we saw in the case of the prisoner dilemma/chicken game above, the generation of cooperation under the rules of game theory can be very difficult, relying upon quite restrictive preconditions. But supposing we begin from a slightly different starting point, accepting that trust/cooperation is already in existence or operative at some level. The point here is to recognize that cooperation and trust are preconditions for any form of collective existence. Thus at some level they must already exist. The analytical problem then becomes one of specifying the conditions in which, or under which, *greater trust* or *greater cooperation* can be generated, or different relationships between cooperation and trust can be established. Alternatively, the different starting point can be used to ask how relationships can become more cooperative or more trusting. How can countries/governments become more deserving of trust (more trustworthy) or more disposed to cooperate and more cooperative? Now, while some of the above formulations do pose these issues, in the main they are wedded to a conceptual framework that does not allow these more realistic problems to be either the most important ones or those foregrounded in the analytical situation. In the world of growing cooperative integration, we are in a world of already existing integrations and cooperations. The problem is not how to start integrative cooperations – these already operate. Rather, it is to encourage these to develop further in similar or different directions with respect to different policy issues or areas and with respect to new arenas or country groupings, and so on. This is the currently existing complexity that needs to be addressed and which provides the bedrock for the analysis in the following chapters.

Chapter 2 begins this process immediately. It serves a double purpose; on the one hand to outline the contours of that entity called 'Europe' that is the object of the analysis in this book, and on the other to discuss the manner in which that object has evolved over the post-Second World War period. Before we can get too far into the detail of the present integrationist moves, the historical record on this needs to be confronted since it informs the present debate with a certain legacy from the past. The history of integration, and the way it has been analysed, is discussed in Chapter 2. But in so doing, the chapter also more formally examines the question of whether it is the 'repeat transactions' of post-war European interactions that have secured a new attitude towards integration in the present. Thus in Chapter 2 we are 'testing' the Axelrod thesis outlined above; we are asking whether a secure cooperation has now evolved within Europe.

Chapter 3 continues this analysis by asking how we should best think about and analyse the evolution of the managed economy in Europe. It examines this issue in the context of the diverse traditions of economic management typifying the major European countries over the post-war period. The argument is that the effects of these traditions still linger in the emerging European management framework as the movement towards economic and monetary union gathers pace. The emphasis here is upon the *diversity* of management traditions in Europe, rather than upon any presumed homogeneity. A central feature of this assessment is the dual evolution of a neo-liberal policy programme for Europe, as opposed to one stressing the continued virtues of consensus, cooperation and neo-corporatist organized outcomes. In the light of the entry of the European Commission into the management framework, Chapter 3 ends with an assessment of the prospects for an integrated European management approach and the impact this might have on the wider international economic environment.

In what way will the benefits to freer trade and further integration emerge in the European context? Chapter 4 addresses this issue directly. It scrutinizes the European Commission's analyses justifying the moves towards further European economic integration. In particular, it focuses on the way economies of scale have become central to the economic evaluation of welfare gains in the recent Commission assessments. The arguments about both internal economies and external economies are reviewed here. It is suggested that the advantages of economies of scale are exaggerated in the Commission's accounts. The policy implications of this critique are drawn out for both internal and external scale economies. The argument focuses upon the implications of the trend away from traditional mass production process technologies and business strategies, suggesting this requires a radically different approach to trade and scale issues and one largely ignored by the Commission.

Chapter 4 looks at the real economy. Chapter 5 switches attention to the monetary economy. This is the area that has received the most attention in the contemporary integrationist literature, dealing as it does with the issues of a possible complete monetary union in the near future. In particular, the post-Maastricht institution-building, convergence criteria and timetable are scrutinized. These are placed within an explicit macroeconomic framework in the chapter. Of particular importance, it is argued, is the outcome in terms of labour market organization, and it is here that the issue of neo-corporatist labour market arrangements is returned to. The dynamic of monetary union is examined to ask whether this is both possible in the timetable sketched out and desirable in the manner which has been suggested. A neglected set of problems associated with monetary analysis is confronted in this chapter, though the overall argument is not against further economic and monetary union.

Many of the issues examined in the previous chapters have major implications for the future industrial structure of Europe as a whole. Chapter 6 confronts the implications of the analytical results of previous chapters for industrial management and industrial policy. It examines the present transitional characteristics of production process technologies and asks how European business is likely to react to these as the national economies of Europe begin to integrate in earnest. The chapter is concerned with highlighting the challenge of the new production process technologies for the enhancement of Europe's international competitiveness. Amongst other things, this includes the characteristic nature of the labour market and the financial market in Europe. While the previous chapter dealt with the labour market, Chapter 6 concentrates on the equally important financial market and the forms of financial calculations that are commensurate with the new production process technologies and an enhanced manufacturing competitiveness.

It would be impossible to write a book about Europe in the mid-1990s without devoting a chapter to the momentous developments happening within what used to be termed Eastern Europe and the Soviet Union. Chapter 7 looks at the question of these developments in terms of their consequences for the integration process and the emergence of a new Europe. The chapter first describes and critically examines the main contours of the transition in the ex-Soviet-type economies and then goes on to assess the possible trajectory for these economies in the context of an expanded European Community. This serves to raise again the issue of the widening and deepening of the Community and its own trajectory of integration as events in the East themselves accelerate with possible prolonged disruptive consequences.

The final chapter returns to issues raised earlier in this chapter; an explicit reconsideration of the political economy of competition and cooperation. The analysis in Chapter 8 tries to sum up the contemporary nature of the forces pressing towards further cooperation, as opposed to those that might be leading away from this and, by implication, towards a renewed competition. This analysis is conducted in terms of centrifugal and centripetal tendencies within Europe. It explicitly raises issues of the nature of possible political union. It also examines afresh the theoretical frameworks outlined in the first part of this Introduction, re-assessing them in the light of the analysis in the rest of the book.

A final few introductory points are in order before we move into the substantive analysis.

The first refers to the attempts at integrating the concerns and themes of the chapters of this book. As the book develops, a conscious attempt has been made both to discuss something different and fresh in each of the chapters and to pick up on themes and issues that have been raised and partly dealt with in previous ones. This means that, as a deliberate policy, there is some slight overlap between the discussion in the chapters as they unfold.

Secondly, the chapters are each designed to combine a judicious mix of theoretical analysis, 'thick' descriptive investigation and policy discussion. The emphasis is not exclusively on any of these in the singular. While some chapters might have a little more of one than the others, overall a balance between all three elements has been kept uppermost in mind.

Thirdly, the assessment in the chapters is meant to be a critical one. This means that the luxury of a distance from the main orthodox intellectual analytical traditions has been maintained, and the approach has gone for a heterodox stance. Sometimes such a critical approach becomes an end in itself and leads to a rather unsatisfactory agnosticism. That is not the case in this instance. Where possible, for instance, the policy implications of the critique are developed in detail, and a series of alternative suggestions is made. But the analysis is also a realistic one. Often there is not much further to say as a direct consequence of the critical approach adopted, because the reality of the situation dictates an outcome, however antithetical to the sentiments of the critique, that must simply be accepted.

Lastly, and connected to all these introductory points, the question of the book's general stance on European integration is posed. There is a thesis in the book. It is that further European integration is both desirable and feasible. It is desirable because it will enable Europe to do things as a whole that its individual countries just could not do on their own. It is feasible because of the political momentum built up in the late 1980s and early 1990s. But – and this is a large but – at the time of preparing the book (mid-1992) events are moving at best temporarily in the wrong direction and at worst in a manner destined to undermine all the positive achievements thus far attained. The reasons for this rather negative assessment will become clear as the analysis in the following chapters unfolds. A final summing up in the concluding chapter provides an overall assessment.

NOTES

1. Representative examples of the American new institutionalists in the international political economy literature are Keohane (1984) and Gilpin (1987). Hall (1986 and 1989), discussed in Chapter 3, also represents this position (see Thompson 1987c). An example of the more conventional neoclassical approach to political economy would be Buchanan (1979). The Marxist and neo-Marxist position on international political economy is represented by Gill and Law (1986) and Chase-Dunn (1989).
2. A different example of the means of competition operating between countries at the political level, but this time definitely not involving cooperation, would be the conduct of wars between nations. Clearly, this particular outcome is very unlikely amongst the Europe of the EC at least.
3. T is the temptation to defect while the other player cooperates (4); R is the reward for mutual cooperation (3); S is the sucker's pay-off when the other player defects (1); and P is the punishment for defection (0).

2. What Is Europe?

INTRODUCTION

In this chapter we look at the forces shaping the moves away from competition between the nations and states of Europe and towards the organization of their cooperation. This chapter is partly historical as a result. In particular it focuses on the post-Second World War period, a period during which the contours of the contemporary integrationist tendencies within Europe were first laid and then consolidated. The analytical background to this process is the point about cooperative evolution discussed in the previous chapter. The question posed for this chapter is how far has a genuinely cooperative attitude evolved within the European Community as it has reciprocally interacted in the post-war period? Thus in a way we are testing in this chapter the Axelrod hypothesis in the case of Europe.

As we shall see below, the nations of Europe have gradually evolved into a cooperative framework, initially without this being 'imposed' by a single central authority, or so it would seem. Indeed, the issue explored in this chapter is the interaction between a set of non-coercive decentralized inter-relationships on the one hand, and the evolution of supportive institutional developments that increasingly took the form of a 'centre' on the other. This itself involves a further set of questions concerning the place the new 'co-operating Europe' as a whole begins to occupy within the evolving international arena. The growth of European integration has posed the question of how Europe might act in its own right in international affairs. For instance, where has Europe fitted into an international economic order? While this might seem a straightforward question to answer, it requires addressing a set of preliminary questions about which there is room for considerable debate, ambiguity and controversy. What is the time period over which we might judge the importance of Europe? With which other parts of the globe should Europe be compared? Indeed, what is meant by the term 'Europe' anyway? Furthermore, the economic order can be measured in relation to a number of different dimensions. Also, is it wise to address the economic position of Europe without at the same time looking at its political or cultural role and at how these might connect to the economic realm?

Table 2.1 Structure of Community trade

	Share in total EC imports	
	1958 (%)	1990 (%)
Developed countries: of which	48	60
EFTA	14	23
USA	18	18
Japan	1	10
Eastern bloc	6	9
Other countries	46	31
Total	100	100

Note: Eastern bloc includes Albania, Bulgaria Czechoslovakia, the GDR, Hungary, Poland, Romania, the USSR, China, Cuba, Mongolia, North Korea and Vietnam.

Source: Eurostat.

These questions form one of the strands for the analysis in this chapter. A preliminary way of showing the importance of Europe can be seen from Table 2.1. The data here report a measure of European trade in its international context; they show the share of the European Community's imports from various countries or regions in 1958 and 1990. Broadly speaking, in 1990 the 'developed countries' accounted for 60 per cent of these imports, the 'developing countries' for 31 per cent, and the 'Eastern trading area' for the other 9 per cent.

But note how 'Europe' is defined for the purposes of Table 2.1. Here it comprises the 12 member states of the EC in 1990. As is indicated by the data, however, a number of other European countries, in a geographical sense, are separately accounted for as either members of the developed country group (for example, the European Free Trade Association – EFTA), or as part of the Eastern trading bloc. One of the main problems encountered in the analysis that follows is thus where exactly to draw the boundary around Europe as an economic entity. And this problem is not solved by simply appealing to the EC as representing the logical centre for the European economy. The EC has changed its geographical boundaries over the years, and it could enlarge them again very soon, as indicated by the analysis in a number of the following chapters of this book.

In the next section the changing conception of Europe as an economic entity, and its accompanying character as a political entity, is focused upon as a prelude to a discussion of its place in the wider international environment, the analysis of which is extended in Chapter 3. A theme of this section is the multi-dimensional character of 'economic Europe' – particularly its political establishment and regulation, and the geographical extent and embrace of these twin defining features. How did we get to a point where we can discuss 'Europe' as defined in relation to Table 2.1, for instance? What exactly is it that is cooperating both within 'Europe' and between it and other areas that relate to that 'Europe'?

WHAT IS THE EUROPEAN ECONOMIC SPACE (EES)?

Is the contemporary economic space of Europe the same as the one possible to describe one hundred years, 60 years or even 30 years ago? Clearly, the characteristic features shaping the European economic space in various historical periods are themselves likely to be diverse and contingent. We can assess these against the background of what have been momentous worldwide transformations, as well as those that impinge more exclusively on the EES itself.

There are two possible routes to follow in the analysis of the EES. The first is to take an overtly *institutional* focus. In this case we would trace the evolution of those institutional mechanisms in which the idea of Europe as an economic unit figured directly, or was implicated by dint of geo-political presence. The other main way to tackle this definitional problem is to look at the characteristic *patterns of economic interaction* which the European states, or private economic actors residing within them, developed between themselves. The first focuses upon a more 'political' approach. It involves charting the definition and redefinition of those typical European-wide consultative, regulatory and administrative mechanisms and their practices which implicate some notion of Europe in their operations. The latter is perhaps a more obviously 'economic' approach. It implies an analysis of the progressive development and reconstruction of market mechanisms to trace growing patterns of trade, investment, production and technological and other economic relationships between the countries of Europe.

Now, while these might look to be different and separate approaches, a moment's reflection indicates that they represent a different emphasis only. They mirror the main analytical issue posed for this chapter; the relationship between a cooperative centralizing process and the evolution of such cooperation as a result of the decentralized relationships of reciprocity and repetition. As the chapter unfolds these twin focuses will be progressively drawn together; they are deployed in combination. But it is still analytically useful to begin with them separately.

THE INSTITUTIONAL MATRIX OF ECONOMIC EUROPE

Taking a broadly defined 'Western Europe' first, this is largely how the EES came to be known over the 50 years from the end of the Second World War up until the late 1980s. In that period it was pitched against a perhaps even less clearly demarcated 'Eastern Europe', but more of this later.

In an economic sense Western Europe included those 16 liberal-market economies that originally set up the Organization of European Economic Cooperation (OEEC) in 1948, and which subsequently expanded to include first the Federal Republic of Germany and then Finland and Spain to make the present European nations in the Organization of Economic Cooperation and Development (OECD).

Alternatively, we could trace the origins of Western Europe to the ten signatories of the statute setting up the Council of Europe (COE) in 1949, which itself subsequently expanded to include 23 members 40 years later. The OECD has retained an explicitly economics brief – to foster the development of liberal-market economic relationships between its members. It does this as a consultative and information-gathering institution, carrying out individual country economic assessments, dealing with issues of common economic interest, and disseminating the results. On the other hand, the COE and its sister body, the Western European Union (WEU), represented the political and military sides, respectively, of pan-(Western) European cooperation in the post-war period, weak though the reality of this political aspiration and military cooperation remained for much of that period.

In addition to these essentially cooperative and consultative institutional mechanisms, post-war Western Europe also saw the emergence of a set of more integrationist and coordinatory organizational formations. Even while still in exile, the governments of Belgium, the Netherlands and Luxembourg (in London in 1944) set up a customs union beginning on 1 January 1948 to be known as Benelux.[1] This developed into an early prototype for the wider economic unions that were to follow. But as early as the end of the 1950s Benelux achieved the elimination of all remaining trade barriers, the free movement of capital and labour and an important agricultural accord between the countries involved. In March 1948 France and Italy also set up a customs union (Francital) which embodied similar provisions and which, by the middle 1950s, had achieved much the same result (though not on agricultural activities).

In retrospect, probably the most important of these early cooperative efforts was the ECSC established by the Treaty of Paris in 1951 (which became operative the following year). Involving France, West Germany, Italy and the Benelux countries (the United Kingdom did not join even though it had participated in the negotiations to set up the ECSC), this Community eliminated tariff and quantitative restrictions on trade (including subsidies) relating to coal and steel between its members. The ECSC had a considerable symbolic effect on subsequent integrationist tendencies within Western Europe though, as will be discussed later, its immediate effects upon the coal and steel sectors within the Community members themselves were limited.

Rudimentary though they were, the early economic cooperative and coordinatory relationships fostered by these institutions (and other important organizations that are discussed more fully in a moment) culminated during the second half of this century in the development of the original EEC of the six (expanding to the EC of the 12 by 1986). Alongside this was the European Free Trade Association (EFTA). This originally comprised nine member states but subsequently shrunk to six (Austria, Finland, Iceland, Norway, Sweden and Switzerland) as the UK, Denmark and Portugal left to join the EC.

Broadly speaking, these developments represent the main institutional contours of the Western European economic space after the Second World War. In a later section the evolution and importance of the EEC/EC will be more fully discussed. But it is worth reiterating at this point that the particular economic space formed over the past 50 years is not the only way of looking at even the restricted scope of the Western Europe economy in an historical sense.

Clearly, the integrating, institutionalized economic space of the post-war period did have a certain geographical continuity and logic. This was centred on the industrial heartland of northern Europe bounded by the Saar and Ruhr and stretching southwards to northern Italy. In addition, for much of the pre-1914 period Germany occupied a pivotal position within central Europe, producing the manufactures which were then exchanged for agricultural produces from Eastern and other central European countries.

How different this was to the previous 'European' economic spaces of the Mediterranean basin in Antiquity, or the North Sea and Atlantic Ocean maritime states of the 16th and 17th centuries (England, the Netherlands, Spain, Portugal and France). These earlier periods of European pre-eminence established their own typical regimes of economic relationships where, in a sense, the EES was extended to areas and regions far beyond the borders of continental Europe itself. In a way, then, the EES has for much of its history not been confined to just the countries of the European continent. It has had a global presence, something developed in the next section and one which, in its contemporary form, this book analyses further.

Indeed, the period since the Second World War has seen a further way in which the EES could be defined, at least in part. This involves the role of the United States of America in particular, and the institutional matrix it was instrumental in developing and supporting after 1945. The term 'Western Europe' as an economic conception owes much to the USA and to US-sponsored developmental agencies, particularly those established immediately after the war. Originally these had in mind a broader Europe, conceived by the United Nations as part of its plan for post-war reconstruction. But the intensification of the Cold War during the late 1940s left this wider conception moribund. The work of the US-sponsored UN Economic Commission for Europe would have included 'Eastern Europe' and the Soviet Union in that reconstruction package, but it required that those benefiting from assistance should agree to promote a system of liberalized multilateral free trade as they recovered, something the USSR could not agree to. Thus although the Eastern European countries were offered Marshall Aid (as it came to be known), this was more or less vetoed by the USSR.

Instead, the main institutional instrument of US-led reconstruction efforts centred upon those 16 countries that set up the OEEC in 1948 to administer the European part of the Marshall Plan (named after the American Secretary of State in the 1940s, General George Marshall, who was responsible for administering the programme). By most accounts the Marshall Plan was a great success.[2] The Plan was a specially formed programme with its own separate institutional apparatus. Originally it was intended to operate for only four years (1947–1951), but it continued into a second phase to well after the Korean War (which ended in 1953). The Plan involved $US 3 billion of official (World Bank) loans and $US 17 billion of direct US government gifts (in total reaching some 3 per cent of US gross domestic product in 1948 and 1949). The Marshall Plan significantly contributed to a modernization of European infrastructure and the reconstruction of its productive industries, but it also enabled rearmament to take place at the same time. It provided for the 'dollar shortage' at a vulnerable time for Europe, helping the OECD countries to finance their severe balance-of-payments deficits. In addition the Plan, particularly in its second phase, envisaged increasing intra-European cooperation, as quota and tariff barriers to trade were to be lifted. In this the immediate outcome was less successful. Thus to some extent the stimulus for post-Second World War European integrative cooperation *did* originate from an organized centre, though that centre was not a part of Europe as such.

It is clear, then, that US concern with European economic reconstruction and integration was very much set within the framework of its wider strategy of containment. The Cold War and a hostile attitude towards the Soviet Union's presumed expansionary intentions in Europe (and elsewhere) drove the policy. But there was another, if secondary, reason involving relationships *within* Western Europe, and between France and Germany in particular. It was anticipated that the form of economic and political reconstruction in Europe after the war would solve once and for all the 'German problem' – it would lock (West) Germany into a system of liberal-market relationships, *and* into a system of constitutional arrangements with its neighbours that would prevent a repeat of the inter-war experience in continental central Europe. This is a theme we return to below, since it has been reactivated in the context of the contemporary moves towards further European economic and political integration.

If the Western European economic space was constituted by a number of different determinations and overlapping institutional frameworks, then defining the Eastern European economic space turns out to be nearly as problematical. As a response to the rejection of the US initiatives in Eastern Europe in the context of the Marshall Plan, the Soviet Union set up its own reconstruction package – the Cominform and the Molotov Plan (1947). These were later extended to become the Council of Mutual Economic Aid (CMEA or Comecon – set up in Moscow in 1949), which assumed the role of premier instrument for the construction of an integrated economic system amongst the centrally planned economies (CPEs) under Soviet tutelage.

After Stalin's death, Comecon developed as a mechanism for national and sectoral economic specialization amongst its members (a kind of socialist international division of labour), though the extent of intra-Comecon trade remained relatively weak as the basic autarkic national development strategies of the socialist countries failed to fully break down. However, in certain key sectors a *de facto* country specialization did emerge. In addition, within the Soviet Union itself, a highly integrated specialization emerged, indicated by the data produced in Table 2.2. The republics of the USSR evolved to trade a very high proportion of their output between themselves. These interdependencies proved a major problem as the Soviet and Eastern economic bloc began to disintegrate in the late 1980s/early 1990s, something further discussed in a later section and more fully in Chapter 7.

To sum up this section, we have seen how the idea of an EES is not easy to define in a consistent institutional sense. It has been the subject of a number of determinations and transformations. A complex overlapping framework emerges, especially for the area of Western Europe and the old Soviet Union. In addition, 'Europe' as an economic object should not necessarily be confused with the geographical limits of what is normally understood as Europe (for instance Greenland and the Faroe Islands have associated status as members of EFTA; the USA/Canada operated as an adjunct of Europe

Table 2.2   Soviet Union: exports by republic

Republic	Exports (percentages of net material product)[a,b]	
	To other republics	To other countries
Russia	29.3	7.5
Ukraine	39.1	6.7
Uzbekistan	43.2	7.4
Kazakhstan	30.9	3.0
Belorussia	69.6	6.5
Azerbaijan	58.7	3.7
Georgia	53.7	3.9
Tadjikistan	41.8	6.9
Kirghizia	50.2	1.2
Moldova	62.1	3.4
Lithuania	60.9	5.9
Turkmenistan	50.7	4.2
Armenia	63.7	1.4
Latvia	64.1	5.7
Estonia	66.5	7.4

Notes:
(a)   Data are for 1988.
(b)   Excludes 'non-productive' services.

Source: International Monetary Fund, World Bank, Organisation for Economic Co-operation and Development and Bank for Reconstruction and Development, 1991. *A Study of the Soviet Economy,* vol. 1, 206, 225, 231. Paris: International Monetary Fund.

immediately after the Second World War; and the 68 African and Pacific states signing the Lome Convention have a privileged associate status with respect to the EC). What is more, 'Eastern Europe' presents another set of definitional problems, the characteristic limits of which are equally ambiguous. (During the 1950s Mongolia, the People's Republic of China, North Korea and North Vietnam became associate members of Comecon – Mongolia, Cuba and Vietnam later becoming full members – see the definition of the Eastern bloc in Table 1.1.) Where exactly does Europe geographically end in the east and Asia begin? Turkey has candidate membership of the EC, but is it a genuine part of Europe? Bearing these points in mind we can now move on to review briefly the pattern of economic interactions that has characterized the institutional spaces of Europe since the Second World War.

PATTERNS OF EUROPEAN ECONOMIC INTERACTIONS

In an influential analysis of the reasons for the post-Second World War 'long boom' in economic activity, Matthews (1968) argued that this was less the result of a (publically inspired) Keynesian demand management of the European and American economies, but more the result of the (privately inspired) dramatic increase in investment and trade between the countries of the 'West'. It is on the importance of trade and investment that we concentrate in this section.

The crucial impediment to the rapid re-establishment of international trade amongst the main capitalist countries after the Second World War was the 'dollar shortage', particularly amongst the countries of Europe. This was solved by a combination of (a) the Marshall Plan and its associated aid and loan arrangements (discussed above); and (b) the inauguration of the European Payments Union. This latter body acted to conserve the available dollar and other official reserve holdings used by the European countries to settle international payments between themselves. It also enabled a more effective use of these reserves in financing the trade and balance of payments of the participants with the outside world.

With the immediate crisis of the dollar shortage easing, it was the devaluations in 1949 that set the European countries on the route to their dramatic increases in international trade. This major realignment of 26, mainly European, currencies against the dollar (by around 30 per cent) secured a competitive advantage for Europe *vis-à-vis* the USA that lasted to the early 1970s. The European economies were effectively transformed into export-oriented economies almost overnight by this move.

The historical record of European economic growth, compared to that of the USA and Japan, is shown in Table 2.3. The period of rapid growth to the early 1970s is clear to see. From the middle 1970s the growth rate fell. Note that over the entire period Europe showed a marginally better growth record than the USA, but a remarkably worse one compared to Japan.

The second part of Table 2.3 gives information on the investment record for the three main country groupings. In terms of gross capital formation, Europe achieved a better result than the USA, and quite a consistent one, but again this compares unfavourably with that of Japan. This striking difference is confirmed if we look solely at investment in machinery and equipment, the basis of investment in the traded goods sector. Perhaps one of the main reasons for the poorer European (and to an even greater extent US) perform-

*Table 2.3   Comparative European growth, investment and trade record,
1960–1988*

	1960–67	1968–73	1974–79	1980–88	1960–88
Real GDP growth (yearly % changes)					
OECD Europe	4.7	4.9	2.6	2.2	3.5
USA	4.5	3.2	2.4	2.8	3.3
Japan	10.2	8.7	3.6	4.1	6.5
Gross capital formation (as % of GDP)					
OECD Europe	22.9	23.5	22.4	20.3	22.1
USA	18.0	18.4	18.7	17.8	18.2
Japan	31.0	34.6	31.8	29.2	31.4
Investment in machinery and equipment (as % of GDP)					
OECD Europe	9.2	9.0	8.9	8.6	8.9
USA	6.7	7.3	8.0	7.9	7.4
Japan	[n/a]	14.4	10.8	10.5	12.3
Net savings (as % of GDP)					
OECD Europe	15.3	15.9	11.9	9.1	12.6
USA	9.8	9.2	7.7	3.6	7.3
Japan	21.2	25.1	20.2	17.8	20.7
Trade balances (as % of GDP)					
OECD Europe	–0.1	0.3	–0.5	0.4	0.0
USA	0.7	0.1	–0.4	–2.0	–0.5
Japan	0.2	1.5	0.4	2.0	1.1

Note: Figures for the EC rather than OECD Europe do not differ significantly except for the case of trade balances, where the EC does marginally better.

Source: Compiled from *OECD Historical Statistics 1960–1988*, 1990, Paris.

ance in all categories of investment is that savings are low in these two economic areas. A dramatic collapse of saving in the US economy over the 1980s is evident from Table 2.3, the fuller consequences of which are discussed in Chapter 3. The remarkably high savings ratio in Japan, and its relative robustness over the period, is also something we take up below. The record of the OECD Europe on savings falls somewhere between these other two.

The final part of Table 2.3 gives one indicator of the trade performance of Europe compared to the USA and Japan. Over the period as a whole the position of Europe has been more or less neutral in terms of the balance of trade. The USA, by contrast, fell into a negative balance on its trade account after 1974, while Japan strengthened its positive position in the 1980s.

If we now move on to just European direct investment, Tables 2.4 and 2.5 indicate the historical position in terms of OECD investment flows. What is significant about these data is the continued dominance of the UK economy

Table 2.4   Inward and outward European investment amongst the OECD countries, 1971–1989

Country	Outward direct investment flows from selected European countries as a percentage of investment by the OECD countries							
	1971/80	1981	1982	1983	1984	1985	1986	1989
France	4.6	9.28	13.20	6.57	5.53	3.68	5.26	18.1
Germany	7.7	8.24	12.00	10.73	11.45	7.95	9.67	14.1
Italy	1.2	2.82	4.42	7.20	5.19	3.01	2.85	2.0
Netherlands	9.2	9.52	14.31	12.75	13.28	5.21	4.50	11.1
Switzerland	n.a.	n.a.	n.a.	n.a.	2.96	7.56	1.46	6.9
United Kingdom	18.0	24.25	30.08	27.54	21.07	18.72	17.93	35.3

n.a.   Not available.

Country	International direct investment flows to selected European countries as a percentage of the inward investment received by the OECD countries							
	1971/80	1981	1982	1983	1984	1985	1986	1989
France	9.0	5.94	5.21	5.19	6.21	6.25	5.83	9.5
Germany	7.4	0.83	2.75	5.72	2.15	2.05	2.90	6.7
Italy	3.0	2.81	2.12	3.79	3.65	2.84	–0.36	2.5
Netherlands	5.8	4.34	3.77	4.54	4.88	3.24	4.41	6.3
Switzerland	n.a.	n.a.	n.a.	0.91	1.51	2.97	2.98	1.9
United Kingdom	21.6	14.43	17.62	16.34	–0.68	16.04	16.85	28.7

n.a.   Not available

Source: International Direct Investment and the New Economic Environment, Tables 15 and 16, 1989, Paris: OECD and *Industrial Policy in OECD Countries, Annual Review 1991*, Tables 24 and 25, Paris: OECD.

Table 2.5 Cumulative outward and inward direct investment flows as percentage of total flows, 1971–80 and 1981–89

	1971–80	1981–89
Outward flows		
USA	44.4	139.7
Japan	6.0	137.8
France	4.6	58.6
Germany	7.7	62.9
UK	18.2	167.3
Inward flows		
USA	30.0	307.0
Japan	0.8	1.5
France	9.0	34.1
Germany	7.4	15.0
UK	21.6	89.2

Source: As for Table 2.4, adapted from Tables 4 and 5 (OECD, 1989) and Tables 24 and 25 (OECD, 1991).

in terms of the proportion of OECD direct investment it either attracts or originates amongst the European economies. The UK economy is a highly penetrated one as far as international investment flows are concerned. This makes the economy particularly vulnerable to decisions of international investors, whether made at home or abroad. Within the rest of Europe, the Netherlands has also traditionally been heavily involved with international direct investment. Despite its size and importance, the German economy was relatively less involved with international direct investment up to the middle 1980s, particularly as a destination for inward investment. Clearly, an important implication of these statistics is that the advanced industrial countries are becoming increasingly interdependent in terms of direct investment flows and holdings. However, in addition to direct investment, the European economies are heavily involved in international bank lending. The stock of bank lending for 1986 and 1991 is shown in Table 2.6, which indicates once again the continued dominance of the UK amongst the European countries as a source of international bank lending.

So much for investment. We can now look at trade more closely. We can begin with the distribution of total world trade as shown in Table 2.7 . This compares the position in 1958 with that in 1990. The remarkable feature of these data is the overwhelming significance of 'Western Europe' in world

Table 2.6   The stock of external bank lending, 1986 and 1991

	1986 (US $ billions)	1991 (US $ billions)
UK	21.8	16.3
Japan	10.5	15.1
USA	14.4	9.4
France	6.2	6.6
Switzerland	3.3	6.3
Germany	4.4	6.1
Luxembourg	4.3	5.0
Belgium	3.6	3.2
Netherlands	2.7	2.9
Italy	1.8	1.5

Source: *BEQR* Table E, p. 193, May 1992.

*Table 2.7   The structure of trade by country and region in 1958 compared
              to 1990*

	Exports (%)		Imports (%)	
	1958	1990	1958	1990
Intra-EC trade	37.2	61.0	35.2	58.8
Other European OECD countries	13.7	12.0	10.1	10.9
Total: 'Western Europe'	50.9	73.0	45.3	69.7
Centrally planned economies	4.3	2.8	3.8	3.7
Total: 'Western Europe' plus centrally planned economies	55.2	75.8	49.1	73.4
USA	7.9	7.1	11.4	7.6
Japan	0.6	2.1	0.7	4.1
Developing countries	27.4	12.5	29.5	12.8
Rest of the world and unspecified	8.9	2.5	9.3	2.1
World total	100.0	100.0	100.0	100.0

Source: *European Economy*, Annual Report 1991–92, calculated from Tables 44 and 45, p.
257.

trade. This accounted for 73 per cent of exports and 70 per cent of imports in 1990. If the old centrally planned economies are added into this total (the vast bulk of trade for this group being conducted by the European CPEs plus the USSR), then the importance of 'Europe' increases even further. The other big trading group is the developing countries, but their significance has declined over the period.

Another major point to emerge from Table 2.7 is that not only is Western Europe the main contemporary player, but it was also the most significant in 1958. For all practical intents and purposes 'international trade' can be considered as intra-advanced industrial country trade. The intra-EC trade alone accounted for 60 per cent of the world total in 1990. Interestingly, tracing this further back in time shows that in the inter-war period intra-European trade (defined as between Belgium, France, Germany, Italy, the Netherlands and the UK) was, even then, as much as 70 per cent of Europe's foreign trade; before it then declined immediately after the Second World War (Milward, 1984, Table 25, p. 214).

Concentrating solely on the Eastern European economies for a moment, it was mentioned above that these economies were (a) not as well integrated into the global economic mechanism in terms of trade; and (b) not as well integrated between themselves as the Western European economies had been (Drabek and Greenaway, 1984 – the exception being the case of the republics of the USSR – see Table 2.2). As Table 2.8 demonstrates, comparing 1970 with 1989, the proportion of the Eastern European economies' intra-country trade had actually *declined*. Instead they had increased their trade with the 'West', and with the 'Other' category. A similar result emerges if we look just at the Soviet Union's trade.

Returning to the Western countries only, the trends in trade flows here since the 1960s have been towards ever greater integration between the economies involved. As a proportion of GDP, trade increased from between 15 per cent to 25 per cent in 1960 to between 40 per cent and 55 per cent in 1990 for the main European economies. The average external trade for EC countries individually was just over 46 per cent in 1990. It was during the middle 1970s that the most significant boost to foreign trade took place for these countries.

However, an important point in contrast to the situation amongst the EC countries has been the much lower and steadier level of trade penetration in the USA and Japan. In the 1960s international trade comprised 10 per cent of GDP for the USA and 18 per cent of GDP for Japan, rising to 17 per cent for the USA by 1990, but remaining the same for Japan at 18 per cent (Hirst and Thompson, 1992, Figure 3). Again, it was during the 1970s that trade penetration really developed for the US economy, nearly doubling over that period as a proportion of GDP. One further important point, however, is the

Table 2.8   Structure of Eastern European and Soviet Union trade: 1970 compared to 1989 (% of totals)

	Exports		Imports	
	1970	1989	1970	1989
Eastern Europe's trade with:				
ECE East[1]	63.7	50.6	63.2	49.9
ECE West[2]	26.7	37.8	28.8	39.1
Other	9.6	11.6	8.0	11.0
Total	100.0	100.0	100.0	100.0
Soviet Union's trade with:				
ECE East	52.8	46.5	56.5	48.8
ECE West	21.7	27.0	25.7	31.0
Other	25.5	26.5	17.7	20.2
Total	100.0	100.0	100.0	100.0
Eastern European and Soviet Union trade with:				
ECE East	59.2	48.3	60.7	49.2
ECE West	24.6	31.6	27.6	34.3
Other	16.2	20.1	11.8	16.5
TOTAL	100.0	100.0	100.0	100.0

Notes:
1. European Commission for Europe East comprises: Bulgaria, Czechoslovakia, German Democratic Republic, Hungary, Poland and Romania.
2. European Commission for Europe West comprises: Western market economies plus Japan.

Source: *Economic Survey of Europe in 1989–90*, UN, calculated from Appendix, Tables C.4 and C.5, pp. 409 and 410.

remarkable similarity in trade to GDP ratios if the three main economic blocs are looked at together. The extra-Community trade of the EC as a whole was 18.6 per cent in 1990, very close to the US and Japanese levels.

THE EVOLVING EUROPEAN ECONOMIC ORDER

The European economy now displays a high degree of interdependence between the countries involved, but combined with their continuing economic autonomy in policy-making. Important in the history of this development has been the increasing role of markets in breaking down the barriers to interdependency, whilst decision-making autonomy has remained. A wide range of economic actors comes into play here, cutting across divisions around nation-to-nation relationships. This creates the potential for a tension between the sovereignty of the nation state on the one hand and the activity of private economic agents who need not respect that sovereignty on the other. It is in this context that the moves towards new forms of economic cooperation and coordination between countries within Europe can be productively assessed. It also raises the acute tensions within many of these countries, which have become jealous of their national sovereignty as it seems to be swept aside, not only by economic interdependencies but also by political regulatory and governance mechanisms created at the pan-European level.

The European states now have highly internationalized financial markets. In particular they increasingly display integration of trading on their currency and equity markets. They are typified by an increasing volume of trade in manufactured goods between themselves – most markets for major industrial products are now international and the major economies both import and export significant volumes of such goods. They have seen the development of transnational production organizations which operate in many different countries, which may mean they cease to have a clear home-base. This has all raised subtle relationships between international and domestic economic policy-making (see Chapter 1). For instance, when German interest rates rise this has dramatic potential effects for other EC economies. So much so that pressures begin to be put on the German authorities by other Community governments to devise their monetary policy with this potential effect in mind. Similarly with devaluation policies.

The response at a world level to these trends has been the development of multilateral organizations of economic governance. The Bretton Woods regime (which includes the World Bank and the GATT system of trade negotiations) inaugurated a system of multilateral 'liberal' trade and other economic interactions, evolving within a system of (semi)-fixed exchange rates.

The immediate aftermath of the collapse of the exchange rate part of the Bretton Woods mechanism in the early 1970s resulted in a short period of totally floating rates. But in 1979 the EMS was established by the EC to provide a 'regime of stability' in exchange rates between the European member countries and the US dollar in particular (which originally operated without the participation of the UK; it having decided not to join the exchange rate mechanism (ERM) in 1979 and only later joining in October 1990 but floating out of it again two years later in September 1992). In addition a more general retreat from a totally free-floating system emerged in the middle 1980s as the advanced industrialized countries of the G-10, G-7 and G-5, set up a series of regular meetings from which a new system of 'international economic coordination', centred on exchange rate stabilization, developed (Artis and Ostry, 1986; Funabashi, 1988).

As mentioned in the Introduction, one of the ways in which the development of the European political and economic order has traditionally been thought about is in terms of whether it is the result of some 'grand design' on the part of a set of visionary political leaders, bureaucrats, key country groupings and so on, or whether it is best thought of as an evolving response to a series of essentially *ad hoc* and incremental problems that have produced particular, if often highly innovatory, institutional development. Has the 'dynamic' of European integration been a 'planned' one or a 'spontaneous' one? Has it been the subject of detailed advanced preparation with the long-term goal of a unitary state or federal Europe always in mind, or has it been the result of stumbling along with no particular destination in sight (Wallace, 1990)?

This characteristic way of posing the question of European integration helps to capture an essential feature of this chapter's analysis; it enables an assessment of the relative strengths of the 'market mechanism' and the 'political calculations' of those involved in building a more united Europe. At a slightly different level it is another way of posing the question of the evolutionary character of cooperative European development in contrast to the idea of its necessary creation by a single and central authoritative body. To look at this takes us back to a further discussion of, first, the ECSC in the 1950s and then the evolving EEC that was built upon it.

As we have seen, the European economies emerged from the Second World War in a battered state, initially dependent upon the USA for capital goods, financial assistance and markets. The productive potential of the economies was not completely devastated, however. Perhaps surprisingly, significant amounts of capital remained intact, it having been the social and economic infrastructure, often publicly owned, that had suffered the most damage. But the problem was to modernize and reconstruct the productive base that remained as quickly as possible. The question was 'how was this to be done?'.

The immediate post-war period was one in which a number of reports and 'plans' were suggested for the future of Europe, associated with those now famous historical names of European integration; the Marshall Plan, the

Schuman Plan, the Monnet Plan, the Tinbergen Report and more besides.[3] A technicist ideology pervaded both the conduct of the war and its aftermath in terms of 'planning' for the future. Any problem was amenable to a rational and technical solution – even the evolution of social and economic relationships.

The Schuman Plan for a European Coal and Steel Community was one such successful manifestation of this trend. Along with the Monnet Plan for the restructuring and modernization of the French economy, it captured the mood of the times.[4] These twin plans developed in tandem and became the prototypes for the formation of the EEC in 1957. Tinbergen later added some intellectual refinement with his distinction between 'negative integration' and 'positive policy integration', referring respectively to the removal of barriers and obstacles to integration on the one hand and the development of common new policies on the other (Tinbergen, 1954). The Tinbergen approach suggested that it would be the mechanism of *harmonization* that provided the main means to reach common policies in the European context. Existing different national treatments needed to be harmonized around an agreed EC-wide common set of standards and rules.

Planning Coal and Steel and the European Community

The ECSC, set up in April 1951 and becoming operational in July of the following year, was both an economic and a political organization. In this way it exactly prefigured most subsequent European institutional developments. On the economic front it was designed to promote free trade and a rationalization of the coal and steel sector, and to secure a regular supply of these vital materials for economic growth. On the political front it was designed to 'settle' the long-running dispute between France and Germany over the territory of the Saar and the Ruhr, and the natural resources located there. In today's climate it is probably difficult to appreciate fully how important an issue this was felt to be in the immediate aftermath of the war.

The important feature of the ECSC from the point of view of subsequent developments was that it established an Executive High Authority to manage community relations – the first supranational unit in the post-war history of European integration, and one with its own budget. This became a prototype for the much more ambitious Commission of the European Communities (CEC), set up by the Treaty of Rome establishing the EEC in 1957.[5]

It was the exclusive sectoral focus of the ECSC that was partly responsible for the relative lack of its success in achieving its immediate economic aims. The coal and steel industries could not be 'managed' independently from the rest of the European economy. The EEC was designed to remedy this defect by creating an organization with an economy-wide focus. The history of the EEC is well known, and there is no need to recount it in detail here.[6] The EEC has always been more than a pure customs union, though this was its first and foremost function. The Treaty provided a framework for the formation of an evolving Community, and this is probably the best way of viewing its development.

Planning Agriculture

The other almost defining institution of the EEC was the Common Agricultural Policy (CAP). Hardly ever out of the public eye, the history of this aspect of the Treaty of Rome is one of its most controversial. But it is important to remember that the CAP was originally regarded as the cornerstone on which the whole of the European integration process was to be built. The crisis of the 1930s had to a large extent been driven by moves towards agricultural protectionism, and the framers of the Treaty of Rome were determined this experience would not be repeated. An integrated agricultural policy would ensure uniform prices across Europe, even if that meant that these were, at times, higher than world prices. Internal agricultural prices would be set by the Community in the light of the need to provide farmers with a guaranteed satisfactory income (just as it was hoped the other measures embodied in the Treaty would lead to satisfactory incomes for other sectors of the working population). The system would include control over imports of agricultural products from outside (via special import duties), the manipulation of the internal agricultural market (the buying of market surpluses at guaranteed minimum prices), and thus the installation of a comprehensive subsidy arrangement for the sector as a whole. The system was phased in between 1964 and 1967.

The CAP is generally agreed to have been one of the Community's least effective policy initiatives. An early problem (in the Tinbergen mould) was deciding around which country's prices harmonization should take place. Germany had the higher prices, and harmonization took place around these, to the initial benefit of other countries' farmers (German agricultural prices fell a little while those in other countries rose substantially). The principle of common financing meant that the net food-exporting nations of the Community received subsidies from the net importing members. The result is that France, and latterly also the Netherlands, Denmark and Ireland, receive large inward flows of foreign exchange. The original formulation of the CAP was often seen as another trade-off between Germany and France; the preservation of French agriculture and a stimulus to German industry via lower food prices there.

The central policy tool of the CAP remains price support. But this has become expensive. In 1990 the OECD estimated that the total CAP programme had cost taxpayers and consumers up to 100 billion ECU. The agricultural budget regularly takes over 60 per cent of the EC annual budget. Disputes over funding have been a major distraction from other important and serious issues of European integration. The form of the CAP also served to maximize the possibility of trade disputes with third parties, the most notorious contemporary instance of which is that revolving around the Uruguay round of GATT negotiations, which dragged on for nearly ten years while CAP reform was being mooted.

As CAP intervention prices have been raised, EC food prices have generally overtaken world prices. Thus who now benefits from the CAP? Other than the ever-present 'bureaucrats in Brussels', those involved in storing, trading and transporting the food surpluses, and large farmers, are the most obvious candidates. Large farmers have prospered under the CAP, while smaller farmers have only survived under it.

It is in the context of the GATT negotiations that some serious reform of the CAP now seems likely. Indeed, only if there is some reform does it look as though these stalled talks will move towards anything approaching a successful conclusion. The 1991 MacSharry Reform proposals (named after the Irish EC Commissioner for Agriculture, Ray MacSharry) suggested a significant price cut along with a transitional direct subsidy to small (that is, poorer) farmers to ease their adjustment problems. It is the complexity of these reforms, however (they are closely tied in with so-called 'set aside' policies that take land out of production), plus the coincidental GATT negotiations and the pressure from the USA, that could result in undermining their adoption (Rollo, 1992). Nor is it clear that overall expenditure would necessarily be cut. The British government (and to some extent the Dutch and the Danes) came out against the MacSharry proposals, since it is their large and efficient farmers who would disproportionately carry most of the burden of the adjustment. Thus the British seemingly reversed their policy, since they had been arguing for subsidy and price cuts for at least 20 years. This demonstrates how difficult it still remains in the EC for genuine 'co-operative' outcomes while a narrow national interest continues to drive much inter-governmental negotiation.

Planning for the Single Market

A policy initiative that the British did go along with, at least initially, was the single market programme. The signing of the Single European Act in February 1986 (entering into force in July 1987) marked a further important event in the history of cooperative relations within the EC. The Single Act introduced some modification to the Community's decision-making processes; in particular it opened the way for (qualified) majority voting on certain matters where strict unanimity had been demanded before. This produced the possibility of novel country coalition formation in the Council of Ministers; under certain circumstances the 'poorer' countries being able to out-vote the 'richer' ones. But from the point of view of economic relations the most important outcome of the Act was the move towards the single market in 1992.

The original 1957 Treaty establishing the Community had signalled the emergence of a customs union where all tariff barriers between the members would be eliminated and a common trade barrier regime erected around the Community as a whole. This was substantially realized by 1968. The Community then went on to form the EMS in 1979, which has successfully worked to link at least the main member currencies together (around the German Deutschmark) and to reduce the exchange rate fluctuations between them. It also provides a mechanism to cushion the Community currencies against the vagrancies of the international financial system beyond – particularly to provide a stability *vis-à-vis* the US dollar.

The aim of the single market programme was to build on this stability by tackling *non-tariff* barriers to trade. However, this is essentially a purgative programme – a case of what Tinbergen called 'negative integration' (see above). The idea is to cleanse the system of its impurities, where these impurities are seen as those that present obstacles to the full rigours of market operation. Thus the accompanying EC competition policy has as its main and overriding objective the removal of all the 'inefficiencies' to the operation of the EC so that the market can properly dispense its benign virtues 'automatically' and with as little regulation as possible. That, at least, is the declared, almost rhetorical, intention.

As the question of the single European market and the particular form of competition policy to support it has developed, however, the sentiment has shifted against further harmonization of European rules and standards. Rather, a new criterion has emerged; the recognition of *national treatments.* Mutual recognition and reciprocity are now the order of the day as far as integration is concerned (Bressand, 1990), along with the idea of subsidiarity, which is discussed in a moment. While there still remains the objective of reaching a 'level playing-field', this is to be assessed in this different, more 'realistic' political context. Harmonization is now increasingly considered as a lowest common denominator criterion by which to set minimum standards or rules only.

But as in any economic situation, the building of a single market requires the establishment of a new institutional structure to manage those economic relations so fostered. This remains the site of some major disputes between the EC members as the further drive towards economic and monetary union gathers momentum. It was the objective of the Maastricht Summit in December 1991 to consolidate this institution-building process by initiating definite moves towards closer political union. The outcome of this meeting remains ambiguous. The initial intransigence of the British authorities over further political union, and their refusal to pre-commit to either full monetary union or the Social Chapter aspects of the Treaty, may have undermined the whole process and stalled its momentum. In addition, the Danish and French referenda results added to the uncertainty over the whole ratification process of the Treaty's provisions. The prospects here as we enter the mid-1990s are further discussed in Chapters 5 and 8.

One preliminary point to recall is that the EC is already highly integrated in an economic sense, as the statistics presented in the previous sections testify. There is thus a question over whether there are many additional benefits to be gained solely from the single market programme, or whether they are as extensive as suggested by the Commission. These issues are analysed in detail in Chapter 4. But in the meantime it is important to note other major developments that could interrupt the smooth transition to a fully integrated market in the EC. These involve the possibilities of membership expansion as the Eastern European economies queue up for admission, along with the Scandinavian countries, and Austria and Switzerland (and possibly Turkey in the longer term). Already the absorption of (East) Germany into the EC has had a significant effect on the (West) German economy – in 1991 Germany went into deficit on its current account. In addition, inflationary worries re-emerged in the united Germany as the government's budget deficit soared in response to the social and economic readjustment costs associated with the transformation of the newly absorbed eastern part of the economy (Chapter 7). It is possible that these costs will continue for a number of years, and they may even increase. The pivotal role the German economy occupies within the EC implies that these problems are likely to affect all the member countries in one way or another. We return to this below.

Integrationist Political Forces

Mention of the role of the German economy within Europe prompts further discussion of the political forces that have driven the moves towards greater cooperative integration since the Second World War. Chief amongst these must be Christian Democracy, a widespread European political movement (though one conspicuous by its absence within the UK), but one that has drawn its greatest strength from the West German CDU Party. The CDU (in conjunction with the Christian Social Union (CSU), and at times in coalition with the German Liberal Party (FDP)) provided the crucial political impetus for what was initially seen very much as a Western European integrative solution to the problems besetting the continent. In particular, its hostility to the Soviet Union and the Eastern bloc focused the Party's political attention on the integration of Germany into a strong economic and political mechanism founded on liberal market principles.

As we shall see in the next chapter, this did not take the form of a commitment to the unregulated *laissez-faire* favoured by conservative forces in the UK. Rather, it took the form of constructing a consensual democratic distributive coalition around the notion of the social market economy. Similar consensual coalitions developed elsewhere, particularly in the Netherlands. (Christian Democracy is a strong political force in the Netherlands and also in Italy.)

The most recent example of the CDU success was during the tumultuous period in 1990 when it effectively reversed its position on East Germany, threw caution to the wind by wholeheartedly embracing the East Germans and reaped the reward of a stunning all-German election victory under the leadership of Chancellor Kohl. The old East Germany was, as a result, fully *politically* absorbed into the EC very rapidly. The economic consequences of this are discussed in Chapter 7.

Finally, it was Christian Democracy that provided the key term under which much of the discussion of wider European political union was being couched in 1992 in an attempt to put the ratification of the Maastricht Treaty back on course. *Subsidiarity* – a concept with a range of interpretations (but usually defined as the principle that things should only be done at a higher level when they cannot be done at a lower one), and which looks destined to dominate the discussion of the form of any political institution-building in the immediate years to come – was first systematically enunciated by Pope Pius XI in his 1931 Encyclical Letter, *Quadragesimo Anno* (Wilke and Wallace, 1990, p. 12). Subsidiarity encompassed a moral precept in the case of the Encyclical Letter. It embodied an ethical principle stressing the intrinsic link between the individual and the social order in which there are certain domains of action that should not be subjected to interference by either the state or society. It has come to express a certain position in social philosophy, a mutual relationship between higher and lower levels of society in which social cohesion and social integration are stressed as virtues.

The problem has been to give some operational and constitutional definition to this emerging key concept of subsidiarity. It is in respect to the relationship between the German *Länder* and the federal government that the concept in its German formulation (*subsidiar*) has achieved most development. It helps demarcate the competences of the different levels of government. It is also implicated in Swiss constitutional discussion and in the case of Dutch Christian Democratic political ideals (which stress 'justice', 'solidarity' and 'stewardship'). Until recently the British government and commentators were antagonistic towards the concept of subsidiarity. Vibert (1990) accuses it of lack of precision in defining institutional responsibilities and as an inadequate basis for Treaty legal provisions (pp. 118–19). It was thought just too philosophical for the practically minded British. But with the advent of John Major onto the European arena in the post-Danish referendum period, the British began to put this principle forward in a more positive light. Major emphasized, however, that it meant only the return of certain powers to the competence of *national governments,* not a thorough potential decentralization to national, regional, federal or local levels of public *or* private governance, as the term implied in its true Christian Democratic sense. One way or another, however, it looks as though subsidiarity is destined to play an enhanced role in the future political integration of Europe (if there is to be any), as the difficulties in ratifying the Maastricht Treaty multiplied in late 1992.

If one looks for a parallel political movement in the other great integrationist power of Europe, France, it can probably be found in the form of 'Gaullism'. This mirrors in many ways the Christian Democratic tradition in terms of its emphasis on a European solution to Europe's problems. But the emphasis here is different. Gaullism pressed more for an *exclusive* European focus, and was hostile to the USA in particular and to powers such as the UK that stressed the virtues of an 'Atlanticist' alliance. The German Christian Democrats, by contrast, were never that hostile to the US presence in Europe, nor to a continuation of close economic and political ties between the USA and Europe. If the German Christian Democracts represent the pragmatic face of European integration, then the Gaullist tradition represents the more dogmatic face of the same movement. Both shared similar objectives in Europe, though the French, in both their domestic and their external policies, have tended to support rather more programmatic schemes for European integration and domestic economic advance (see Chapter 3).

With the relative demise of Gaullism as a strong political force in France, the French socialist tradition adopted many of the European integrationist credentials of its political rivals. François Mitterrand embodied this position perfectly, while Jacques Delors has become the strongest proponent of subsidiarity within the Commission, attempting to establish a Christian–socialist reconciliation around the doctrine.

The Expansion of Europe

A final topic for this section concerns the issue raised earlier of the expansion of the European economic space. If the EC is to advance it will have to both deepen and widen its institutional base. If it does not succeed in deepening its institutional base, the Community is in danger of slipping back into something approaching an elaborate customs union which will increasingly come under the dominance of the German economy. The EC could emerge as little different to the North American Free Trade Area being constructed by the USA in the early 1990s. This means it would not be in a position to provide the mechanisms by which new members could be equitably admitted into the Community, particularly those on its eastern flank. It could simply become an increasingly inward-looking 'exclusive club' of the rich (Chapter 7).

Of those countries queuing up to gain admittance, the likes of Sweden, Switzerland, Finland and Austria (with Norway to follow?) would present little problem in terms of ease of accommodation. They already have advanced economic status, and their consensual political approach, with its semi-corporatist features, would only add to the existing decision-making structure in a positive manner. On the other hand, the countries of middle and Eastern Europe present significant difficulties. They have neither the economic base nor the political traditions to fit easily into the existing EC structures. Thus there needs to be some mechanism created that would ease these countries into a position to make a successful full entry without this undermining the existing EC framework, itself so carefully built up over the last 30 years.

Perhaps a new 'Marshall Plan for Eastern Europe' could fit this bill? To create this would require a major political commitment on the part of the Community, and it would be costly. It would have to be installed in an environment where there was no perceived threat to the very existence of the contemporary European power structure, as had been the case in the late 1940s. In addition, the original Marshall Plan involved outright grants (not loans) to Europe of the equivalent of $US 20 billion – comprising 3 per cent of US GDP in the late 1940s. The existing European Bank for Reconstruction and Development, created in 1991, had only approximately US$ 12.3 billion paid in capital and was to operate on strictly commercial lines with high returns expected from its investments in Eastern European ventures. The *total* level of contemporary advanced economic developmental assistance is, for the most part, still well under 1 per cent of GDP, minimal compared to the original Marshall Aid figures.

INSTITUTIONS FOR MANAGING THE EUROPEAN REGIONAL ECONOMY

A further issue for which the deepening of the European institutional mechanisms could prove to be crucial involves the management of the newly evolving regionalized economy, a point that was introduced briefly above. In particular this concerns the establishment of effective European-wide economic management mechanisms to carry through the programme of monetary and economic union. The form this union might take, and the institutions devised to foster it, were the subject of intense debate in the early 1990s. Of particular importance in this respect would be the characteristics of monetary union and the role of the European Central Bank (ECB), which is to be discussed in greater detail in Chapter 5.

Behind the manoeuvres on the nature of the central bank lay deep differences over the pace and character of wider monetary union. The Delors Report (Committee for the Study of Economic and Monetary Union, 1989) had suggested a three-stage process for moving towards full monetary union. The first stage involved all the member countries joining the ERM and adhering to the narrow band of exchange rate variation. The second stage involved the gradual establishment of a central banking mechanism and the movement towards close financial and monetary cooperation by the individual national authorities. The third stage would involve the establishment of an irrevocably fixed system of exchange rates between the participant countries, the introduction of a single currency within the Community, a central banking system conducting monetary policy (implying a single European interest rate, or spectrum of interest rates), and most probably a highly coordinated or even single fiscal policy as well. In effect this final stage would mean that individual governments would no longer have control over their monetary policy (and possibly their fiscal policy as well – though see Chapters 3 and 5). The Maastricht agreement (HMSO, 1992) set 1997 as the target date for the introduction of a central bank and moves towards monetary union – to which the UK could later join if it so wished.

The Maastricht Summit may mark a watershed in these negotiations. A rather complex compromise outcome emerged from the meeting. The Treaty, and the subsequent difficulty in ratifying its provisions, may have enhanced the likelihood of a 'two-speed' (and possibly 'two-tiered') Europe (see Chapter 5). With the UK opting for non-participation in the immediate development of EMU and the so-called Social Chapter, while the other 11 EC members (plus new entrants) proceed more speedily towards further economic and political integration, this could be one dimension along which the two tiers emerge. Another possibility, considered at greater length in Chapter 5, could be the emergence of a hard core of closely integrated countries (centred around Germany and France), while the weaker peripheral countries continue in a second tier.

The social dimension to future European integration proved a particularly difficult stumbling block to unanimous agreement at Maastricht. Eventually the UK completely opted out of this section of the Treaty. Thus the UK authorities clearly see a different future for Europe than do the other member states. In a period of significant economic dislocation, the EC has become a site of major economic restructuring (see Chapter 6) and a very attractive destination for economic migrants (Chapter 7). The provisions of the Social Chapter part of the Treaty try to put a floor under the EC labour market by introducing minimum guaranteed working conditions, minimum health and safety standards, possibly minimum wages, and various co-determination conditions. Without these there is a strong likelihood that the European economy will be tempted down a route of low wages, low productivity and low value-added production. Without a floor under the labour market, wages and working conditions are liable to be continually 'rendered down' in the name of increased competitiveness, particularly as lower skilled migrants enter from the east and south. This was something that the UK authorities deliberately urged for Europe as a whole, as they had done on the purely domestic front. The other members of the Community see the future in terms of high productivity and high value-added production, which implies a high wage economy.

But a possibly more important consequence of the fracturing of the unity of the EC at, and immediately after, the Summit is that further serious European political unity is stifled in the longer run. This was clearly another objective of the British Conservative government at the time, and it could be one of their most significant achievements. A clear political momentum had been built up behind further political integration before the Summit, and this could have been dissipated and dissolved by its outcome. In the absence of any political integration to 'govern' and regulate the Common Market, a neo-liberal *laissez-faire* outcome seems more likely in the long run, with all its attendant inequalities and uncertainties. However, this rather pessimistic scenario for political integration is not clear-cut. It is too early yet to judge the final outcome. This is discussed further in the next chapter and in the concluding one.

Whatever the precise longer-term developments and arrangements, the most likely immediate outcome for the 11 core states still looks to be a single market, with a single economic policy-making body, managing a single currency: the ECU. How would such a regional economic entity as this fit into the overall global economic framework? This is one of the major issues tackled in the next chapter. However, before moving to this we can sum up the implications of the analysis conducted in this chapter on the nature of European integration and cooperation.

CONCLUSION

One of the objectives set for this chapter was to assess the changing nature of the notion of 'Europe' as a coordinated economic space, and to place this in the context of the evolving contours of its relationship to the international economy beyond. The argument has been that in the post-war period the interdependencies between the European national economies developed to such a degree that cooperative policies were increasingly called upon to manage those relationships. But without the continued political will to foster these relationships, even the existing EES could either stagnate or fragment.

One difficulty has been to provide a consistent definition of the 'European economic space'. The founding and evolution of those mechanisms of European integration arising since the Second World War served to provide a way of posing the issue of a truly European-wide economy, organized around institutional developments on the one hand and market-driven interactions involving trade and investment on the other. Whilst at the beginning of the period considered here, there existed a clear alternative centre of political, military and economic power – the Soviet Union – which stimulated much of the early European integrationist moves, by 1991 this had totally collapsed.

These momentous events have, as yet, no clear impact on exactly what course the newly constituting European economic space will take. Indeed, they are combined with an internal debate within the European Community and its immediate candidate members as to the future course of political and economic union amongst the members that is potentially almost as momentous as the events taking place to the east. Europe is in the middle of one of those historic periods of transformation that few could have envisaged, even in the mid-1980s.

But whilst great uncertainties with respect to the immediate, let alone the long-term future, remain, certain trends from the past look likely to continue in one form or another. These trends have also been focused upon and analysed in this chapter. For the foreseeable future, despite its immediate difficulties, it is the German economy that is likely to continue to dominate in Europe, even in an extended European Community. In addition, there is unlikely to be an interruption in the growth of interdependencies between either the national economies of Europe or between Europe itself and other centres of economic power. Within this complex structure, the EC as a whole looks set to play an increasingly important role. Whether the EC is politically equipped to play properly the role increasingly marked out for it in terms of its economic integration remains another uncertainty. The question of whether the global economy could be easier to manage as European economic integration gathers momentum is a major issue for the next chapter.

Finally, what about the issue of the evolution of genuine cooperation within Europe along the lines of the Axelrod thesis? The verdict here ultimately depends upon whether the undoubted achievements registered so far with respect to European cooperation are secure enough to suppress the possible re-emergence of new competitive pressures consequent upon an upsurge in nationalist sentiment and a renewed emphasis on the national interest. Can the institutions established to manage and regulate the European economic space withstand the contemporary moves against any further 'centralizing' tendencies? This chapter has examined the mechanisms developed to establish and then further cooperative arrangements amongst the European states. For the most part these have not been overtly centralizing. Indeed, the argument has been that they represent an overlapping set of partial institutional arrangements without an obvious centre that can impose its will. Although the European Commission has undoubtedly become more important in recent years, the rest of the analysis of this book argues that the present structure of European integration could open up the space for its more decentralized political regulation. The challenge is to perceive these opportunities before they slip away. The elaboration of these possibilities is the task set for the following chapters.

NOTES

1. A customs union between just Belgium and Luxembourg, the BLUE, had been in operation since 1921.
2. There remains some controversy here. For a positive recent assessment see Hogan (1989), for a more sceptical view see Milward (1984).
3. See Milward (1984), Chapter XII for a discussion of all these reports and plans. In the period of the early 1950s they included the Meyer Plan (1952) for a European army, the Beyer Plan (1955) for economic unification, and the Spaak Report (1956) on a common European nuclear energy programme. Later versions of the same trend would include the Werner Report (1970) on economic and monetary union and the Delors Report (1989) on a similar theme .
4. A more Anglo-Saxon inflection of this trend is associated with the Keynesian policy programme of macroeconomic demand management. This is discussed at length in the following chapter.
5. The Treaty of Rome established: (a) the Commission, which could formulate initiatives for European integration and monitor the way the objectives of the Treaty were being implemented; (b) the Council of Ministers which had final decision-making authority; (c) the Court of Justice which deals with legal issues associated with the Treaty and its implementation; and finally (d) the European Parliament which has remained advisory rather than legislative. This set of arrangements may be dramatically modified or completely revised as a result of the Inter-Governmental Conference on political union which completed its work in late 1991. These developments are discussed in Chapters 3, 5 and 8.
6. For a good recent British description of the EC and other European institutional arrangements see Nicoll and Salmon (1990).

3. The Evolution of the Managed Economy in Europe

INTRODUCTION

How can we best think of the evolution of the managed economy in Europe? This is the main issue confronted in this chapter, and it continues a theme examined in the previous one. Although the chapter is partly methodological, it also raises some theoretical issues about the nature of the managed economy since the Second World War. In addition it provides an analysis of the political framework in which the management of the European economy can be thought under contemporary conditions. The argument here is that the European economy is being, and will continue to be, 'managed'. In an era – within an Anglo-Saxon intellectual culture at least – where there is a reaction against notions of active economic management, it is argued that *all* economies *demand* to be managed and that whatever the political or rhetorical intention, the temptation to intervene managerially is overwhelming.[1] Thus the issue is the *character and form* of interventionary/management practices rather than whether they are present or absent in some absolute sense.

This chapter emphasizes a number of features when dealing with the managed economy in Europe which it is worth outlining at this stage. The first is the difference in historical tradition of management style in the main economies of Europe since the Second World War. This chapter concentrates upon the experiences of France, Germany and the United Kingdom. The problem is to deal with the continued importance of these diverse traditions for the presently emerging European management structure. Does the impact of these divergent traditions still linger on in the present debate to help frame the structure, or have they been swept aside by the emergence of a new and universal neo-liberal intellectual and policy culture since the mid-1970s?

Secondly, and partly as a response to this first point, the analysis emphasizes institutional developments in the European management context. Here, the argument is that it is the institutional particularities and continuities/discontinuities that must be foregrounded in any analysis of the evolutionary nature of European economic management. Nationally specific institutional structures still characterize the present context, along with the old and new institution-building processes developing at the European level (as discussed in the previous chapter). The impacts of all these, it will also be suggested, continue to co-exist uneasily within the main European economies. Although the specifically national form of these institutions may act as an obstacle to the full development of the European-wide ones, as we shall see below the former may also enhance or help to enforce the latter.

The final theme of this chapter, though this operates very much as a background issue, concerns the nature, effects and consequences of economic changes since the mid-1970s for the evolution of the European managed economy. Here the issue can be summed up as the relationship between continuity and change in both the style and content of approaches towards economic management on a European-wide scale. Perhaps it is the issue of structural discontinuity versus cyclical change that best captures the theoretical problem at stake here. Has there been a dramatic discontinuity in the nature of capitalist economies, reflected in the changes since the mid-1970s, or are these merely the result of a cyclical process of recession soon to be followed by a new era of managed growth much like the period from the 1950s to the early 1970s?[2] Although this represents a major theoretical issue of general importance, the analysis that follows only touches on it in passing. A rather more pragmatic approach is adopted, detailing the consequences of the changes since the mid-1970s on economic management institutions, styles and practices without systematically relating these to possible structural features.[3]

NATIONALLY SPECIFIC INSTITUTIONAL DIFFERENCES: FRANCE, GERMANY AND THE UNITED KINGDOM

When looking at the history of the managed economy in Europe, it is the diversity of approaches and institutional mechanisms deployed in attempts to manage national economies that is immediately striking. Now, this may seem odd to those raised squarely in an Anglo-American intellectual culture. In that milieu the triumph of a single institutionalized management technique is widely celebrated, namely Keynesianism. This system of demand management is often thought to have hegemonized (and thereby also homogenized) the policy management framework of all advanced industrial economies in the post-war period, at least up until the mid-1970s, particularly those of Western Europe and the USA. But we need to review this afresh in the context of the present process of developing what could become genuinely trans-European practices of economic management. A point that should be re-emphasized is both the historical and contemporary diversity of embedded national institutionalized management practices. We shall try to assess the consequences of this for the evolving European mix of contemporary developments.

As we shall see, this is no easy task. Any impact of the rich historical detail can get lost in the debate and specifics of contemporary economic argument. In addition, not every important aspect of past economic management practice gets taken up in the present formulation of new institutional governance mechanisms. There is no necessary connection between the past effectiveness of particular mechanisms and their contemporary relevance or attractiveness. What is more, a further theoretical issue arises here: how far does an analysis of the present need to take account of the past? Clearly, we still live in an intellectual climate where the analysis of the past is widely thought to be an indispensable tool for the correct analysis of the present. But how far is this the case?

Despite some reservations about this latter issue in particular, it will be argued that an attempt to show the extent of the historical importance of institutional differences for confronting the present problems facing the European economy is valid and worthwhile (see also Chapter 2). Thus the point of the above remarks is to register a certain scepticism over the significance of historical factors alone, not to argue for their total unimportance.

Perhaps a good starting point for this kind of investigation is a book edited by Peter Hall. In *The Political Power of Economic Ideas: Keynesianism Across Nations* (Hall, 1989), the problem posed is how 'economic ideas are diffused across nations and acquire influence over policy' (Preface). The case taken is that of Keynesianism, and the mode of analysis is to ask why Keynesianism *did* or *did not* take hold in various countries within Europe and elsewhere. The issues posed in earlier parts of the book are the conditions necessary for the adoption of a Keynesian management policy. The subsequent analyses go on to enquire whether these conditions were or were not met in various countries, and to discuss the history of their development where they occurred.

Perhaps the main problem with this approach is the (implicit) presumption that Keynesianism is the 'natural' macroeconomic regulatory mode, so that the issue becomes one of explaining why it was taken up only weakly, or not at all, in various countries. Indeed, a more basic (implicit) presumption is that Keynesian ideas would have taken hold in *all* the countries considered, and directed policy in each, if only certain obstacles at the level of ideas or institutions could have been cleared away in advance.

In fact this is a rather harsh judgement on what is in many ways an excellent book. But it is accurate to a surprising extent (Tomlinson, 1991). What is interesting about the book is that some of the essays included in it speak against its central approach. Thus, for instance, the essay on Germany contributed by Christopher Allen shows that Keynesianism was unimportant to the German post-war macroeconomic management environment, except for certain short and rather unusual periods (for example, at times during the Grand Coalition, particularly between 1969 and 1972). Even then however, a heavily qualified Keynesianism operated (Allen, 1989, pp. 277–8).

It was remarked above that the way Hall approaches the problem in *The Political Power of Economic Ideas* is surprising. The reason for this surprise is because of the way he had set up the analysis of European economic management in his previous well-known book, *Governing the Economy* (Hall, 1986). In that book, dealing mainly with a comparison between the United Kingdom and France – though with Germany introduced at times for added contrast – it was the diversity of institutional conditions that was concentrated upon from the outset, and which consistently drove the analysis that followed in the book (Thompson, 1987c).

If we are to take diversity seriously and look to differences as being as important as similarities, if not more so, then a reformulation of the history of the managed economy in European countries becomes necessary. Even noting the institutional differences and proceeding along these lines may not be enough. Rather, a thorough exploration of those politico-economic configurations which might be termed 'Monnetism' for France and 'Eucken/Erhardism' for Germany, remains the central problem (Tomlinson, 1991). These might then be contrasted to a 'liberal Keynesianism' for the UK and a 'consensus Keynesianism' for Scandinavia.

MONNETISM

To sketch what Monnetism means is not that difficult. Between 1946 and 1952 Jean Monnet was the High Commissioner of the French reconstruction plan – The Plan for Modernization and Re-equipment. Subsequently, from 1952 and 1955, he became President of the High Authority of the European Coal and Steel Community. In 1956 he founded the Action Committee for the United States of Europe (Mayne, 1972). The Monnet Plan acted as the precursor of the ECSC, placing particular emphasis on the reconstruction of French (and by implication German) steel and coal output. As discussed in Chapter 2, the ECSC was the first post-Second World War trans-European economic management organization and is generally credited with providing a model for the founding of the EEC in 1957 by the Treaty of Rome.

One well-known consequence of the Monnet Plan was the setting up of the *Commissariat Général au Plan* in 1947, along with the lesser known *Commissariat Général à la Productivité*. These two organizations encompassed that characteristic French suspicion of the ability of industry to modernize itself and the vision of the state as industrial guardian (*Etat tutelaire*).

The various plans initiated by the *Commissariat Général* embodied what came to be known as 'indicative planning' – a pervasive feature of French economic regulation until this planning mechanism went into decline after 1965 (Estrin and Holmes, 1983).[4] Though a number of important and innovatory developments in the planning mechanism took place during the late 1960s and through the 1970s, the Plan began to lose its significance within the overall panoply of macroeconomic regulation. Large-scale econometric models were developed, and economic policy was increasingly centralized within the Ministry of Finance. The Finance Ministry promoted budgetary policy as against indicative planning, and the Plan lost its organizational function in economic development. There is also some question over the effectiveness of indicative planning, even during the height of its influence (Hall, 1986).

Formal planning in France flourished when the economy was growing and went into decline as sustained economic growth slowed in the 1970s. It also flourished in a period when the economy was relatively closed, but came under increasing pressure as the economy became more internationalized and open. Thus it may be that 'planning', or comprehensive macroeconomic governance/regulation of any kind, can only be sustained in periods when the 'costs' of these methods are relatively low. As the costs of trying to move against the grain of the market rise, so comprehensive 'planning' goes into a terminal decline. The socialist government after 1980 tried to rescue some notion of planning, but this was quickly undermined by the international constraints on the French economy and was rapidly abandoned.

Despite this, however, it is important to note that planning, and particularly intervention in industry, has retained both a strong symbolic significance as well as an operational significance in France. Nor were the econometric models introduced during the 1970s and the development of budgetary policy orthodoxly 'liberal Keynesian' in inspiration.[5]

An important adjunct to the economic indicative planning elements in Monnetism must be the political ideology of Gaullism (Chapter 2). Monnet was a personal ally of de Gaulle, and Gaullism served as a perfect complement to the *dirigiste* style of French economic management. Indeed it reinforced it, with its acute suspicion of anything Atlanticist and its promotion of French (and later European) 'national champions'. The promotion of such national champions was eagerly embraced by the socialist government that inherited the Gaullist mantle in the early 1980s.

These features have left a strong legacy on contemporary French economic management. One of the enigmas associated with this is exactly how to characterize the present state and structure of the French economy. The country's economy still remains heavily regulated at the industrial level (for example, the work of the *Agence Nationale pour la Valorisation de la Recherche* implemented through the *Fonds Industriel de Modernisation* (FIM) programme – see Salais, 1988; Storper and Salais, 1992). But there may be *many* French economies rather than a single one, operating within quite different models. An undynamic, low wage, but highly flexible rural industrialization of the 'new east' can be contrasted to the design-intensive and craft-based metalworking and mechanical sectors of the Rhône-Alpes region; to the large-scale, high-tech manufacturing and service centres of certain areas in the south (for example, around Toulouse); and in turn to the small-scale but high-tech, craft-based sectors in the Ile-de-France area around Paris. In general, France would seem to have a technologically competent, though not very specialized or dynamic, mix of industrial sectors and branches, which are heavily brokered by powerful national and local state political structures and organizations. Internal organization of production tends to be both hierarchical and closed (Storper, 1991).

To a large extent this characteristic history of French intervention in the economy, along with the present structure of French industry – despite the considerable variation it displays – can help account for the position France tends to adopt within negotiations on the future of trans-European economic management structures. Although Monnetism as such no longer remains the fulcrum around which economic policy is organized, the objectives it embodied still live on: an overriding concern with industrial modernization; the forging of a secure relationship between the French and German economies; a suspicion of anything tying French hands too closely with the USA; support for 'national (now European) champions', and a significant continued public ownership presence in the economy.

As far as labour market organization is concerned, it has been the French socialists who have stressed the importance of underpinning this with progressive and interventionary 'social' policies. The French system of labour relations is marked by a low level of trade union membership and a fragmented peak structure. As a result the socialists have attempted to compensate with a system of 'concertation without labour' at the national level; *implicitly* involving the labour movement via their own legislative programme and policies.

EUCKEN/ERHARDISM

Walter Eucken was the noted theorist of the Freiburg School of liberal economics in Germany which had a considerable influence on Ludwig Erhard. Erhard was the CDU Minister of Economics between 1949 and 1963, German Vice-Chancellor (1957–63) and subsequently Federal Chancellor from 1963 to 1966. Eucken/Erhardism is a summary term for that constellation of economic policies and Christian Democratic political ideals that is often termed the 'social market economy' (*Sozialemarktwirtshaft*). Descriptions of the social market economy in English abound, and it is not my intention to repeat another one here (see Peacock and Willgerodt, 1989a and 1989b, and the references cited therein). Geoffrey Pridham (1977) provides a comprehensive analysis in English of German Christian Democracy. Erhard's relationship to this configuration is discussed in Erhard (1958). Some preliminary analysis of this configuration has also been offered in the previous chapter.

Two different emphases can be discerned within *Sozialemarktwirtshaft*: its *ordo*-liberal wing and its *neo*-liberal wing (Allen, 1989, p. 282). The *ordo*-liberals stressed the organized nature of capitalism – they wanted an orderly market framework where it was the (limited) role of the state to provide a stable legal and social order (*Ordnungspolitik*), including adequate social security and infrastructure developments. The *neo*-liberals stressed an open international system in which the German economy as a whole should be the object of regulation, and where German exports were seen as the engine of economic growth. Competition was favoured, but only operating within the bounds of acceptable cooperation. Both wings emphasized monetary orthodoxy and a strong politically independent central bank. This would ensure a stable money supply, thereby making (interventionary) anti-cyclical policy unnecessary (see Chapter 5).

Exactly how important the ideas associated with the Christian Democratic-social market economy have been to the *actual* development of the German economy remains an open and heavily debated question, particularly in the context of the early reconstruction and the first two decades of post-war 'super-growth' (*Wirtschaftswunder*) (Abelshauser, 1982; Dumke, 1990). But a number of genuine achievements and legacies of the 'supply-side' aspects of this management style can be elaborated which are less controversial.

In the first place the importance placed upon exporting has driven the characteristic German attachment to a relatively undervalued Deutschmark. Secondly, the independence of the central bank is generally credited with a major impact on the traditionally low levels of German inflation (though see Chapter 5 for some caveats to an exclusive emphasis on this aspect). Thirdly, and perhaps most importantly in the context of this chapter, the emphasis on social order and consensus has led to the careful construction of institutional mechanisms to foster these. This has resulted in a remarkably resilient package of labour market measures which has been particularly conducive to relatively successful industrial relations and wage restraint.[6] The measures have also resulted in active labour market policies, particularly in terms of training, something admired and envied in much of the rest of Europe.

Of course not all of these effects are the direct result of government policy. Some are as much the result of autonomous activity by private agents and corporate bodies (the organizational structure of the trade unions, the role of the commercial banks, the effectiveness of German productive 'technik'). But the broad objective of consulting and negotiating with the 'social partners' to reach agreement, aligned with a vigorous defence of industrial interests, but a hesitancy in becoming too directly involved with industrial ownership or restructuring, provides a different model of economic management to either Monnetism or liberal Keynesianism. Even during those brief periods when German governments flirted more seriously with Keynesian policies – the Grand Coalition (1966–1969), and the centre-left governments under Willy Brandt (1969–1974) and (to an even lesser extent) Helmut Schmidt (1974–1982) – *Konzertierteaktion* (tripartite discussion of a 'Keynesian form') remained the order of the day.

A number of authors working in the mainstream English-speaking tradition have now recognized the importance of these kinds of neo-corporatist social, political and economic institutional factors for the successful conduct of economic management, adjustment and growth under contemporary conditions (Calmfors and Driffill, 1988; Carlin and Soskice, 1989; Layard, Nickell and Jackman, 1991; Soskice, 1991; Tolliday and Zeitlin, 1991). Comparative economic performance is markedly better where neo-corporatist institutional arrangements prevail. These crucial points, about the labour market in particular, are raised again and analysed at much greater length in Chapter 5, while Chapter 6 deals with their implications for the operation of capital markets.

But it is important to recognize that the success of the German economy is not just because of its labour market characteristics, central though they may be to a sensible wage determination regime. The industrial structure also contributes significantly to this success. Again, the German economy may be best viewed as a number of economies, but not so markedly as in the French case. Germany is still driven by large-scale oligopolistic firms, however these may be under a current process of transformation.[7] These oligopolistically organized firms have traditionally relied upon a wide range of small and medium-sized subcontracting and supplier firms, which according to some sources are forming new industrial districts and regionally-based economies within Germany (Sabel, 1989, Sabel *et al.* 1990). However, the craft sector in Germany does not seem that dynamic and nor is there a strong growth of small firms (Weimer, 1990). Obviously, this picture is being complicated by the absorption of the old German Democratic Republic *Länder* into post-1990 Germany proper, something discussed in detail in Chapter 7.

Although one would need to be cautious, these typical experiences and styles of economic management were again important in explaining the particular position Germany adopted within the debates about the European-wide economic management structures that arose again in the 1980s. The well-known German insistence on a stable European currency and the importance it attaches to a politically neutral European Central Bank are obvious cases in point (Chapter 5). But Germany has also been at the forefront of arguments for a consensual politico-economic order at the European level, where the interests of the European 'social partners' are properly represented. How far this might be achievable in the near future is discussed later in this chapter, and the prospects for the longer term in Chapters 6 and 8.

'LIBERAL KEYNESIANISM' AND 'CONSENSUS KEYNESIANISM'

In this section we discuss liberal Keynesianism and consensus Keynesianism together, since these are probably the most well-recognized management configurations. Liberal Keynesianism involves the usual emphasis on budgetary policy and demand management, with the dominant objective to maintain full employment, but set firmly within an ideological commitment to the overriding virtues of the market mechanism. The classic examples of this management complex were to be found in the USA and the UK during much of the post-war period, though up until the mid-1970s the commitment to the market remained strong but rather implicit in these countries. The Keynesianism that operated, while attempting to manage the market, was always subservient to its dictates. Set within the long-boom period, it cost little to maintain full employment, something akin to the position in France with respect to industrial intervention.

As Matthews (1968) and Tomlinson (1981) have both persuasively argued in the case of the UK, the 'long boom' was mainly fuelled by private investment and the growth of international trade, not by the budgetary interventions on the part of government. These were predominantly *de*flationary in the period to the mid-1970s . According to Tomlinson's (1981) analysis, even the full adoption of a Keynesian policy within the UK must be treated with caution. This is certainly so if it is the acceptance of Keynesian policy *ideas* that is seen as the main constraint on the formulation of policy. Fundamentally, the 'long boom' was not initiated or 'managed' by governments, but was an effect of the decisions made by private economic agents with

respect to their assessment of market-driven opportunities. Thus the
Keynesianism operating here was a *liberal* Keynesianism. This is not to say
that government activity was totally unimportant. It operated at times to
smooth out the short-term business cycle in the interests of full employment.
But if and when this policy package came up against the full rigours of the
market, the policy package collapsed. Such was the case in times of balance-
of-payments/exchange rate crises, as well, of course, as when the 'long
boom' finally came to an end in the early 1970s.

An important adjunct to the liberal Keynesian policy package has been the
inability of the economies involved to establish effective and robust supply-
side industrial policy interventionary mechanisms. Even nationalizations
were only tentatively secured and were the subject of intense political struggle. Those institutional mechanisms that were explicitly formed to conduct
industrial policy broadly conceived, particularly as initiatives with respect to
identifying gaps in the productive cover and attempting to fill these with
publicly funded activities or which took training as their objective, were
never properly supported or secured and were easy to undermine quickly.

The political counterpart to the liberal Keynesian economic policy package, something that makes it a politico-economic configuration in the terms
used above, is a form of debased social-democratic conservatism. This seemingly contradictory ideology is just that, a combination of conservative and
social democratic sentiment that is almost unique to the UK centre-left and
centre-right political traditions. It is a tradition quite different to continental
Christian Democracy, and to that equally particular combination of neo-
liberalism and neo-conservatism that might be thought to have swept all
before it in the UK and the USA since the 1970s (more on this later).
Furthermore, liberal Keynesianism was never consensual in a deeply committed sense; it only accepted this as a contingent necessity.

Another contrast to liberal Keynesianism has been the consensual
Keynesianism of Sweden in particular, but which can also be found amongst
other Nordic countries and as an element in German/Austrian social democracy. The Swedish Social Democrats ruled the country almost uninterrupt-
edly from the 1930s to the 1970s (sometimes in coalition). Their
countercyclical fiscal policy was itself predicated upon an independently
established theoretical formulation that slightly pre-dated Keynes's own writings (the Stockholm School). Its post-war development in the context of the
Rehn Plan stressed a 'solidaristic' wages policy, an active manpower policy
and a set of other 'supply-side' measures to encourage investment (special
investment funds and taxation incentives) which were designed to both
maintain full employment and to encourage the modernization, competitiveness and flexibility of Swedish industry. Thus the Swedish model emphasized its own particular mix of demand and supply-side measures, set within

an overriding commitment to a solidaristic and consensual ideological style of policy-making. By and large this seemed to have worked and to have stood the test of time, at least up until the mid-1980s. The Swedish model also emphasized social policy measures to a greater extent than did the liberal Keynesian variant.

A COMPLETE TRANSITION IN THE 1970S AND 1980S?

The previous section gave only the briefest outlines of those politico-economic configurations that have been the most typical and important to the post-war European national economic management regimes. Most of that discussed above is well known. The point of it, however, is to stress the diversity of management traditions within the main European economic powers, set against a common presumed homogeneity articulated around the single term, Keynesianism.

But have these variable traditions now completely collapsed in the face of the rise of a new neo-liberal socio-economic order which, since the end of the post-war 'long boom' in the mid-1970s, has swept all before it? This is something that many have argued for strongly, and which even more have been tempted to agree with. But we need to sound a strong note of caution here.

First, it is necessary to define carefully that structure thought to have displaced the variable traditions analysed above. Elsewhere it has been suggested that this is far from homogeneous, even within the UK or the USA (Thompson, 1990). In particular, it involves an unstable but dynamic mix of (often contradictory) theoretical positions and policy prescriptions; economic neo-liberalism, monetarism, 'supply-side' economics, public choice propositions, political neo-conservatism, *laissez-faire* sentiments, and more besides. These cannot all be reduced to a single monolithic neo-liberalism. The 'New Right', for instance, is far from homogeneous.

Secondly, the conduct of economic policy is not just the result of a change in theoretical and policy ideas, as the above discussion of the advent of Keynesianism in its various guises has demonstrated. The embedded structure of institutional differences, politico-policy styles and contingent constraints is of equal, if not more, importance. For instance, the analysis by Fritz Scharpf (1991 – originally published in German in 1987) of the way the social democratic regimes in Austria, Great Britain, Sweden and the Federal Republic of Germany reacted to the economic recessions of the 1970s, shows that reaction was variable, and the subject of definite choices on the part of those involved. The outcome was also variable according to

Scharpf, although he does tend to over-homogenize the final resolution of this period of crisis in the form of an 'end to the Keynesian interlude'.

What Scharpf emphasizes in his richly textured analysis is the variable manner in which fiscal policy, monetary policy and wages policy were coordinated within the economies he deals with. This follows a broadly institutionally specific approach, where it is the ability to manage the evolving policy trade-offs that have to be made in an era of heightened economic tension that turns out to be crucial. In particular the relationship between wages policy and the other two areas is the key, he suggests, to the maintenance of some continued semblance of social democratic purchase on the policy programme. As the ability to manage this conflict was either internally eroded by the dynamic of domestic politics, or by the activity of international forces and constraints, or by some combination of them both (see Chapter 1's formal analysis of the relationship between internal and external policy mixes), so social democracy as traditionally understood in those countries, itself went into decline (the 'win set' for social democracy collapsed).

The lesson to be learned from this type of analysis is that institutional variability counts. And in as much as it is 'structurally' embedded, it is very difficult to shift. A good deal of 'superficial' changes in policy objectives, instruments of regulation and styles of policy-making can be accommodated within such embedded structures. Like a lot of other things in life, economic policy is fashion-driven to a certain, if not large, extent. It can come and go in a cyclical manner. This is not to argue that things have remained unchanged since the mid-1970s in European economic management regimes, only to register once again a scepticism. It is to emphasize that not necessarily *everything* has changed. Deep continuities in attitude and structure may be more important than remarkable transformations .

Finally, given that there remain the differences outlined above, and that these country-specific approaches to economic management in a broad sense have been introduced into the contemporary arguments about the evolving European-wide management mechanisms, there is no need to assume that the *least* effective of these sentiments will *necessarily* win out in the current negotiations. The possible implications of this kind of an argument are taken up in a moment.

It is clear that the peculiarly Anglo-American variant of neo-liberalism took hold earlier in the UK than in the other countries of Europe. Indeed, for all practical intents and purposes, Keynesianism in whatever form no longer has credibility in the UK policy context. But a number of the other features of what was above termed the liberal Keynesian configuration continue to exist in the UK, notably the ever-present celebration of the market mechanism. But the new conservatism in the UK does not just comprise an uncritical commitment to the market. To start with its 'neo-liberalism' is articulated with a new 'neo-conservatism' that is quite hostile to the 'full rigours of the market' when and where this latter threatens other more important shibboleths of conservatism. 'Sovereignty' is a case in point; the national integrity of the UK, and with it what is seen as an organic relationship between the citizen, *his* property (and it is a deliberately masculine form here) and the 'national soil', comprises a powerful motif for the new neo-conservatives in the UK (Scruton, 1984).[8] No doubt similar instances could be given for other European states, and the recent rise of the *Front Nationale* in France and the right wing Republican Party in Germany point to the threats posed for serious European economic integration if a more nationalistic political environment matures towards the later part of this decade. Again we leave a more thorough analysis of this possibility to Chapter 8.

But interestingly, the neo-liberal embrace in the UK – which has celebrated deregulation, liberalization and competition with an intensity seen in few other countries – has rather contradictorily led to new forms of extensive economic *re-regulation* (Thompson, 1990; see also Majone, 1989). Significant parts of the financial system, and all the denationalized public utility companies, have been subject to substantial re-regulation during the period of conservative rule. Thus even the UK 'neo-liberal conservatives' are not necessarily adverse to intervention. The doctrine of monetarism also involves a new form of control – control of the money supply – which, if taken seriously as a management technique, would lead to new forms of interventionary regulation (Chapter 5).

There is little doubt that since the mid-1970s a broad advance of deregulatory, pro-competition and less interventionary policy sentiment has strongly appeared in the other countries of Europe discussed above. But once again, the advance of this has not been consistent and it has taken very variable nationally specific forms. Even the very recent demise of the social democrats in Sweden has not yet heralded the complete dismantling of either the welfare state or the basics of the traditional Swedish approach to industrial support (though it may lead to this in the longer run, of course).

ENTER THE EUROPEAN COMMISSION

Bearing these points in mind, we can now go on to assess the emerging European-wide economic management structures. There is little doubt that the European Commission has taken the initiative here – a political initiative in the first instance – to re-energize the European integrationist bandwagon (see Chapter 2). The signing of the Single European Act in 1986 and the

Delors Report of 1989 marked the beginning of the present offensive. Both of these embody definite neo-liberal credentials.

The single market programme is designed to proceed along explicit pro-competitive lines. As mentioned in the previous chapter, the dominant metaphor under which this policy package is being pursued is a *purgative* one (Grahl and Teague, 1989, p. 40). The economic system is seen as one inhabited by obstacles and impurities which impede the full rigours of competition by barriers to trade, impediments to efficient size operation, and obstacles to full market competition. The implication is that once these 'inefficiencies' are eliminated or cleared away, the system will *automatically* generate the benefits.

As analysed in greater detail in Chapter 4, the Commission's document, *The Economics of 1992* illustrates this approach perfectly (European Commission, 1988). It is driven by the new trade theory, stressing an oligopolistic market structure and unrealized internal economies of scale. As the single market emerges with the sweeping away of non-tariff barriers to trade, transactions costs will be reduced and European firms will move down their long-run average cost curves to reap the latent economies of scale. In addition, the expansion of the market will increase beneficial competitive pressures, eliminating the least efficient firms, dynamizing the others, and leading to a virtuous growth of research and development expenditure, investment, new product innovation and output.

The Delors Report adopts much the same approach, but this time in the realm of money and finance (Committee for the Study of Economic and Monetary Union, 1989). This was mentioned in the previous chapter and is discussed at greater length in Chapter 5. The Delors Report is, above all, concerned with the control of the money supply and, in true monetarist style, via this with the control of inflation. Indeed, the control of inflation has become the single dominant objective during the present round of institution-building for European economic management. A politically independent central bank that will have as its main objective the control of European money supply and inflation looks likely as a result. Quite secondary to this are other legitimate economic policy objectives. In addition, as Chapter 5 emphasizes, it is not clear that *just* the establishment of an independent central bank and a sound money supply will be enough to control inflation at the European level.

In the subsequent Commission documents justifying economic integration – the successor documents to *The Economics of 1992* – the theme of the benefits from the proposals for economic and monetary union are developed. In *One Market, One Money* (European Commission, 1990a) and *The Economics of EMU* (European Commission, 1991), while the neo-liberal approach again dominates, it is the new growth theory that drives the analysis of the 'real' benefits to be derived from EMU. New growth theory stresses the endogeneity of technical progress along with the idea of external economies of scale. Again, a virtuous spiral of investment and growth emerges from EMU in this analysis. This suggests previous estimates of the benefits to be derived from the 'one-off' purgative programme embodied in the single market were severely underestimated.[9]

An interesting feature of these analyses emanating from the Commission is that they are uneasily combined with a continued plea for social solidarity, consensus and a bargaining between the 'social partners' (Chapters 2 and 5). This is shown in a concrete manner by Table 3.1, drawn from a Commission document dealing with the prospects for structural adjustments in the European Community. Note how under the heading of 'Prerequisites', 'competition' appears with 'economic and social cohesion'.

Table 3.1   The character of structural adjustments

Prerequisites	Catalysts	Accelerators
Competition	Internal market	Research,
Economic	Commercial policy	development,
context		technology,
Educational		innovation
level		Training
Economic		Small and
and social		medium-sized
cohesion		enterprises
Environmental		Business services
protection		

Source: 'European Industrial Policy for the 1990s', *Bulletin of the European Communities, Supplement 3/91*, Brussels, 1991, p. 23.

Thus while the strictly economic analysis stresses a very straightforward neo-liberal view of the benefits to be had from more competition, more deregulation, more liberalization and more individualized incentives – that is, from strictly market-driven operations that mirror the analysis of neo-classical economics – this is heavily qualified by a neo-corporatist desire for social cohesion, order and solidarity. And this latter position is not one that just pertains to the European 'industrial policy' or 'social dimension'; it pervades the Commission's general pronouncements about the economy as much as about social and industrial policy, broadly conceived.[10]

Thus there is a dilemma or schism – and possibly even a contradiction – between these two priorities. The driving analytical motif seems to be at odds with the desired politico-economic frameworking device. Indeed, it is the dynamic set up by the tension between these two overriding objectives that is propelling debates at the European level. And these are not unconnected to the history of the development of economic management techniques within the European countries, as discussed above. What is more, this schism is itself far more complex than indicated by the simple dichotomy indicated here. Each element within it has its own nuances and subtleties, again as indicated above. The different traditions and experiences live on within the present conjuncture. Exactly how these tensions will be resolved – whether they threaten an explosion or an accommodation – will be decided by the concrete negotiations now proceeding at the European level, something we take up again in the concluding chapter. But, to summarize the contours of this negotiation at this stage, there is a clear neo-liberal programme at stake, but one that itself involves a number of variants; the new UK (or Anglo-American) neo-liberals are not to be totally confused with their older German counterparts for instance. In addition, there is a clear neo-corporatist programme involved which, again, is not a homogeneous one. The German neo-corporatist tradition, that to be found in the Scandinavian countries and in Austria, and even elements of the French approach, all present slightly different agendas. Furthermore, the continued French commitment to a more explicitly interventionist outcome at the European level can be found in the so-called 'Cresson clauses' attached to the Treaty on Economic and Monetary Union (the Maastricht Treaty – HMSO, 1992) supporting a European industrial policy. The next section is designed to highlight some additional features and consequences of the debate initiated by these programmes and approaches.

MANAGING THE NEW EUROPEAN ECONOMY

What are the prospects for a progressive management of the European economy as the current institutional reform and development takes place amongst the existing 12 members of the EC? This section tries to lay out a number of features of such an analysis in a preliminary way. For the most part, it avoids those areas dealt with at length by conventional analysis; in particular the likely form of monetary management. This aspect is explicitly addressed in Chapter 5. Clearly, the relationship between monetary policy and fiscal policy is going to be at the heart of the European management debate, and this relationship is equally likely to be shaped in conventional terms. In as much as this element in the debate cannot be avoided, the analysis presented here tries to raise some additional neglected aspects, as well as those which are particularly relevant to issues of the 'neo-corporatism versus neo-liberalism' dilemma pointed to above. However, the points made below are not meant to be comprehensive.

Taking fiscal policy first, the emergent orthodoxy is that monetary policy should take precedence and that fiscal policy should occupy a secondary and supportive role (for example, Meade, 1991, amongst a vast range of other similar analyses). But Begg (1990) points to the need to 'decouple' fiscal policy from monetary policy. Indeed, this would seem a sensible position given (a) the way fiscal policy would otherwise be tethered to a very conventional monetary orthodoxy (constrained to support the fight against inflation as the *only* objective along with an inability to finance any independent public sector fiscal initiatives); and (b) the extreme unlikelihood that fiscal policy can be coordinated at the European level under present conditions (Boltho, 1990).

For a proper coordination of fiscal policies the need is for a true fiscal federalism at the European level. This is where tax revenues can be raised by local, state and the federal (national) government, with the states redistributing a part of their revenues to the localities, and the federal authorities doing the same to the states. The rationale for this is the existence of externalities between areas – the external benefits of expenditures extend across jurisdictions. It also acts as an insurance policy, redistributions occurring from regions or jurisdictions with permanent or temporary higher incomes to those with lower ones. These adjustments are important for a monetary union, since the possibility of devaluations to adjust for differences in the income/competitiveness of different regions or jurisdictions is ruled out under these circumstances. In the late 1980s in the USA, the states were receiving over 20 per cent of the revenue for their expenditures from the federal government, and the local authorities some 34 per cent of their revenue for expenditure from state and federal sources (Eichengreen, 1990, Table 7, p. 140). Taken together, tax and transfer adjustments in the USA were estimated to eliminate as much as 40 per cent of the decline in regional incomes consequent upon region-specific demand shock effects.

The difficulty for the EC is the low levels of inter-governmental fiscal transfers. The Community budget rarely exceeds 1 per cent of EC GDP. Important redistributive vehicles such as the regional fund receive less than 10 per cent of this budget, and a significant share of its expenditure goes to projects in the high income countries. Agricultural price support traditionally gets 60 per cent of the budget, and this is not particularly redistributive. The Social Fund (designed to aid labour market adjustment problems brought about because of integration) remains very underdeveloped. In addition, the EC's existing tax-revenue base (mainly VAT, customs duties and agricultural levies) is not particularly 'stabilization sensitive' in a redistributive sense (Eichengreen, 1990, p. 142).

The question all this poses is whether the post-Maastricht economic and monetary union will inaugurate a development of the EC budget, and whether in the long run political developments will lead to a federal European state. In fact, the Maastricht Treaty is much more concerned with limiting the fiscal powers of individual governments than it is with dealing with an enhanced Community budget (see Chapter 5). The fiscal powers of the Community as a whole are largely ignored in the Treaty. As far as the idea of Europe becoming a federal state is concerned, it is argued in the final chapter that this is very unlikely.

But maybe these points do not matter that much. There are, within a monetary union, other mechanisms that can bring about adjustments between regions or countries. With the absence of any capital controls, capital flows can quickly and easily flow into countries or regions to alleviate temporary difficulties caused by a loss of their competitiveness or a fall in their demand. A permanent loss of these features will eventually call for wage and spending adjustments to restore an export and import equilibrium but, again, these will be easier to accomplish as factor markets integrate and mobility increases, it is argued. Quite whether these 'automatic' adjustments will work in such a smooth manner is in doubt, however, when one looks at the permanent regional income differences that exist within long-established currency unions and unitary nation states.

However, in many ways the move towards monetary union could enhance the 'independence' of fiscal policy for the EC nations separately. During the 1970s and 1980s it became difficult to argue for the independence of fiscal policy from monetary policy on an individual nation-by-nation basis (as the French found to their cost after 1980). But with the European Community as a whole increasingly taking responsibility for the monetary policy of its individual members (which will involve interest rate, money supply and exchange rate policies), to a certain extent this unlocks the relationship between monetary and fiscal policy. As monetary policy is organized and conducted from the centre, individual countries could be given some greater flexibility in the conduct of their own fiscal policies. Indeed, this may be an absolute necessity to cope with any internal or external shocks that have a differential impact on the countries of the Community. While the countries or regions of Europe remain differentiated in terms of their economic structure and their ability to cope with systemic shocks, the case for fiscal flexibility remains.

Clearly, against this assessment is the requirement under existing European statutes to harmonize certain tax rates (VAT and indirect taxes on expenditure, for instance). But the Commission is only pressing for the introduction of minimum tax rates, allowing for the possibility of variation above these and for a more general 'fiscal competition' between Community governments (which may have negative destabilizing effects, however). In addition, there are the Maastricht convergence guidelines on fiscal deficits (3 per cent of GDP) and government debt ratios (60 per cent of GDP) which are to be met before economic union in the late 1990s. As is argued in Chapter 5, however, these may turn out to be no more than 'aspirations' and be more flexible in practice. No doubt pressures could grow for a tighter interpretation of these agreed rules and for further tax harmonization, particularly if the orthodox monetary and fiscal policy marriage-makers have their way. But this is not inevitable. Thus, for instance, it might be worth thinking about imaginative ways for conducting a more independent set of taxation policies.

As the European economy becomes slowly more integrated, economic factors will be able to move across Europe with increasing ease. But not all the elements in a possible tax base are necessarily mobile. There are, rather, degrees of mobility. Capital is probably the most mobile factor, and will become increasingly so as European capital and money markets integrate further. Thus profits and savings will become more difficult for individual governments to tax effectively. If we look at expenditure, then where people will conduct their purchases could again be influenced by the tax regime in place. But will people be either prepared to or able to travel long distances to conduct all their purchases? Thus there may be more scope for differential consumption taxes. As far as taxes on personal incomes are concerned, this depends crucially on how extensive and how quickly the labour market integrates. It is the better-off professionals who will probably be the most mobile in the European context. But a lot of work overseas for this group tends to be temporary, as it does for any overseas skilled and unskilled jobs. The majority of indigenous European workers will continue to be relatively immobile in job terms, if nothing else, for cultural and language reasons. Country income tax differentials could still be effective, therefore. Finally, the least mobile 'factor' of all is probably property. Thus there could be scope for some imaginative tax initiatives with respect to this element within a tax base. This could become increasingly attractive as a source of tax revenue for governments.

In general it is worth pressing for considerable individual country autonomy in the conduct of fiscal policy. This would allow for a diversity of policy preferences. It would also give flexibility with respect to the pursuit of economic policy objectives other than the single-minded concern with the control of inflation. The case of employment is an obvious one, but this can be extended to independent public sector investment and other expenditure initiatives such as industrial policy (Chapter 6).

The case of Italy is an instructive one. While it might not be appropriate to support every aspect of Italian economic management over the last 20 years, that country has been surprisingly successful in terms of its real economic performance. The recession of the mid-1970s and early 1980s hardly affected the Italian growth rate, and the country built up a very robust manufacturing export sector. To a large extent this is the direct result of the buoyant internal demand within Italy, produced by the consistent budget deficits over the period, and one fostered by the active industrial policy Italy has been able to pursue because of this. Whatever its other undesirable effects (and one suspects these are exaggerated by conventional analysis), without a continued fiscal independence this kind of strategy would no longer be possible.

If we now turn to monetary policy proper, it is worth stressing what is likely to happen in the private financial sector if monetary union ever gets seriously under way. Orthodox economics is almost single mindedly focused upon the public domain and the character of the central bank (see Chapter 5). But how would the private banking sector react to EMU? One of the first things needed would be a European-wide private payments mechanism. Thus we might expect to see close liaisons, if not outright mergers, developing between banks in different countries. At a minimum this could involve something like the AMEX Bank combining with a large UK and German bank. Other banks would also be likely to develop close liaisons.[11] Thus the European banking sector could very rapidly become highly oligopolistically organized on a European-wide scale. This would pose acute problems for the supervision and regulation of such 'conglomerate banks', something the EC has largely ignored in the run-up to EMU (see Chapter 5).

The above remarks point to a more general issue of the role of competition policy within Europe. This is an area where the present infatuation with neo-liberalism is most prominently displayed. However, a number of careful analyses of the progress of European deregulation have pointed to the limits of this trend (for example, Montagnon, 1990; Woolcock *et al.*, 1991). Although the British have pressed this most consistently, and are continuing to do so, there is no reason to believe that the Germans and others will necessarily capitulate to that pressure. It is the German characteristic and continuing insistence on *Ordnungspolitik* – as indicated above, involving a clear and consistent regulatory framework, often anchored in statutes, within which market forces are allowed to operate – that sets the limits as to how far they are prepared to see deregulation go, according to the analyses mentioned above.

Of course, it is with respect to labour markets that the most obvious differences between the neo-liberal programme and the neo-corporatist one can be seen. At the European level the problem for the neo-corporatist model will be the mechanisms by which labour in particular can be represented within any future bargaining and negotiating institutions. Clearly, the interests of the employers and their organizations are less difficult to articulate; though whether they are either ready to cooperate or already have their own lobbying and representational bodies operating at the European level, still remains an open question. However, their interests certainly look more easy to construct.

On the other hand, the organizations of 'labour' and other interested parties (consumers, environmentalists, farmers) still only have a largely national brief, or do not as yet even exist as strong lobbying bodies. Thus bringing the 'social partners' together at a European level will prove extremely difficult, if not impossible, even as those countries such as Sweden which are used to this kind of activity enter the Community. The implications of this argument are developed further in the concluding chapter.

The absence of active labour market policies within the European Community could spell disaster. It was pointed out above how the crucial importance of such policies for effective economic performance was now beginning to be widely recognized (see also Chapter 5). But this could become even more acute in the future. The European Community is an attractive destination for economic migrants. It has a more or less 'open' eastern and southern border. The effect of major migration moves into Europe could be to push down the average price and quality of labour. Without some European-wide policy to put a floor under both the price of labour and working conditions more generally, the European economy could be tempted down a low wage, low value-added, low productivity route (Chapter 7). Clearly, private businesses and some governments saturated by neo-liberal ideology would welcome this outcome. But what might be good for business is not necessarily good for the economy. In as much as neo-classical economics stresses the benefits to be gained by a lower cost of labour for a given level of skill and productivity, it fails to address the *dynamic* tendencies set up by such developments. Institutional reform that provides a proper European-wide response to both migration and working conditions becomes an absolute necessity under these circumstances. The fact that the UK government opted out of these types of arrangements at the Maastricht Summit indicates where it sees the development for this particular economy.

Finally, we can point to the position of the evolving European economy in the context of managing the global economy.[12] As EMU gathers pace the European economy will emerge as a major player in its own right. If the growth estimates of the Commission are to be believed it will become a very attractive destination for inward investment. On the Commission's estimates it will also encourage a vast increase in international trade between the EC and the rest of the world. Generally, with such a large and new player on the international financial stage, with the Commission's intention of a solid, low risk, inflation-free currency, there is likely to be a major increase in demand for ECU-denominated assets. This will have the long-run tendency of pushing the exchange rate of the ECU upwards, particularly if at the same time the USA and Japan were seen to be weakened by these developments. What is more, this might happen at just the time there was added interest in making real direct investment in Europe to take advantage of developments associated with the single market. This would also add to the demand for ECUs.

If these possibilities are not properly foreseen or managed correctly if they do arise, a progressive overvaluation of the ECU and a concomitant loss of European international competitiveness could arise. Such was the position of the US dollar for much of the post-war period up until the late 1960s, with the subsequent well-known consequences for the US economy. But a further possibility is that the increased demand for ECU assets could produce domestic (European) inflation as the money supply expands to accommodate the increase in ECU demand. If the ECU interest rate were raised to try to control this situation, the European economy could be further disadvantaged. These possibilities must be avoided at all costs for the European ECU.

What this analysis reveals is the crucial importance of the management of the global economy for the future of Europe and the other major evolving trading blocs. The possibilities of coordinating economic activity between the three big trading blocs – Europe, the USA/North America and Japan – can be illustrated with reference to the data shown in Figures 3.1 and 3.2 (see also Hirst and Thompson, 1992). I use this for illustrative purposes only, since the actual situation in the late 1990s is unlikely to match exactly the one shown here, but it indicates the possibilities in the run-up to full economic union.

Figure 3.1 shows the proportion of trade to GDP for the three blocs in 1990. Although *individual* members of the EC traded an average of 46.2 per cent of their GDP externally (mostly with other EC countries), the Community as a whole only traded 18.6 per cent of its combined GDP with the outside world. This is a very similar proportion to both the USA and Japan. Thus each bloc is similarly committed to outside trade which, indeed, is still quite modest in extent.

Figure 3.2 shows a measure of international capital flows between the three blocs between 1960 and 1990. The relationship between national savings and investment for the three combined is very close, though it fluctuates widely over the entire period. When disaggregated according to bloc, however, the differences emerge. The EC is in rough balance between savings and investment. Since the early 1980s the USA has shown a divergence,

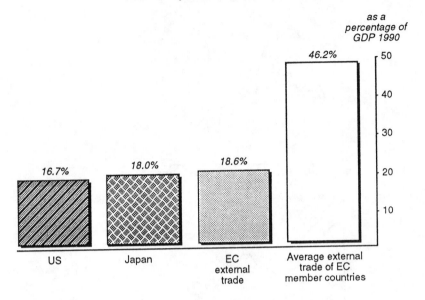

Source: OECD.

Figure 3.1   The structure of trade: EC, USA and Japan, 1990

where investment is much higher than savings. This position was caused by the emergence of the (linked) 'twin deficits' in the USA, one on the balance of trade and the other on the government's budget. Investment to finance these imbalances had to be attracted from abroad. Clearly, it mainly came from Japan (though some of it came from the EC in the mid-1980s). Japan is in the exact opposite position to the USA, with higher savings than investment ratios. Overall, then, there is a certain symmetry between the 'Big 3' on these measures, even though the graphs show significant fluctuations in the overall levels of GDP devoted to investment and savings.

The point about Figures 3.1 and 3.2 is that they show how integrated the three blocs have become in the case of investment and savings ratios, and how similar they are in terms of overseas trade. Thus the three blocs almost 'need' each other. If they do not quite have incentives to manage actively the economic relationships between themselves, at least they do not have incentives to take a totally 'go it alone' strategy.

Perhaps, then, these underlying symmetries might make the coordination and management of the global economy *easier* as Europe itself coordinates further during the 1990s. With the European economy emerging as a single managed entity in relation to the USA and Japan, and the symmetries out-

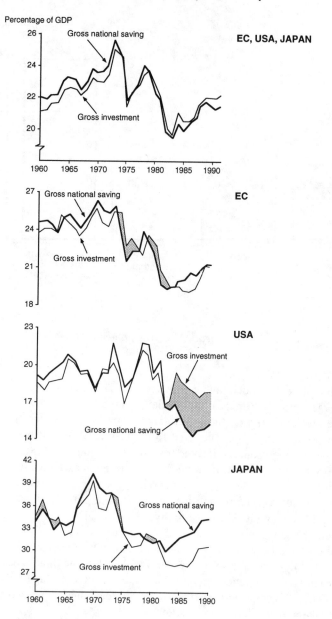

Source: Commission services.

Figure 3.2   *The evolution of savings and investments in the EC, USA and Japan, 1960–90*

lined above in place, there is an added incentive to coordinate between the three parties themselves. They are caught in a relationship from which it would be dangerous for any party to withdraw unilaterally. In addition, gaining agreement between just three players is likely to be easier than between the existing G-5, or G-7 players. The move to EMU, if it does indeed occur, could help secure this beneficial result.

CONCLUSION

There is always going to be a place for the management of the 'domestic' economy in advanced industrialized countries. Governments will not totally abandon their responsibilities in this respect, however rhetorically committed they may become towards market forces, or however internationally integrated their economies might appear. In the case of the EC, a new domestic management arena is being constructed. This combines a complicated and complex amalgam of nationally specific management traditions, experiences, historical conditions, theoretical commitments and institutional arrangements, alongside of which is developing a set of EC-wide institutions and practices.

The main axis around which this amalgam is evolving within the EC is the neo-corporatist and neo-liberal one. Quite how the dynamic set-up between these two programmes will turn out is unclear. But it can be said with some certainty that neither of the two will emerge totally intact or without serious modification of their form or function. Further discussion of this vital issue for the future of Europe is reserved for the final chapter.

NOTES

1. This point is discussed at length in Thompson (1990).
2. Gordon (1988) poses the issue of structural change, and challenges it in the context of the global economy.
3. This wider issue is analysed in detail in Hirst and Thompson (1992).
4. Pierre Massé, the successor to Monnet as *Commissaire* at the CGP between 1959 and 1966 is generally credited with initiating 'indicative planning'.
5. The econometric models tended to emphasize input–output techniques, for instance, while the Finance Ministry emphasized budgetary orthodoxy and financial control. The interpretation here is thus quite different to that of Rosanvallon (1989), who sees a triumph of Keynesianism after the Second World War in France (pp. 183–93).
6. Many commentators prematurely prophesized the demise of this system as Germany experienced its bitterest public sector union-led strikes for 18 years in April and May 1992. But it must be remembered that there had not been such strikes for nearly 20 years, and they were predicated on a unique set of circumstances that seem to be temporary in nature. These points are elaborated further in Chapter 7.
7. There is some dispute as to whether large German firms are 'horizontally and vertically

disintegrating'; see Sabel *et al.* (1990) for a positive argument to this effect. The analysis of Weimer (1990) would seem to lead to a more sceptical assessment.

8.   Scruton gives the most philosophically sophisticated analysis of neo-conservatism. This is elaborated in the journal *Salisbury Review,* which carries some economic analysis from this position. Perhaps the best known politicians to espouse these views are Nicholas Ridley and Norman Tebbit, but Margaret Thatcher has also been an exponent of them at times.

9.   The role of *internal* economies of scale and new trade theory in justifying European integration is assessed in Thompson (1991a). The way the Commission switched from stressing internal to *external* economies of scale and the new growth theory is reviewed in Thompson (1991b). As mentioned in the main text, all this is discussed in great detail in Chapters 4 and 5 of this book.

10.   For instance, see 'Annual Economic Report, 1990–91', p. 22, *European Economy,* **46** (December 1990); 'Intergovernmental Conferences: Contributions by the Commission' (pp. 132–4), *Bulletin of the European Communities,* Supplement 2/1991; 'European Industrial Policy for the 1990s' (pp. 22–3), *Bulletin of the European Communities,* Supplement 3/1991.

11.   Perhaps it is French theorists who have thought through the likely effects of EMU in the most interesting way. While not directly addressing the issue of EMU in its contemporary form, Jacques Riboud (1991) sees the necessity of private agents to combine in the face of an emergent European currency. His particular concern is to construct a constant-value financial asset that could act as a basis for the *private* issue of Euro-money. Thus although directed by a typical neo-liberal/semi-monetarist shibboleth, the analysis has the merit of posing the issue of private financial agent behaviour.

12.   Some of the issues discussed in the following sections are broached in European Commission (1990a).

4. Justifying European Economic Integration

INTRODUCTION

In December 1985 the Single European Act launched the European Community on its drive to create a genuine single market by the end of 1992 via the elimination of non-tariff barriers to intra-Community trade (Commission of the European Communities, 1985). Subsequently, the EC went on to initiate even closer economic ties when it agreed moves towards full economic and monetary union at the Maastricht Summit in October 1991. This programme is scheduled to be completed by the end of 1999.

This chapter examines the way each of these policy initiatives has been justified. In particular it concentrates upon how the notion of economies of scale (EOS) has been used to provide one of the main economic arguments for the twin policy programmes. The idea of economies of scale has a long and distinguished history in the field of applied economics and with respect to policy analysis. An interesting feature of the policy programmes explored here is the central importance attributed to economies of scale in measuring the expected gains from the moves towards freer trade and economic union. As we shall see in a moment, however, an important change in the notion of economies of scale applied in each case.

The process of EC economic union has tended to concentrate upon the monetary and financial side of economic activity; this is analysed in Chapter 5. This chapter explores the real side of the economy, and particularly how the European Commission set about officially justifying further economic integration in terms of its growth effects. The original *Economics of 1992* programme, as presented in the Cecchini Report, stressed the notion of *internal* economies of scale (IEOS) set within new trade theory models (European Commission, 1988). Later analyses, notably those associated with the *One Market, One Money* document and monetary union, switched attention to the role of *external* economies of scale (EEOS) set within the context of new growth model theories (European Commission, 1990; European Commission, 1991a). In addition, the Commission has emphasized the long-wave approach, arguing that the move towards ever-closer economic union in the late 1990s is likely to coincide with the emergence of a new long wave of economic restructuring associated with the widespread deployment of microprocessor technology (European Commission, 1990b). The next section provides a critical commentary on each of these approaches in turn.

Table 4.1 shows the estimated extent of economy of scale benefits for the 1992 single market programme. The central forecast of the Cecchini Report estimated a 5.3 per cent increase in GDP for the seven main Community members, 2.1 per cent of which was attributed to beneficial economy of scale effects, that is nearly 40 per cent of the total GDP gain. Clearly, in this

Table 4.1   Potential gains in economic welfare for the EC resulting from completion of the internal market

	% of GDP
Step 1 Gains from removal of barriers affecting trade	0.2–0.3
Step 2 Gains from removal of barriers affecting overall production Gains from removing barriers (subtotal)	2.0–2.4 2.2–2.7
Step 3 Gains from exploiting economies of scale more fully	2.1
Step 4 Gains from intensified competition reducing business inefficiencies and monopoly profits Gains from market integration (subtotal)	1.6 2.1*–3.7

Total
  for 7 member states at 1985 prices
  for 12 member states at 1988 prices
  mid-point of above
	4.3–6.4
	4.3–6.4
	5.3

Notes:
* This alternative estimate for the sum of steps 3 and 4 cannot be broken down between the two steps.

The ranges for certain lines represent the results of using alternative sources of information and methodologies. The seven member states (Germany, France, Italy, United Kingdom and Benelux) account for 88 per cent of the GDP of the EC-12. Extrapolation of the results in terms of the same share of GDP for the seven and twelve member states is not likely to overestimate the total for the EC-12. The detailed figures in Table 4.1 relate only to the seven member states because the underlying studies mainly covered those countries.

Source: Cecchini (1988), Table 9.2, p. 84. This is a summary table drawn from *European Economy*, no. 35, March 1988, 'The economics of 1992', Table 10.1.1, p. 157.

case IEOS are calculated to significantly generate the welfare benefits of the policy initiative.

The twin policy programmes thus serve to restimulate a debate about the extent of possible economies of scale, whether internal or external. They enable a broad investigation into the continued utility of the concept of economies of scale and its applicability as industrial organization moves away from traditional forms of mass production into a more 'flexibly specialized' production environment. In this case, it is not only possible economies of scope that must be taken into account, but whether the nature of industrial organization is changing so radically that both scale and scope economies offer little explanatory power in understanding current developments.

In the next section some necessary background analysis is presented. This is followed by an analytical section that discusses exactly how the EOS benefits were calculated and the assumptions lying behind them. The arguments advanced against the extent of these benefits are reviewed subsequently, and this is followed by a final main section which raises the issue of wider utility of scale and scope economies. The arguments of the chapter are summed up in the Conclusion.

MODELLING THE GAINS FROM ECONOMIES OF SCALE

The key document in the Commission's assessment of the 'Costs of Non-Europe' programme was the survey of EOS carried out by Pratten (1988). This provided the basic information used in the Commission's other background papers dealing with EOS (Helg and Ranci, 1988; Smith and Venables, 1988 – though not in Schwalbach, 1988) and for its final 'Costs of Non-Europe' project (Commission of the European Communities, 1988; Cecchini, 1988).

Pratten conducted a wide-ranging survey of the evidence for the existence of EOS in mostly manufacturing industries. He is careful to distinguish the various different senses of economies of scale, though he does not have much to say about economies of scope. The main focus of the survey is on plant and firm economies, using engineering study data. There is no econometric cost analysis or any other original analysis in the survey, so the Commission had to rely on others' work and on rather old data. Many of the studies Pratten refers to were completed in the 1960s. Also, there is a reliance on United Kingdom and, to a lesser extent, North American data, with few continental studies.[1] The possibility of diseconomies of scale is raised, particularly with respect to management, but these are dismissed as

Table 4.2   Branches of manufacturing industry ranked by size of economies of scale

NACE code	Branch	Cost gradient at half METS[1] (%)	Remarks
35	Motor vehicles	6–9	Very substantial EOS[2] in production and in development costs
36	Other means of transport	8–20	Variable EOS: small for cycles and shipbuilding (although economies are possible through series production level), very substantial in aircraft (development costs)
25	Chemical industry	2.5–15	Substantial EOS in production processes. In some segments of the industry (pharmaceutical products), R&D is an important source of EOS
26	Man-made fibres	5–10	Substantial EOS in general
22	Metals	>6	Substantial EOS in general for production processes, also possible in production and series production
33	Office machinery	3–6	Substantial EOS at product level
32	Mechanical engineering	3–10	Limited EOS at firm level, but substantial production
34	Electrical engineering	5–15	Substantial EOS at product level and for development costs
37	Instrument engineering	5–15	Substantial EOS at product level, via development costs
47	Paper, printing and publishing	8–36	Substantial EOS in paper mills and, in particular, printing (books)
24	Non-metallic mineral products	>6	Substantial EOS in cement and flat glass production processes; in other branches, optimum plant size is small compared with the optimum size for industry
31	Metal articles	5–10 (castings)	EOS are lower at plant level, but possible at production and series production level
48	Rubber and plastics	3–6	Moderate EOS in tyre manufacture, small EOS in factories making rubber and moulded plastic articles, but potential for EOS at product and series production level
41–42	Drink and tobacco	1–6	Moderate EOS in breweries, small EOS in cigarette factories; in marketing, EOS are considerable
41–42	Food	3.5–21	Principal source of EOS is the individual plant, EOS at marketing and distribution level
49	Other manufacturing	n.a.	Plant size is small in these branches, possible EOS from specialization and the length of production runs
43	Textile industry	10 (carpets)	EOS are more limited than in the other sectors, but possible economies from specialization and the length of production runs
46	Timber and wood	n.a.	No EOS for plants in these sectors; possible EOS from specialization and longer production runs
45	Footwear and clothing	1 (footwear)	Small EOS at plant level, but possible EOS from specialization and longer production runs
44	Leather and leather goods	n.a.	Small EOS

Notes:
[1]   Minimum efficient technical scale.
[2]   Economies of scale.

Source: *European Economy,* 'The Economics of 1992', March 1988, no. 35, Table 6.1.1, p. 109.

being of little likely consequence. Pratten concludes his careful but patchy survey thus:

> For reasons given in this report, estimates of the economies of scale are elusive and many of the estimates which are available are hedged around with qualifications. Nevertheless the evidence reported in this paper does support the hypothesis that economies of scale are a widespread feature of manufacturing industries and to a lesser extent of service trades (Pratten, 1988, pp. 149–50).

The estimates of the potential economies of scale drawn from this report that were used by the Commission are shown in Table 4.2. These data are aggregated into two-digit NACE industry levels from Pratten's three to four-digit technical engineering analysis. This accounts for the range of figures given for cost gradients – these being dependent on the precise product subsector within each branch category. The figures indicate the range of cost savings that would emerge if branch industries moved from output levels of 50 per cent of the minimum efficient technical scale (METS) to full METS output levels.

We can now go on to consider in a little more detail each of the studies that used these estimates. In doing this we also develop a critical assessment of them.

SPECIFIC COUNTRY ANALYSES

The recent history of Italy presents an interesting example of industrial development (Chapter 3). In their analysis of the reasons for the relative size of Italian plants, Helg and Ranci (1988) stick resolutely to the role of the size of the market, export performance and economies of scale in determining plant size. They use single equation cross-sectional econometric models to analyse 14 three-digit Italian industrial sectors (data average 1982–83) and generally conclude that market size and economies of scale are important in determining plant size. The implication is, then, that enhancing the market size after 1992 will have a positive effect on plant size and IEOS. However, the analysis is driven by the *assumption* of the importance of economies of scale:

> All the analysis relies on the assumption that plant/cost curves show increasing returns up to some minimum efficient scale, and constant returns afterwards (p. 20).

It is hardly surprising, therefore, that IEOS are found to be important in determining the results. It is the Pratten survey material which provides the basis for this crucial assumption.

A similar analysis was conducted to determine the reasons for the smaller relative size of West German and United Kingdom plants compared to those of the United States (Schwalbach, 1988). The problem in this case is to explain why plant sizes deviate from minimum efficient size (MES). A range of engineering-based studies was used to determine theoretical MES and the deviations of representative industry plants from it (Schwalbach, 1988, Table 3). It was found that actual plants were, on average, smaller than MES, particularly in Germany. In the Federal Republic, multi-plant operation is preferred. The United Kingdom, by contrast, showed higher plant concentration, and thus presumably operated nearer to the theoretical MES. This is perhaps why the cost gradient variable was highly *in*significant in the United Kingdom regression run, though it was not statistically significant in the German case either (Schwalbach, 1988, Table 4, p. 33). But all the regressions show very low levels of fit as well.

The implications of this analysis would seem to be that: (a) unexploited EOS are minimally important in explaining deviations of actual plant size from MES; and (b) even if they were important, United Kingdom industry would be more efficient than German industry because it was already working with larger plants and nearer to MES. This latter implication in particular is rather counter-intuitive, which perhaps should have led to a scepticism with respect to the analysis. But the results of this were incorporated into the Commission's final assessment, if only in a small way (CEC, 1988, p. 117, p. 183).

IEOS and Equilibrium Modelling

Smith and Venables (1988) incorporated the Pratten IEOS estimates into a partial equilibrium economic model with imperfect competition and IEOS; an explicit reference to the new trade theory as applied to the European example. New trade theory involves oligopoly market structures, increasing returns, product differentiation, entry barriers and the like. It is a form of analysis the Commission adopted widely in its treatment of economic integration. Thus it is impossible to separate completely the discussion of IEOS from the wider context of trade modelling under imperfectly competitive behaviour. As we shall see later, assumptions about the strategic policy responses of firms to the removal of trade barriers, particularly their pricing behaviour, can be crucial to the realization of the benefits predicted by the models.[2]

As part of the calibration of their model, Smith and Venables deployed the Pratten estimates for ten representative three-digit NACE industries, with 1982 as base year for the projections. They argued that the Pratten estimates seemed to indicate an element of 'loglinearity' in the cost function, where marginal costs as well as average costs fall as output expands. A weighted linear and loglinear function is generated for the ten industries in the Smith and Venables analysis (p. 9, Table 1 and Technical Appendix), so IEOS in this case are never theoretically exhausted. Their final cost function was:

$$C(X_i, M_i) = C_i[z\{C_0 + M_i, C_m + M_i, X_i\} + (1 - z)\{M_i, X_i^\alpha\}^\beta]$$

where C is cost, X is output and M is product variety. The linear component of the cost function has weight, z, and the log-linear component the weight $1 - z$. The values of the C_i parameters were selected to be consistent with Pratten's estimates.

In fact the justification of the weights in the cost function look arbitrary and seem to amount to little more than 'guesstimates'. Similar comments could be made about the arbitrariness of the assumed METS (defined as in Table 4.2), for this analysis taken as the size of the average 'representative' firm in the European Community. Finally, economies of scope appear 'rolled into' the cost function by taking IEOS as defined when output changes at half MES (a) keeping the number of product varieties constant, or (b) keeping the output per variety constant, but changing the number of product varieties and seeing what happens to average cost (p. 9).

The results from Smith and Venables show a positive gain to freer trade under various further assumptions about firm reaction functions, pricing behaviour, extent of market integration, and so on, which appear very robust to sensitivity analysis (including various scenarios for the extent of trade barrier reduction). The partial equilibrium, industry by industry, nature of the analysis abstracts from feedback effects on prices of inputed intermediate products, on competitive conditions for primary factors, and on possible exchange rate changes consequent upon the altered trade pattern. It is suggested that the absence of this more general equilibrium framework might underestimate the resulting total benefits.

An assessment of the equilibrium approach
Applied partial equilibrium (APE) models are 'numerical' models. They are not subject to probability testing because they are 'calibrated' at a particular point in time. They are deterministic rather than stochastic. Within these models, markets are presumed to clear – indeed they are made to clear by the algorithms used to guarantee convergence on an equilibrium. There can be no underutilization of resources in such models, which could substantially limit the credibility of this kind of analysis in a policy context .The Commission/Smith and Venables APE model was calibrated for 1982 when European Community-9 unemployment was 8.2 per cent (EC-12, 9.5 per cent). The early 1980s represented a period of intense cyclical downturn for all

OECD economies, probably not an appropriate time to assume full employment in any market or industrial sector.[3] Once 'wrongly' calibrated, however, the reliability of gain estimates also becomes questionable.

The advocates of equilibrium modelling with imperfect competition argue for this because of its added intellectual rigour. But there may be a less subtle reason. In the case of Canadian analyses of the US–Canada Free Trade Agreement, for instance – which deployed a *general* equilibrium modelling framework – the welfare gain emerging from competitive neoclassical approaches to free trade consistently showed negligible or zero gains from free trade. As was tellingly remarked by the main exponent of this form of analysis in Canada, these studies '[had] been of little comfort to economists promoting free trade' (Harris, 1984, p. 1016). Thus the advocacy of free trade seemed to prefigure the analytical techniques devised to confirm its benefits. It is more comforting to use applied (partial) general equilibrium (A(P)GE) models with imperfect competition if economists wish to promote free trade, because the gains from these models far exceed the gains from models assuming competitive constant returns.

It is notable, for instance, that an earlier competitive constant returns AGE model assessing the impact of the United Kingdom's entry into the European Economic Community also predicted negligible impact on United Kingdom national income (Miller and Spencer, 1977). It is increasing return assumptions that make a significant difference to the results of AGE and APE models, and this is their attraction to those who are already convinced of the benefits of free trade.

As mentioned above, a related issue is the pricing and competitive assumptions built into these types of approach. Smith and Venables (1988) consider both (non-collusive) Cournot and Bertrand behaviour in their model. Cournot behaviour (competition on quantities produced) was favoured by them as being more realistic, though it produced slightly smaller final welfare benefits than Bertrand behaviour (competition on prices). Collusive, or part-collusive, behaviour can be very important to the results from modelling with AGE and PGE assumptions (Thompson, 1991a). Although it is not absolutely clear if collusive behaviour is totally ruled out in the Commission's final analysis of the effects of 1992, it certainly does not figure in the Smith and Venables background paper.

The Commission's Overall Analysis and Results

Returning to the main argument about IEOS, both Pratten and Helg and Ranci express caution about the validity of their respective surveys and analytical results, pointing to the uncertainties over IEOS. However, these cautions and reservations tended to disappear when the results of the two studies, along with those of Smith and Venables (1988), were deployed in the Commission's final report on the benefits/economics of 1992. Only once in the Commission's substantive treatment of Pratten's survey material, for instance, is there a negative comment on the likely IEOS benefits (European Commission, 1988, p. 107).[4]

The IEOS estimates figure in both the microeconomic and macroeconomic analysis that the Commission undertook (CEC, 1988, Annex A and B). But they operated most centrally in the microeconomic analysis, particularly in the Stage 3 and 4 calculations of the integration and increased market-size effects.

The Stage 1 analysis concerns the direct economic benefits arising from the removal of trade barriers on final demand goods. The costs of existing non-tariff barriers (border formalities, national diversity of product standards, and so on) are calculated within a partial equilibrium framework assuming perfectly competitive markets, and the gains from their removal for each of the (seven main) countries are calculated and aggregated together. Stage 2 involves a similar analysis, but this time for intermediate goods for the Community as a whole. The welfare gains in both stages are the sum of direct cost reductions (changes in producers' and consumers' surpluses), since perfectly competitive market assumptions rule out anything other than their full pass-on in the form of price reductions.

Stage 3 and 4 effects concern a set of more indirect benefits arising from the realization of economies of scale, from the restructuring of industry, and from the expansion of the market and increasing size of productive operations. Most of these benefits are 'technical' in nature, having to do with production cost reductions in existing sub-optimal-sized plants. The increased trade opportunities enable the larger firms to expand their market shares by absorbing or putting smaller rivals out of business. IEOS estimates figured in both these sets of calculations. In addition, the degree of market integration is important for the final level of benefits, and here the Smith and Venables estimates were used (see CEC, 1988, Chapter 9 and Annex A). When all these levels of benefit are added together, the results in Table 4.1 emerge.

As well as these 'technical' benefits there are 'non-technical' indirect benefits arising from (in particular) research and development cooperation and learning/experience effects. These 'dynamic' economies arise from the completion of the internal market, which is expected to have beneficial innovative consequences, as market competition produces a virtuous spiral of more efficient research and development effort, innovative product design, faster learning, intensified competition and larger firms. Although no direct estimate of these dynamic gains is given in the report, they are argued to be very important to the overall welfare benefits of the 1992 programme.

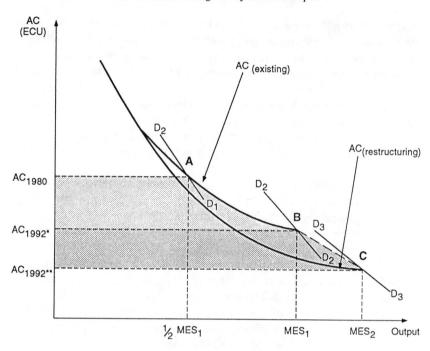

Figure 4.1   The EOS benefits from Europe 1992

In Figure 4.1 the process involved in generating Stage 3 benefits is sketched as the movement down the $AC_{(existing)}$ cost curve from point A to point B (from $1/2$ MES_1 to full MES_1). In effect, then, the Commission is assuming that the demand curve for European manufacturing output will move from D_1D_1 at about 1980 to D_2D_2 after 1992, that is, that there will be a potential *doubling* of manufacturing output in the most efficient plants of those sectors of industry considered in its analysis because of the single market programme associated with IEOS.[5]

In addition to the cost gains from IEOS associated with increasing the size of operations in existing sub-optimal plants, a further set of cost advantages is associated with the restructuring of European industries as a result of the expansion of the market. These benefits were argued to arise in the context of the increasing degree of market integration, leading to increased market share of the most efficient producers as they absorbed or put out of business smaller, less efficient, rivals. Thus there are some hypothesized productivity gains to be made here; the completion of the internal market is expected to have beneficial innovative consequences, as enhanced market competition produces a virtuous spiral of more efficient research and development effort, innovative product design, faster learning, intensified competition and larger firms. These indirect 'competitive' Stage 4 gains and the 'dynamic' gains are shown in Figure 4.1 as shifting the average cost curve from $AC_{(existing)}$ to $AC_{(restructuring)}$. In effect, then, if the firms are assumed to move to the optimal levels of output after this restructuring takes place, the ultimate post-1992 output level will be at point C on $AC_{(restructuring)}$, with assumed demand curve D_3D_3 and MES_2. The overall gain is then shown as the sum of the two effects: the two diagonally shaded areas in Figure 4.1. In the Cecchini Report, the calculated part of this secondary, indirect benefit accounts for another 30 per cent of the overall benefits (Cecchini, 1988, Table 9.2, p. 84 – the Stage 4 gains of 1.6 per cent GDP increase shown in Table 4.1). In addition, there would be the 'dynamic' gains not calculated in the Report. Thus, overall, some 70 per cent plus of the entire potential estimated benefits from the single market programme would be captured by the shaded areas shown in Figure 4.1.

Finally, the results in Table 4.1 were supplemented with a macroeconomic analysis based upon the Commission's two econometric-based macroeconomic models (HERMES and INTERLINK), which gave a total Community medium-term increase in GDP of between 3.2 per cent and 5.7 per cent after the completion of the internal market (CEC, 1988, Table B.5, p. 197).

Assessing the Commission's overall analysis

Clearly, the vision driving the Commission's analysis of the post-1992 European economy in these documents is at least one of generalized, intensified competition involving cross-border mergers, with even larger oligopolistic firms dominating the manufacturing sector. Reaping the potential economies of scale by moving down the average cost curve provides the rationale for this particular vision. There are, however, a number of problems with this assessment.

First of all it is difficult to believe that the 1992 process will lead to a doubling of the EC's manufacturing output in the most efficient plants. This looks optimistic. One problem here is that the process of estimating these gains relies upon the adding together of lots of small oblongs and triangles of welfare benefits, as suggested in Figure 4.1. While these might exist individually, will they appear in the aggregate? The kind of analysis conducted in the abstract around Figure 4.1 would actually involve looking at each firm or industry separately, estimating its individual cost curve slope at 1/2 MES and then moving down those curves to full MES. The gains would then be aggregated across industries and countries. In addition there is the issue of the indirect productivity benefits arising as a result of market rationalization. As we have seen, the EC documents present some rather 'loose' analysis here, and anyway these benefits are all rather speculative (see Peck,

1989). More detailed, though similar, Canadian analyses of this type show not only the difficulty of generating reliable statistics on the indirect and dynamic benefits, but also that they are very sensitive to assumptions about productivity changes (Thompson, 1991a). For instance, in the context of productivity differences between the USA and Canada with the advent of the Canada–US Free Trade Agreement, a doubling of Canadian manufacturing output only produced a 3 per cent reduction in overall costs (Rao, 1988).

Secondly, the Commission seems to have ignored the lessons that might be drawn from the previous period of substantial rationalization and merger activity conducted in the late 1960s and early 1970s. Most studies agree that this was less than a total success. Efficiency did not improve as expected, nor did profitability (Hughes, 1991). A good deal of the merger and take-over activity conducted then was done more for reasons of financial engineering than with productive investment in mind. Recent history suggests that there is little reason to think things have dramatically changed since then (see, in particular, Chapter 6).

Thirdly, in the business school literature in particular, *diseconomies* of scale (and scope) have been stressed from the late 1970s onwards, not economies of scale. This has to do with a reassessment of the nature of business organization, emphasizing the competitive advantage of the smaller and more focused firm over the large-scale producer of standardized products. As pointed out above, the Pratten survey relied upon older studies – some undertaken as far back as the 1960s – which perhaps pertain to a different era as far as productive structure is concerned. The debate about the 'end of mass production' and its possible replacement by an era of 'flexible specialization' just did not figure in the Commission's analysis. While one might want to treat much of this form of theorization with a certain caution, the perfunctory way the Commission dealt with it in *The Economics of 1992* – confined to a single short footnote on page 107 (see note 4) – seems inadequate. If the documentation and analysis is meant to look towards Europe's future, then a proper assessment of a likely industrial structure that does meet the needs of the new flexibility would have been expected. As it stands, this is completely absent. Below and in Chapter 6 we review this issue in greater detail.

In the United Kingdom, Geroski (1989a and 1989b) has made a number of telling criticisms against the likely IEOS outcomes predicted by the Commission/Pratten analysis. To start with he points to the actual limited extent of unrealized MES cost gains. Nearly 90 per cent of industries surveyed by the Commission showed MES of less than 10 per cent of the Community market, and three-quarters were less than 5 per cent (CEC, 1988, Table 6.1.2, p. 110; Geroski, 1989b, p. 31). In addition, against the Commission/Pratten interpretation, he suggests the size of the cost penalty looks fairly modest (Geroski, *ibid.*, p. 110). The way the Commission defines MES, as 50 per cent of theoretical output, implies a doubling of manufacturing output to achieve the full EOS benefits shown in Table 4.2. The Commission's methods had the tendency to add up a lot of very small gains. The question is whether expansion of the market will actually lead to the realization of all these small gains. As Cutler *et al.* (1989, p. 65) suggest, a doubling of the market size looks very unlikely.[6]

Even within a well-developed domestic market such as the United Kingdom, a large number of sub-optimal plants continue to operate. A similar result is likely to typify the European market. There are a number of reasons for this. First, the Commission's results depend on theoretical questions about what cost levels would be like if certain technical conditions held (Cutler *et al.*, 1989, p. 64) – they are not empirically grounded with respect to organizational and managerial constraints. As both Geroski and Cutler *et al.* point out, the problems of managing large plants have demonstrated that the merger strategies of the 1960s and 1970s, designed to exploit IEOS, largely failed in terms of efficiency results. There is no reason to believe a new round of cross-European mergers will be any more successful.

Geroski (1989b) highlights the trade-off between scale and diversity in contemporary production decisions, seeing the balance shifting decisively towards the diversity pole in the European context. This is exemplified by the manifest diversity of preferences and non-homogeneity of tastes in Europe as a whole. Cultural and linguistic differences reinforce this. Significant and persistent price differences for similar product ranges in different countries are indicative of these differences, Geroski suggests. They indicate subtle differences in product specification and reflect continuing specificities of demand on a country-by-country basis. Under these conditions the large increases in product runs needed to reap EOS benefits are unlikely to emerge. Indeed, the trend may be the reverse: to highlight even greater diversity and open up new ranges of non-standardized demands.

We must be careful not to press this point too far, however. In the Smith–Venables/ Commission analyses 'diversity' is, in part at least, internalized into the models of cost via the product-variety 'scope' element that comprises part of the total cost function in each case. In addition, product differentiation is a feature of the trade models deployed in the analysis. Thus these models do not hypothesize a strict output elastic one-product cost function (*contra* Cutler *et al.*, 1989, p. 63).

But, as is correctly stressed by Cutler *et al.* (1989), the Commission decided first to eliminate non-tariff barriers and then to set about justifying this. The programme of analysis it initiated was entitled 'The Costs of Non-Europe', which indicates the way the decision determined the approach. Also, the programmes were *purgative* in character (Grahl and Teague, 1989,

p. 40). The dominant metaphor under which both programmes are proceeding is one of purging a system of its impurities, where the impurities to be cleansed are the barriers to trade, the obstacles to MES operation, the impediments to market competition, and so on.

The problem is that there is likely to be a continued demand for quite specific and subtle differences in product characteristics across Europe, even if its market is formally 'unified'. Subtle differences in taste will remain well after 1992, if nothing else for cultural reasons. Thus a productive structure that celebrates and embodies the large-scale production of standardized outputs for the whole European market could quickly come unstuck. In addition, this vision deflects attention away from other, perhaps much more important, ways of reducing costs, such as the elimination of factory waste, the reduction of stocks and the improvement of quality. Business strategies based upon these principles are the ones leading to competitive advantage. In general, there is a serious lack of any consideration of business strategy in these documents, or of the importance and innovative dynamic attributed of late to the smaller and medium-sized firm.[7]

FROM IEOS TO EEOS

However, perhaps all this does not matter that much, since soon after *The Economics of 1992* was published, the Commission effectively turned its back on the central analytical technique embodied in that document. If we now turn our attention to the way the moves towards monetary and economic union (rather than the 1992 programme) have been justified, the Commission seemed to abandon any further mention of IEOS, as it quickly embraced the idea of EEOS instead.

The two key documents that embody this shift in emphasis are *One Market, One Money* (European Commission, 1990) and *The Economics of EMU* (European Commission, 1991a). The latter document presents the background papers to the analysis contained in the first. They explore the use of the 'new growth models' developed by Paul Romer, Paul Krugman and Richard Baldwin, amongst others. In addition they rely heavily upon the analysis of Caballero and Lyons (1990, 1991), which found no unrealized IEOS within Europe but pointed the way to the existence of substantial EEOS.

As we have seen, one of the contentious issues with the single market programme analysis concerns the question of structural readjustment and the dynamic gains this engenders. As the Commission's original analysis of the IEOS benefits came under criticism, it switched the emphasis of its assessment away from the *internal* economies to the *external* economies of the

1992 process, which implicate specifically dynamic welfare gains (Italianer, 1990, pp. 28–9). The analysis of Caballero and Lyons (1990), while again pointing to the absence of widespread unrealized internal economies of scale in Europe, found some evidence of external economies of scale, especially in France and Belgium (though not in the United Kingdom and Germany). External economies – in Caballero and Lyons's case, inter-industry, external economies (see below) – arise in a rather indistinct way as a possible consequence of 'public intermediate goods'. External human capital effects of the 'learning by doing' variety, and other informal interactions between economic agents, are mentioned as possible sources of these effects.

EEOS and the New Growth Theory

This analysis was developed by Baldwin (1989) in an attempt to quantify and justify the dynamic long-term growth implications of the 'one-off' 1992 purgative programme. In a model which generates a non-steady-state *per capita* growth path, technological progress is endogenized (rather than appearing exogenously as 'manna from heaven') via new investment, research and development, innovation and a declining capital–output ratio (which generates the economy-wide increasing returns).

Put simply, the basic new growth theory model deployed by Baldwin can be expressed as follows (Baldwin, 1989, pp. 247–81):

[% change in GDP in the long run] = [% ↑ in GDP because of one-off gains] × [e], where e is made up of EEOS.

This equation can be further subdivided as follows:

[% ↑ in final GDP] = ([% ↑ in one-off GDP] + [medium-term growth % of GDP]) × [e],

so that e is related to a one-off 'static' effect and a medium-term growth effect as well.

The traditional (neoclassical) growth models of the Solow type assume decreasing or constant returns to scale, so that any one-off increases in an accumulatory factor eventually come up against decreasing returns to the non-accumulatory factor, and a new steady-state growth rate is achieved.

However, if we encounter economy-wide increasing returns this is not necessarily the case. The result will be continued dynamic growth. This could greatly increase the potential benefits from the one-off EC 1992 programme. Indeed, Baldwin suggests that the 'static' analysis of *European*

Economy no. 35 could underestimate the beneficial effects by as much as between 300 per cent and 450 per cent (Baldwin, 1989, p. 269).

This result emerges from the 'endogenous growth model' of Romer and Krugman. This can be developed from an economy-wide Cobb–Douglas (C–D) production function as follows:

$$GDP = A(K)^{a+b} (L)^{1-a}$$

The Cobb–Douglas function is 'dynamized' by the factor '*b*', which represents the external economy effect.

Clearly, the value of the coefficient *a+b* is crucial:

if *a+b* < 1 we get the *usual result* (a new steady-state growth);

if *a+b* > 1 we get *accelerating growth* (which is ruled out on empirical grounds).

Only if *a+b* = 1 do we get the new dynamic growth rate.

A good deal of analysis in the background papers dealing with EEOS is devoted to explaining why *a+b* is likely to be equal to 1 on existing estimates.

In the Baldwin model, the one-off growth effect is based upon the orthodox C–D analysis. The medium-term growth is also based upon the C–D approach. The long-term growth comes from endogenizing innovations and technical progress (which are usually specified in terms of a time trend).

The *medium-term growth* effects arise from a number of sources. First, there is an increase in *firms'* profitability due to the Europe 1992 programme, which leads to an increase in investment and then to an increase in GDP. Secondly, there is an increase in *consumer* welfare because of Europe 1992, which leads to an increase in savings, to an increase in investment, and then to an increase in GDP. The overall medium-term impact is a result of both these aspects working together. The *long-term growth* effects arise because of an increase in the market size due to the Europe 1992 programme, leading to a reduction of the unit cost of innovations because of the increase in the size of the market and more competition. This then leads to a 'dynamic' growth of innovations and technical progress, and finally to an increase in output.

Assessing the new growth theory results

All this begs a number of questions.

In the first place, why should *a+b* conveniently equal 1? A careful scrutiny of the arguments and estimates advanced in the background papers justifying this reveals them to be rather speculative and subjective.

Secondly, one of the features of the model is an increase in firms' profitability, leading directly to an increase in investment. This then acts as the link to an increase in productivity and output. But here a number of well-known problems arise, particularly in the case of the UK economy (though these are general problems not confined to any single national economy). For instance, the assumed link between profitability and (real) investment can be tenuous, since firms have the option of either financial investment or the distribution of additional surpluses to workers or owners. Also, the 'quality' of any additional real investment is likely to be very important. Clearly these are empirical questions, which are likely to be nationally specific. Detailed estimates and calculations would be needed before a sensible result could emerge, rather than the aggregated 'guesstimates' supplied by Baldwin.

Similar points can be made about the role of innovations. To start with the relationship between innovations, product development and marketable output is highly country-specific. Even within Europe there is great variability in the efficiency of the process, the time taken for it to occur and its success. What is more, better results seem to emerge in some sectors rather than in others, and in cases where small and medium-sized firms are involved, rather than the large ones exclusively considered by the Commission. These kinds of speci..cities were not considered in the analysis.

Fourthly, consumer income increases are hypothesized to lead directly to increases in savings (and then to increases in investment, and so on to an increase in output). But again, and not just in the case of the UK, this could merely manifest itself in increased consumption rather than in savings. Such an increase in consumption often takes the form of increased imports, which causes balance-of-payments difficulties. Thus there could be a hidden cost involved which would need to be taken into account in any thorough investigation.

It might be argued that, while valid in their own right, the previous four points are unfair since the growth model analysis is first a highly aggregated one and secondly not meant to be empirically rich. But against this, Baldwin does make some large claims about the implications of the approach for actual European economic growth, as pointed out above. If we were to take the Cecchini Report's mid-point estimates of GDP growth for the 1992 programme (5.3 per cent) as our 'one-off' gains and relate these to the estimated percentage underestimate of between 300 per cent and 450 per cent of GDP growth, as suggested by Baldwin from his growth model, the resulting long-term effects of the one-off 1992 programme would be (approximately) 16.5 per cent and 24 per cent growth of European GDP. Once again this looks optimistic.

But here we encounter a slight difficulty, which is partly of a technical nature. The problem is that the estimates from one analysis are used to undermine or bolster the implications of another, but are they necessarily compatible? For instance, the Caballero and Lyons analysis of internal and external economies of scale, on which Baldwin and the Commission built a lot of their own assessments of European growth (see below), derives its estimates of EEOS on an *inter-industry* basis for *individual countries* only. This is then used to criticize the Cecchini Report's use of IEOS because Caballero and Lyons do not find any evidence of unrealized IEOS at this inter-industry level. However, the original Pratten survey for the Cecchini Report provided estimates of IEOS at the *plant or firm* level, using *engineering data* for the most part.

Thus the first point is whether it was statistically legitimate to aggregate the 'raw' Pratten data into branch industry data, as the Cecchini Report itself did. Subsequently, as just mentioned, Caballero and Lyons conducted an aggregate industry-level analysis and found no IEOS, which was then used to argue against the Cecchini results. But is this quite legitimate given the differences in the manner in which these two types of study were conducted? Furthermore, when it comes to the long-term growth model of Baldwin, the nationally specific inter-industry EEOS that Caballero and Lyons do claim to have isolated are deployed at another level of aggregation: for Europe as a whole. In this case it would seem to be *intra-European industry* EEOS that are at stake, not nationally specific inter-industry ones. But in their explicit attempt to isolate these particular intra-industry EEOS at the European level, Caballero and Lyons were unsuccessful (Caballero and Lyons, 1991). This must at least cast further doubt on the Baldwin estimates. In fact, as Smith notes, the non-statistical significance of the intra-industry EEOS coefficients in Caballero and Lyons might also invalidate their estimates of inter-industry EEOS (Smith, 1991). However, this did not prevent Caballero and Lyons from providing non-IEOS but enhanced EEOS estimates of the growth benefits of the 1992 programme based upon the original Cecchini work, which in fact resulted in a reduction in the overall estimated growth effects (Caballero and Lyons, 1991, p. 47).

While bearing some of these warnings in mind, but rather ignoring them for a moment as do the authors quoted above, we can look into some other deployments of the results from one study as used to bolster another. Taking again the base 1992 programme results of a 5.3 per cent increase in GDP, on the Caballero and Lyons (1990) results, this now includes 2.1 per cent IEOS benefits that they claim no longer exist. In addition, though this is controversial and not totally clear (Peck, 1989), some of the Cecchini Stage 4 benefits mentioned previously (1.6 per cent GDP) – due to rationalization and restucturing productivity changes and the like – would appear also to constitute part of the EEOS benefits derived by Caballero and Lyons. Thus in estimating the long-term growth effects of 1992 with EEOS we should first adjust for these possibilities of double-counting. Using the Caballero and

Lyons (1990) estimate of an EEOS coefficient, e of 1.4, we get the following recalculated results for the Baldwin long-term growth model:

First, take the base position:

[% ↑ in GDP growth] = [5.3] × [1.4] = 7.4% long-term GDP growth;

But supposing we take the 2.1 per cent IEOS away from the 5.3 per cent, then we have:

[% ↑ in GDP growth] = [3.2] × [1.4] = 4.5% long-term growth;

Further, supposing we take away all the Stage 4 benefits (1.6 per cent) as well, then:

[% ↑ in GDP growth] = [1.6] × [1.4] = 2.2% long-term growth.

To find the overall long-term GDP growth we need to add these figures to the original 'static' Cecchini results. Thus, this could vary anywhere between 12.7 per cent (7.4 + 5.3) and 7.5 per cent (2.2 + 5.3), considerably lower than the figures suggested by Baldwin. To relate this approach to EMU, the specific 'one-off' benefits of that particular programme would first need to be estimated and then a similar exercise completed.

Finally, what exactly are EEOS? They tend to be rather vaguely specified in the papers referred to here. But they include such items as the effects of education and training, cooperation in production of various kinds, technological spillovers and the like. An argument made about EEOS in distinction to IEOS is that the former rule out the beneficial effects of targeted industrial support that the latter have traditionally been used to justify. And with no remaining unrealized IEOS in Europe, targeted industrial support is pointless anyway. But if EEOS do actually exist, these could form the basis of beneficial economic multipliers. One implication on the policy front would be to make an argument for an increase in *aggregate demand* in Europe to take advantage of the EEOS by stimulating spillovers and so on. This is not something considered by the Commission, however.

Another aspect of new growth theory used to provide optimistic assessments of the Europe 1992 programme is that these models can be quite easily combined with hysteresis effects (Baldwin and Lyons, 1991). Thus an argument can be developed for 'self-fulfilling growth'. If there are a number of steady-state equilibria that the economy could 'choose' on the basis of expectations of agents, the one actually chosen could be affected by the changed expectations resulting from the widening of the market and the

EEOS expected to result from this. The European economy could move very rapidly, therefore, from 'Euro-pessimism' to 'Euro-optimism'. External economies will actually emerge because there is an expectation that they will. Exactly how seriously these arguments can be taken remains, of course, another matter.

The Long-Wave Approach

The final way the Commission has approached the issue of the likely growth effects of the recent moves towards closer economic integration involves the long-wave approach associated with the Kodratieff cycle. In the Commission's Annual Economic Report for 1990–1991 this appeared alongside a presentation of the Baldwin model as constituting the two main ways the Commission was dealing with these growth effects (European Commission, 1990b – this presentation was itself based upon Reati, 1991).

In many ways this approach is the most unorthodox of the three, and it is also perhaps the most controversial. This controversy refers to the actual existence of such a cycle, though the Commission presentation insists that new statistical filtering techniques have provided conclusive evidence that a long-wave cycle of some 50-year duration does indeed exist (European Commission, 1990b, p. 96). The initiation of these cycles is associated with technological revolutions, clustered around innovations in processes and products. Each cycle is characterized by a new leading sector; the latest one being associated with the technological revolution in computer and information technologies which started in the 1970s. Tracing out the evolution of aggregate value-added and profitability, sometimes also in respect to key sectors, for a number of leading European countries, Reati argues that these add up to a coordinated upswing commensurate with the new long wave. Thus it is the coincidental coordinated upswing in the short-run business cycle of a number of leading countries that provides the main evidence of the beginning of the new long cycle.

It is difficult to know exactly how to evaluate this kind of analysis without a detailed scrutiny of both data and techniques. To a sceptic, it might look nothing more than wishful thinking: supposing the business cycle takes a coordinated downturn in the near future, which it is threatening to do? The problem with all technologically driven theories of the economy is that they seem to give a spurious certainty to economic behaviour when that behaviour is radically dependent upon behavioural relationships between active agents. From a different perspective it might be argued that the main industrial economies are still caught in a recessionary downturn, the exit from which is difficult to forecast. Indeed, a real possibility remains a much more serious *depressionary* downturn.

One thing about the long-wave theory as described by the Commission, is that it does not give any hard and fast empirical estimates of the extent and level of future GDP growth, unlike either the IEOS or the EEOS/new growth theory models. On the other hand, it is a highly aggregated model like the new growth theory; it rather abstracts from the detail of comparative industrial structure in those economies included in its assessment. However, both the new growth theory and the long-wave theory produce very optimistic scenarios as far as the immediate growth prospects for Europe are concerned. In general the Commission is upbeat about the future for European growth in all these documents. Perhaps that is to be expected from an organization that has led the arguments in favour of ever-greater European integration. But in our critical assessment these forecasts are far too optimistic. This is not an argument against further European economic integration, but one that suggests that integration needs to be secured on a more solid foundation than present policies are allowing (see Chapter 6).

MASS PRODUCTION OR A FLEXIBLE FUTURE?

One of the problems with the analyses of both the Europe 1992 programme and that of EMU is that they essentially look 'backwards' to the conditions of the post-war period for likely indications of the future course of economic events. They are caught in a rather conventional set of tried and tested economic arguments, that may turn out to have little or no purchase on contemporary radical changes in the economic environment to which businesses in the future are going to have to react.

At the centre of this type of criticism of the programmes would be an argument about the continued importance of mass production process technology and the idea of economies of scale that it supports. Put simply, the argument is that the era of mass production is rapidly coming to a close as businesses come face to face with the demands of a more flexible production process technology and economic environment. This embodies a quite radical challenge to the way economic development will be understood in the future, and to the practices of firms and public authorities in relation to this new flexible era.[8]

These are bold claims. Put this way they have been used polemically to open up a debate on fundamental issues involving the characterization of contemporary transformations in the production process technology of advanced economies. This is not to say that these possible trends have gone totally unrecognized in the official literature on the 1992 programme. But they have appeared as footnotes to the main exercise of justifying free trade on the basis of EOS. Nor is it to say that a settled idea of what constitutes a flexible production process technology and its consequences has been generated, even by those who have been engaged with the idea and who generally support it.[9] In what follows I outline some of the features of this debate, pointing to its implications for the idea of EOS in particular.

One of the main contemporary critiques of EOS has its origin in management literature dealing with the reasons for the decline of the American manufacturing sector, but this is also pertinent in the European case. The argument here is that it was an over-reliance on size and EOS, along with the deployment of discounted cash flow (DCF) techniques, that had been one of the major reasons for this decline.

The Harvard Business School authors in this tradition stressed various forms of *diseconomies* of scale operating along the following dimensions:

1. Distributional diseconomies which arise because of the increasing cost of distribution to dispersed customers as production becomes more centralized – total delivery costs may increase, as can the time taken to deliver, which itself undermines competitive advantage and a flexible response.
2. Bureaucratic diseconomies arising from increased size and difficulties of management.
3. Diseconomies of confusion which emerge in the context of increasing numbers of products, processes and specialists within a given plant.
4. Diseconomies of vulnerability to risk – multi-plant operation increases the possibility of interruption of supply if one plant becomes inoperable for any reason (Hayes and Wheelwright, 1984).

Although this represents a rather condensed list of scale and scope effects, it offers a comprehensive critique of the usual focus on IEOS. Against the emphasis on larger size, these authors introduce the idea of a 'minimum economic-sized' plant: one that is the smallest size possible commensurate with competitive and operational viability, and that has a highly 'focused' manufacturing function.

With respect to DCF techniques, which these authors link with IEOS, the argument is that these cannot adequately deal with strategic investments which involve either the strong likelihood of retaliatory moves by competitors, which imply a chain of further interdependent investments, or which have hidden 'soft' investment consequences such as necessary programming and working capital implications. At best, DCF leads to short-term 'patching' investments of a defensive type (Myers, 1984; Hayes, Wheelwright and Clark, 1988, Chapter 3.). When used to justify large-scale strategic investment it has failed to come to terms with the diseconomies noted above or has led to the ignoring of possible retaliatory moves by competing firms.

A second, related, line of argument against IEOS suggests that they concentrate too much on the idea of size as being the only, or most important, means for reducing costs. Going for supposed size advantages tends to ignore all the other managerial and operational ways of reducing costs which are not necessarily related to size in any direct way. For instance, study of Japanese manufacturing techniques shows that these concentrate upon eliminating stocks as a prime way of eliminating costs and waste in the factory (Williams *et al.*, 1989a and 1989b). The use of flexible manufacturing systems (FMS) and just-in-time (JIT) techniques serves to cut down on the amount of stock holdings, and at the same time it highlights possible improvements in the design of the production process overall, thus serving a double function in improving competitive edge (see also Chapter 6).

A further but more ambitious critique of IEOS stems from the idea of 'flexible specialization' (FS). Here the argument is that new forms of production organization are being created in the wake of the break-up of the mass production paradigm; these are summarized by the term 'flexible specialization'. FS represents a new paradigmatic business strategy, one that needs to face up to a new degree of differentiation and uncertainty in the field of consumer demand. No longer can manufacturers look forward to stable, long-run, standardized demands for their products, but rather these are increasingly being fragmented into specialized niche markets. The challenge to manufacturing under these circumstances is to provide a means by which a flexible response in the production environment can be generated to meet these changed consumer purchasing patterns.

One response is to develop extensive subcontracting networks that are both closely supervised by the main assembly firms but where, at the same time, the subcontracting firms are themselves not totally dependent on any one of the main firms for all their business relations. This provides a desirable flexibility to cope with both rapid change and the avoidance of operational difficulties when a downturn comes in one sector or in one of the main firms. Under these circumstances, industrial districts or regional economies can be formed composed of complementary but competitive activities. The emphasis here is on small- and medium-scale organizations, but using the most up to date and efficient manufacturing techniques which can be flexibly configured to meet *expected* rapid changes in demand. Tying the company to a single standardized commodity with a long production run will not be an adequate business response under these presumed circumstances. Thus networks of mutual support and trust are built up in this new flexible environment. These do not rely upon 'cut-throat' competition on the basis of price as their motivating principle (Thompson, 1993).

Even in large multi-product firms, it is argued, the need to respond to these changes is appearing in the form of 'quasi-vertical disintegration' (for example, Sabel, 1989). A centralized and (inflexible) control of production is being displaced via a break-up into semi-autonomous production departments and units, which operate much as independent businesses would – contracting and subcontracting their activities as suits their purpose, within and outside the firms, and subject only to a more or less tight technical or financial control by the centre. Flexibility is introduced internally to the firm in this way, and reliance on a traditional notion of EOS within the plant or firm is undermined as a result. It should also be remembered that simply introducing various forms of flexible manufacturing systems (FMS, JIT, CAD–CAM, CIM (computer integrated manufacturing) and so on) does not constitute a 'flexible specialized' production environment in these terms. This requires a complete change in business strategy designed to cope with a radical fracturing of established demand patterns and the systemic uncertainty this engenders.

Perhaps a number of these developments could be understood in terms of EEOS as discussed above, however. For instance, the network of interdependent main and subcontracting firms can be discussed under the heading of 'external' or agglomeration economies (Scott, 1988) – which could be accommodated with the idea of external economies as discussed above. The main object of the FS critique of scale economies would seem to refer to plant and firm economies. The difficulty with these has also to do with the level of aggregation that traditional IEOS analysis invokes. As we have seen, two- or three- (and sometimes four-) digit NACE/SIC branch divisions are the usual level at which the analysis is pitched. But as Luria (1990) has shown, testing the FS hypothesis really requires a much more disaggregated product-by-product approach. Since this level of disaggregation is not available in official statistics, advocates of FS tend to be confined to their case study approach. Also, traditional IEOS analyses tend to exclude small and even medium-sized firms for similar informational reasons.

One thing all these slightly different critiques of traditional notions of EOS would stress is the shift of emphasis from price competition to non-price competition. This constitutes another dimension to criticisms of EOS and the kind of trade models deployed in the discussion above, which rely on price competition and cost minimization to support them. Increasingly, however, it is rather nebulous factors such as quality, design, reliability and continuity of supply, delivery dates, after-sales service and effective marketing that determine consumer choice, rather than price as such. There is no necessary relationship, as a result, between lower cost and greater market share.

CONCLUSION

This chapter has concentrated upon how the notion of economies of scale served to justify the economic assessment of the two most recent programmes for European real economic integration. The way EOS entered the two assessments was via the economic models devised to quantify the impact of the moves towards freer trade. Since the publication of the original Cecchini Report, a number of further analyses of the EOS benefits likely to arise from the 1992 programme have emerged which embody a more elaborate and innovative approach. These embody the notion of external economies of scale.

Size economies only shift the firm along any cost curve. Thus, with a move onto the lower cost curve the welfare gains would not be due so much to increased size of plants, but rather to better productivity. In fact, the gains here were found to be highly sensitive to the hypothesized 'dynamic' productivity changes. But (a) these were always heavily dependent on a rather speculative calculation of their extent; and (b) the resulting overall welfare improvement looked likely to be small anyway.

As far as EEOS gains are concerned, it was noted that these rely heavily on the possible barrier-reducing trade benefits of 1992, not on average cost reductions because of the expansion of industrial branches as such. For instance, EEOS do not necessarily imply gains from mergers or acquisitions designed to increase the scale of production internally to plants or industries. They are also more compatible with a general increase in aggregate demand as a stimulus to external economies, or of greater emphasis on education and training. But a problem for the external economies argument in the European context is that trade integration is already so well developed that even the non-tariff barrier (NTB) programme behind 1992 is unlikely to have a significant additional impact (Neven and Roller, 1990).

There are a good many criticisms that can be levelled at the FS and the other critiques of EOS analysed in the subsequent part of this chapter (these are discussed with respect to FS in particular in Thompson, 1989a and 1989b). But the point of bringing them into focus in this chapter is to highlight a set of criticisms of IEOS and EEOS that just did not figure in the official discussion of the 1992 programme. In their eagerness to justify free trade in each case, official assessments overlooked some necessary caution. In the Commission's analyses the evidence looks thin for IEOS benefits in particular, and exaggerated for EEOS. At best they remain only a hope.

But there is also a possibly more serious consequence of the type of analysis presented in each of the cases. The European economies may misjudge the nature of the adjustment processes needed to compete in the evolving contemporary economic environment as they concentrate once again upon IEOS and large size. The ability of these strategies to produce their benefits may be fast approaching their limit, or their time may have already passed. Picking up on new trends and challenges remains the problem if the European economies are to revitalize themselves for the future. Chapter 6 explores these issues further.

This chapter has not presented a full empirically grounded alternative set of calculations for the programmes it has analysed. Rather, it has brought together a set of criticisms and arguments that should lead to a healthy scepticism of the officially calculated benefits to be derived from the programmes. As is hinted in the discussion, conventional economic theory may no longer be able to provide a credible analytical framework for thinking sensibly about these matters. If we are moving into a more 'flexibly specialized' era, what are the implications of this for trade policy? As it stands, the official assessments discussed here remain caught in a fundamental tension between explicitly advancing competition on the one hand, and implicitly encouraging concentration on the other, to reap economies of scale.

NOTES

1.　West Germany is the main continental country considered, see Schwalbach (1988) and Owen (1983).
2.　For instance, free entry equilibrium assumptions can rule out the possibility of *dis*economies, while firms 'protect' unrealized economies because of distortions such as tariffs and non-tariff barriers.
3.　This also seems difficult to reconcile with the European Commission's explicit recognition of less than MES operation for much of European industry.
4.　This appears as one sentence on p. 107 of the main report: 'Yet certain industries now see the reappearance of small firms, which are adapting faster to technological change by using new production processes (flexible manufacturing systems, faster cutting, etc)'.
5.　In the background paper produced by Aujean (1988) Community *trade* is assumed to increase by 25 per cent as a result of this process.
6.　In a later Commission paper, Geroski's criticisms are dismissed as resulting from a muddle over 'realized' and 'potential' IEOS effects (Italianer, 1990). This paper stresses the abolition of non-tariff barriers to the potential benefits of the 1992 programme, collapsing the specifically IEOS benefits to only between 10 per cent and 30 per cent of total benefits (Italianer, 1990, p. 8).
7.　The only gesture to business strategy is a formal and abstract imperative to reap unrealized internal economies of scale on the one hand, combined with the competitive thrust of restructuring on the other.
8.　Amongst a large literature the seminal text is Piore and Sabel (1984).
9.　These issues are discussed in Hirst and Zeitlin (1989), Thompson (1989b), and in Zeitlin (1989).

5.   Economic and Monetary Union: Problems and Prospects

INTRODUCTION

This chapter examines the moves towards economic and monetary union in the period leading up to the Maastricht Summit. The emphasis is upon macroeconomic considerations, and particularly the controversial issue of monetary convergence and monetary union. As of mid-1992, full monetary union for the EC was scheduled to begin after a summit in 1997, and to be completed before the beginning of 1999 (Stage 3). A crucial element in the movement towards these deadlines is the 'convergence criteria' agreed in 1991 at Maastricht and embodied in the Treaty (HMSO, 1992). Since these are likely to act as the benchmark against which the whole process will be judged, we concentrate upon them immediately below. One point to note about these criteria is that they involve, more or less exclusively, attention to monetary variables.

Alongside the expected movement towards monetary convergence will go the creation of the European System of Central Banks (ESCB, or Euro-Fed). This will inherit the responsibility of controlling the monetary side of the unified European economy after 1999. Before then, a European Monetary Institute (EMI) will prepare the ground (during Stage 2) by monitoring the convergence criteria and developing the operational mechanism that the European Central Bank (ECB) will inherit. It was the precise nature of this ESCB that exercised politicians, policy-makers and analysts in the run-up to the Maastricht Summit, and which threatens to continue as a major issue during the transition period. We discuss the prospects for a successful development of this Bank below, both in terms of its emergent nature in the transition period and how it might operate in a monetarily unified Europe. The ESCB is the most important example of economic institution-building that the EC is likely to undertake before 1999.

The third feature of EMU discussed in this chapter involves an analysis of the macroeconomic aspects of the process. As a prelude to this, a preliminary clarification is made of elements in monetary analysis that are important for an understanding of the specific problems facing those organizing EMU under contemporary conditions. The argument here is that recent changes in the financial system are presenting policy-makers with a new set of problems that are not sufficiently recognized by conventional analysis.

Finally, the dramatic events regarding the ERM and monetary union occurring in September 1992 are reviewed separately near the end of the chapter. This chapter was prepared well before these events happened but, as will be seen, its analysis substantially prefigured and anticipated them. Thus the assessment near the end explicitly draws on the previous analysis and explores the possible future of the ERM and monetary union in the light of the position in late 1992.

THE MAASTRICHT CONVERGENCE CRITERIA EXAMINED

The question posed by the convergence criteria as they emerged from the Inter-governmental Conference on EMU, and as confirmed by the Maastricht Treaty, is whether they can ever be met in the time specified or by a large enough group of countries to make the whole process viable. These criteria were laid down as being necessary for the EC countries to achieve before they could advance to full monetary union. The idea is for the respective EC governments to monitor their economies and work towards meeting these criteria before the summit scheduled for 1997. We can briefly look at each of these criteria in turn:

1. The most important criterion centred upon inflation. The target here for each country was agreed as an inflation rate less than the average of the lowest three rates in existing EC countries, plus 1.5 per cent. As shown in Table 5.1, almost half of the EC countries would *not* have met this criterion had it been operative in 1991.
2. A second important criterion involved the position on budget deficits and government debt. Yearly budget deficits are to either less than 3 per cent of GDP, or less than the level of government investment (defined as general government gross capital formation), while the outstanding gross government debt criterion is set at less than 60 per cent of GDP. As can be seen from Table 5.1, seven EC countries met the budget deficit criterion in 1991, but only five the government debt figure.
3. An additional monetary convergence indicator was set on interest rates. Long-term interest rates are to be less than 2 per cent, plus an average of the lowest three country rates. A fairly large group of eight of the 12 members met this criterion in 1991.
4. Finally there was a set of further indicators on monetary conditions involving commitments to the ERM. Currencies are to have been oper-

Table 5.1 Convergence criteria for the EMU, 1991

EC countries	EMU Criteria of the Maastricht Treaty					ERM performance	EMU performance
	Inflation rate <4.4%[1]	Budget deficit <3.0% of NI[2]	Government investment ratio[3]	Government debt <60% of NI[4]	Interest rate <10.6%[5]		
Belgium	3.2	6.4	1.6	132.3	9.3	+	−
Denmark	2.4	1.4	2.0	60.6	10.1	+	−
Germany[6]	3.5	3.2	2.4	41.8	8.6	+	−
Greece	19.5	16.1	3.1	82.9	16.6	−	+
France	3.2	2.2	3.5	48.6	9.0	+/−	−
Ireland	3.2	1.9	1.9	101.2	9.2	+/−	−
Italy	6.4	10.2	3.4	102.7	12.9	−	+
Luxembourg	3.1	−2.0	6.1	6.9	8.2	+	−
Netherlands	3.9	2.6	2.3	77.3	8.9	+	−
Portugal	11.4	6.1	2.9	64.7	17.1	−	−
Spain	5.9	1.5	5.2	46.3	12.4	−	−
United Kingdom	5.9	2.8	2.0	36.5	9.9	−	−

Notes:
1. Consumer prices (OECD, Economic Outlook, December 1992, Table 5.7).
2. General government financial balance (OECD, Economic Outlook, December 1992, Table 2).
3. General government share of GFCF as % of GDP (Annual Economic Report 1991–92, European Economy No 50, December 1991).
4. Gross public debt as % of GDP (OECD), Economic Outlook, December 1992, Table F2).
5. Nominal long-term interest rates (Annual Economic Report, 1991–92, European Economy No 50, Table 48).
6. West Germany only.

ating within the 2.25 per cent narrow band of the ERM for at least two
years; there are to have been no devaluations during that time; currencies are to have been trading within normal margins, and there must
have been no 'severe tensions' in maintaining the balance of payments
or currency value.

Clearly, these criteria are meant to be those for entry into EMU only in the
late 1990s. Thus we would not expect them all to have been achieved as
early as 1991. But the figures for that year do point to the tremendous task
set for a number of countries if they are to be in a position to advance to
EMU. In principle *all* these criteria must be fulfilled by each country. However, the task for the likes of Greece, Portugal, Spain, Ireland, Italy, and even
Belgium, looks formidable. Can the targets be successfully achieved in these
countries before the final process begins in 1997? The countries just mentioned comprise *half* of the existing EC membership. In addition the UK,
while meeting most of the formal quantitative criteria in 1991, was still
operating in the wider 6 per cent band of the ERM at the time, and was
hardly operating without 'severe tensions' in its payments position.[1]
 When examined together, then, perhaps these criteria look to be too restrictive to be manageable. If they do turn out to be so, four possible consequences might follow. The first is that the whole process will grind to a halt
when it becomes clear that the targets just cannot be achieved by enough EC
members. Secondly, these criteria might be altered or relaxed as the process
nears its completion towards the end of the decade. Thirdly, there may be a
general extension of the time period before they have to be reached. Finally,
there could be a strong temptation to go down the path of a clear 'two-speed'
EMU, with a band of five or six convergers and a group of others who tag
along beside (or behind) and enter the full EMU if and when they can meet
the criteria.
 The first of these outcomes remains the most worrying for those committed to further European economic integration. The final one looks the most
likely. The other two would seem the most appropriate, but perhaps not so
attractive from the point of those pressing for a rapid advance towards EMU
(see later in this chapter).
 An additional problem emerging in the early 1990s was a slowdown in the
trend towards economic convergence amongst the Community members
(*European Economy*, No. 50, December 1991: Annual Economic Report
1991–92, pp. 11–14). In part, this was the result of the slowdown in growth
due to the recession, which tended to re-emphasize differences. The budgetary situation worsened in Germany and the UK in particular. The external
surplus on the German current account disappeared, and the position deteriorated for the UK and Spain. Community international competitiveness

also deteriorated. The real 'catching-up' process for Spain, Greece, Ireland and Portugal seemed to be slowing.

The problem with the criteria as they stand, and in the light of the strong possibility of widespread default, is that in their attempt to meet the deadlines set, a general deflationary bias will be engendered in those countries singled out above who have to move the furthest to reach the targets. It is well known that there is an asymmetry in situations of this type – when all are trying to converge on a very restrictive set of criteria. The pressures of adjustment are on those who do not yet meet the objectives, while those who have already achieved them feel little pressure to adjust in an accommodating manner. The consequence of this could be a deflationary bias in the system as a whole, since those pressured to adjust are pushed into restrictive policies and those facing little or no pressure are reluctant to undertake the appropriate reflationary offsetting adjustment.

Thus, under the circumstances outlined, it would seem inappropriate to encourage any 'deficit' country to sign up to EMU prematurely or before a genuine adjustment had had time to mature. Indeed, there is likely to be a strong reluctance to do this on these countries' own parts. But in addition the criteria themselves look unduly deflationary and too restrictive to be politically acceptable in the long run. This tends to be confirmed by the analysis of the formal macroeconomics of the transition period conducted below, which we return to in a moment.

THE EUROPEAN CENTRAL BANK

The creation of the European Central Bank has been one of the most controversial and closely contested aspects of the EMU process. Broadly speaking, there have been two conflicting ideas as to how it might be constituted and function. For want of a better terminology these can be classified as a 'political' bank and an 'independent' bank. For the purposes of this exposition the characteristics of each of these are exaggerated slightly to bring out the differences between them and to focus the nature of the debate.

The political bank was initially favoured by the French in particular, but also by certain elements in the British position whilst Margaret Thatcher was still Premier (though she was personally very hostile to the whole notion of monetary union). Such a bank would act directly in the name of the countries of the EC. It would be directed by a board made up of political representatives of all the countries of the union, and would be made politically accountable to them or their governments. By contrast, the independent bank, which was favoured by the Germans in particular, and which was modelled on the *Bundesbank,* would act quite independently of political pressure in the way it undertook monetary policy. With this idea of a central bank there would be less direct political control and accountability.

The differences between these two conceptions were argued to result in a different outcome for inflation. For those committed to an independent bank, the control of inflation remained the top priority. For them, the political bank option was thought more likely to be 'soft' on inflation, as the bank would yield to premature political pressures to reflate. However, the argument from those supporting the political bank idea was that there were other quite legitimate objectives that monetary policy should be sensitive to – levels of unemployment for instance – and that an institution so important as the European Central Bank must be the subject of some form of political accountability. Although nuanced in various ways, these points constituted the main contours of the debate about the form of the Central Bank in the early 1990s.

The outcome of this debate looked to be something of a compromise between the two conceptions, though from the draft statutes of the Central Bank embodied in the Maastricht Treaty, it looked as though the independence option was the one gaining the upper hand ('... [the ECB should not] seek to take instructions from Community institutions or bodies, from any Member State or from any other body. The Community institutions and bodies and governments of the Member States undertake to respect this principle...' Chapter III, Article 7). The precise constitution and organization of the Bank was to be as follows (Chapter III):

A European System of Central Banks consisting of the ECB as the central body, with 12 national central banks as part of the federation. The main decision-making body is to be the Council of the ECB. This is to comprise the President, Vice-President, four members of the Executive Board and the Governors of the 12 national banks. This Council would meet monthly, but the day-to-day operational activity of the Bank would be conducted by the Executive Board. The members of this are to be appointed for eight-year terms by the European Council after consultation with the European Parliament and the ESCB. Great emphasis is placed in the statutes on the constitutional independence of the Bank, particularly from control by governments or elected politicians. But some minimal democratic accountability will be exercised via the link to the European Council and Parliament.

As suggested above, the issue of independence for the Central Bank was predicated on the statutes of the *Bundesbank* that require it to maintain the value of the DM as its main priority.[2] The record on inflation of the German economy over much of the post-war period added to the legitimacy of the German model. But that model is not quite so unambiguous as it might at first seem. For instance, the *Bundesbank* has been subject to successful political pressure on a number of occasions, not least during the recent monetary union with the old East Germany. The *Bundesbank* initially insisted on at least a two to one conversion of the Ostmark to the Deutschmark, but that was overruled by the Kohl government and more generous terms were finally agreed (see Chapter 7). Thus whatever the precise wording of the ECB constitution, there is likely to be political pressure applied at times. Indeed, it would seem absolutely necessary that this be the case. It would be an impossible situation if any central bank, with such wide responsibilities as the ECB will have (see below), could act totally independently of political control and democratic accountability.

OPERATING A CENTRAL BANK IN EUROPE

Central banks have traditionally fulfilled a number of functions which have to do with the regulation of both the monetary unit and the financial system. This is not the place to go into the long history of these issues in detail. Suffice it to say that with the emergence of a strong neo-liberal ideology since the mid-1970s, the traditional role of the central bank has increasingly been called into question. Some of this debate is reflected in the manner in which proposed ECB is planned to operate. Although it is early days and the precise nature of the ECB responsibilities have yet to be defined in detail,[3] the Maastricht Treaty gives some indication of the nature of its expected operating characteristics.

The usual functions attributed to central banks are as follows: a) to act as the banker for the government; b) to be responsible for the issue of money and currency ('control the money supply'); c) to supervise and regulate the financial system; d) to set the discount rate on 'money' ('set interest rates'); e) to act as lender of last resort; f) to manage the exchange rate of the currency; and g) to hold and manage the official reserves of the country.

Not all these functions have at all times become the responsibility of the central bank, nor have such banks always exercised responsibility for all of them. The list above represents those functions that have at one time or another been attributed to a central bank, or become the responsibility of central banks within broadly capitalist economies. Clearly, there is also a good deal of overlap between them. We can use this list as a measure against which the functions suggested for the ECB can be discussed.

It is certainly not the intention of those framing the ECB's statutes to include as one of its responsibilities the role of government banker (other than as its fiscal agent). Indeed, this function has been explicitly excluded for the ECB's proposed tasks. The point here is to prevent the finance of government deficits by extending credit to them and thereby to prevent the supposed inflationary consequences of such practices. As a consequence the

ECB is to have nothing to do with the direct purchase of government debt, at least in theory. But there seems little reason why the ECB could not purchase already existing government debt in the market, for instance. Unless this is explicitly forbidden, which in a financially sophisticated and credit-rich economy would be very difficult to enforce, the ECB could, indirectly at least, finance governments at some level. Formally, however, the ECB is not to be the governments' banker, and it will not be allowed to 'bail out' governments with subsidized loans (Chapter IV, Article 21).

It will be the task of the ECB to issue whatever the European currency eventually becomes. As discussed at greater length below, this will be some form of ECU. But whether the ECB will be able to control the amount of the European money supply remains a moot point. Targeting both narrow and broad monetary aggregates has not been very successful at the national level since the waves of deregulation and liberalization of financial systems in the 1970s. Even if a stable demand-for-money function at the European level can be found, the relationship between the monetary aggregate and inflation and output is still likely to be a weak one.

According to Artis (1992), there may be a stable narrow measure such as M0, or even the broader M2, at the European level. But do these measures adequately represent '*the* money supply' in a financially sophisticated economy? There is no strong evidence, for instance, that limiting the supply of reserve money (even if this could be effectively done), has much effect on the overall money supply and credit expansion. The problem is that credit in all its forms is increasingly becoming money for all practical intents and purposes, and it is private financial institutions that control the level of systemic credit in an economy, not the central bank (Thompson, 1986, Chapter 6). In addition, there have been some recent developments in the designation of money in a modern economy that will complicate, at least, the task of trying to control the money supply. These are discussed in the next section.

Very little is said about the role of the ECB in supervising and regulating the European financial system in the Maastricht Treaty. Formally there is a clause in the draft statutes that gives the Bank some role in this respect. It '... *may* offer advice ... [and] .... it *may* perform specific tasks concerning policies relating to prudential supervision of credit institutions and the stability of the financial system' (Chapter V, Article 25). However, as indicated, this is not a mandatory or binding commitment. So much depends upon the sentiment in the Bank itself. In general, the tone of the statutes is 'narrow' in its definition of regulatory supervision – relating to monetary stability only – not 'broad' in the sense of requiring regulation for financial market stability as a whole. But, given that the model for the ECB is the *Bundesbank,* this is probably not surprising. The *Bundesbank* does not regulate the German

financial system. That is done by a completely separate organizational structure. The small number of large universal private banks in Germany themselves take on the main responsibility of supervising the system. In such a
highly bank-intermediated system as in Germany (see Chapter 6), these
banks clear all the wholesale payments and securities transactions at the end
of each day. With little risk exposure to non-bank financial institutions there
is no need for the central bank to provide either intra-day credit or stand
ready to act as lender of last resort. The big banks know what the overnight
positions of the financial institutions are, and if problems seem to be emerging they, along with the *Bundesbank,* can, and do, act quickly to provide
emergency *ad hoc* assistance. Thus, in fact, the German system is highly and
tightly regulated, but not by its central bank. The problem will be that the
European system as a whole is not going to be quite like the domestic
German one. It is destined to be much more open and deregulated, with
dispersed capital and money markets (though, as argued in Chapter 3, this
should not be exaggerated, as the system is unlikely to be completely
deregulated in a style suggested by neo-liberal ideology).

This lack of a clear supervisory and regulatory requirement relates to
problems with the idea that the ECB will set interest rates by, in the first
instance, setting the discount rate. Clearly, the Bank will have some influence on interest rates, but it will not be able to set these unilaterally. As is
argued below, it is more likely that the financial system will have the larger
influence and will effectively set these rates on the ECU. This is certainly
likely to be the case in the transition period when other already existing
European currencies are operative, and it could extend into the post-union
period when there is a single European currency. This problem is discussed
in greater detail below.

All this links to the other supervisory function conspicuous by its absence
in the documents and the Treaty; the issue of the lender of last resort
function. Nowhere is this mentioned as a responsibility, or potential responsibility, of the ECB. Again, this might have something to do with the dominance of the German model in drawing up the draft statutes. The *Bundesbank*
does not act as lender of last resort, which is consistent with the bank-
intermediated nature of the German credit system.

Finally we come to the issue of exchange rate management, in which we
include the holding and management of the official foreign reserves. In the
draft statutes there are two clauses pertaining to this issue. The management
of the official reserves is unambiguously attributed to the Bank. But the
general conduct of foreign exchange operations is to be done in accordance
with the prevailing exchange rate regime of the Community. It is the Council
of Ministers that will be both responsible for establishing this regime and
for: '... formulating general orientations for exchange rate policy...', after

consultation with the European Parliament, the Commission and the ECB (Chapter 2, Article 109). So the Bank would not be responsible for that regime as such, it would just be required to manage the exchange rate (and the reserves) in the light of it, and in the light of general exchange rate policy decisions (though all this is to be done notwithstanding the objective of price stability). Thus the setting of the ECU exchange rate could remain a more politicized issue, with a clear line of political accountability. Of course, the ECB will have a significant advisory role with respect to the exchange rate, but its room for manoeuvre on monetary policy would be severely constrained, if indeed the ECOFIN were able to maintain its authority over the external exchange rate regime.

Table 5.2   European Central Bank

Function	Responsibility			
	Definitely	Possibly	Unlikely	Not at all
Governments' banker				✓
Issue of currency	✓			
Supervision of FS			?	
Set discount rate		✓		
Lender of last resort				✓
Manage exchange rate		?	✓	
Hold official reserves	✓			

Thus in Table 5.2 we summarize the functions of the ECB as these were emerging in the early 1990s. Since not all of this is unambiguous, a graded responsibility matrix is produced. Overall, however, the ECB looks to be developing a 'minimalist' stance on the usual range of central bank functions.

CONSIDERATIONS OF MONETARY THEORY

This section serves to raise a number of issues from monetary theory and policy that, although largely overlooked by conventional analysis, threaten to have an important impact on the development of EMU. They are discussed here in an attempt to indicate their relevance to, and impact on, the process of monetary union as it matures towards the end of this century. These issues are fairly general and abstract, but their importance will become apparent in later sections of this chapter, where the specifics of the monetary union debate are discussed in detail.

The first of these neglected issues is that modern theories of money are driven by the twin conceptions of the functions of money and money as a representation of the real economy. All modern theories of money are thus 'functional' theories of money on the one hand, and 'representational' theories on the other. It is important to highlight the implications of these features of the conception of money as a prelude to discussing the difficulties of managing a new trans-European monetary unit.

The second overlooked feature of modern approaches to money is the increasing importance of 'interest-bearing money'. No longer is it possible to think of the monetary domain in terms of (non-interest-bearing) money on the one hand and interest-bearing bonds on the other. The breakdown of this distinction has profound implications for monetary theory, not all of which can be explored here.

Representational Considerations

Let us consider the issue of money as representation first. The general conceptual mechanism working here is one of money representing value, wealth or the real economy. Money becomes a 'sign' – a sign of wealth, value or the real economy. In the case of neoclassical economic analysis, for instance, value is given by the utility obtained from the use of any commodity. The amount of money consumers are prepared to pay for a commodity depends upon the utility they derive from it. But that utility cannot be observed directly. It is represented by money, as it remains hidden by it. Money operates as a sign of value (utility) and the real economy.

Another way of making this point is via the Fisher or quantity equation, $MV = PQ$ (where M is the money stock, V the velocity of circulation, P the aggregate price level and Q the quantity of goods and services in circulation). As it stands, this equation is an identity. To render it into an equation of causality requires a theory of the behavioural relationships that links these variables together, and which determines the values they take. In general terms, orthodox monetary theorists of the neoclassical approach read this equation from the left to the right. They stress that it is the stock of money that determines or represents the circulation of commodities via the price level, that is, they argue $MV \rightarrow PQ$ as a causal mechanism.

Non-neoclassical economists, by contrast, stress the mode of causality operating in the other direction. They tend to turn the quantity equation around to read it from the left to the right, that is, $PQ \rightarrow MV$. Under these circumstances it is the circulation of commodities which determines or represents the flow of money. Commodities call forth, as it were, the necessary means of their circulation – or money to represent them – not necessarily in a precise quantitative sense that implies their full circulation in each time period, but in the fundamental sense of the mode of causality operative. Money, being a phenomenal form of value as embodied in commodities, 'realizes' that value as it enables it to appear. It represents it. It represents it via its price.

Thus although the mode of causality is reversed here, the fundamental structure remains unchallenged. The reason why monetary theorists can retain the notion of representation in this form is that they see money as a 'sign'. For neoclassical quantity theorists, money is a 'sign' of wealth and utility (which gives its value), for others it is a direct sign of value, embodied in commodities and the real economy. In both cases the referent of that which is signified by money is 'elsewhere' and subject to a different, but more essential, set of determinations. The analytical problem then becomes one of discerning that hidden 'deeper structure' which gives rise to the phenomena it supports.

But one problem with these theories of money is that they both rely on the notion of representation. Representation makes present an absence. In the theories discussed above, money makes value present in its absence. More generally, money makes the real economy present in its absence. But things cannot be both present and absent at the same time. This is the logical flaw in all theories of representation. To undermine such representational theories is also to undermine the depth model and those 'structural' theories that rely upon it.

Functional Considerations

Now the treatment of money as a 'sign of something else' in these theories of money does not exhaust their specification. They are also characterized by a 'functional' component. Money functions as well as signs. For the neoclassical theorist, money functions as the lubricant that glues the social system of capitalist exchange together. It both lubricates and glues. Indeed, it lubricates *as* it glues, via relationships of exchange (see Codere, 1968; Yeager, 1968; Brunner and Meltzer, 1971; Jones, 1976).

Interestingly, it is Keynesian theories of money that emphasize the functional components of money. In elementary economics textbooks the chapters on money all elaborate the functions of money: means of exchange, measure of prices, unit of account, means of deferred payment, and store of value. Thus money as sign and money as function are inextricably linked in modern theories of money. The distinctive Keynesian twist to these is to add the issue of why agents hold money – what function does it fulfil and thus why is it demanded? Here, the concepts of liquidity preference, transactions demand, precautionary motive and speculative motive are introduced to analyse the process of money demand.

Different monetary theories stress one or other of these functions as being of decisive importance within the context of the general matrix of exchange. It is well known, for instance, that Keynes emphasized the store of value function, while non-Keynesians have emphasized the means of payment function as being the most important. Clearly, these functions can also be grouped together. Those stressing the means of exchange also attach to this the standard of price function – the former implying the latter – and the unit of account function. On the other hand, those stressing the store of value function see money as also acting as a means of deferred payment, and also attach to this a unit of account function. Hence the oft quoted comment of Keynes that the role of money is to link the present with the past and the future, that is, it acts as a store of value and as a representation of the means of deferred payment (credit) in an intergenerational sense.

Some interesting and important theoretical issues are associated with these functions of money which cannot all be properly developed here (see Thompson, 1986, Chapter 6 in particular). I will just point to the most relevant for the analysis of this chapter.

In the first place, a hierarchy of functions is an important problem. This was raised above in connection with the Keynesian and non-Keynesian emphasis. An important argument of this chapter is that money does not fulfil the store of value function in an economy dominated by fiduciary money and credit money. Such a conception rests upon an analysis of money as, on the one hand, a representation of wealth (as discussed above) and on the other as dependent upon a 'prior' and arbitrary periodization of time. To store value is to store it over time, but why should this periodization of time theoretically limit the status of money as a category? The problem with the representation element is that in times of inflation, monetary variables lose their connection to the real quantities they are supposed and required to represent. They lose their capacity to represent over time. They 'sign' but they fail to 'represent'. In fact, this is a definition of inflation in one sense. What is more, this is an endemic feature of all representational theories. In the case of 'orthodox' monetary theories, it is written into their conceptualization and is thus not simply a consequence of inflationary situations (see Thompson (1987a) for an elaboration of this point).

The implication of these remarks is to argue that money has to be analysed primarily through its means of payment function – this gives rise in turn to its measure of prices function, as mentioned above. Money performs the means of payment function precisely because, with generalized commodity circulation, there is a disjuncture, both spatial and temporal, between sales and purchases. This implies that all sales and purchases are not co-terminous and simultaneous. In such a situation, it is this disjuncture that gives rise to the existence of money balances which are held over from one period to another. Thus not all money and commodities will circulate in any period. It is this *effect* of generalized commodity exchange which gives rise to the holding of money balances, not some 'demand for liquidity' or 'demand for money' in its own right. Hence, the idea of a generalized Keynesian theory of money, based upon a general theory of choices by economic agents among money and its substitutes, would be displaced by this kind of a conception.

The second main problem associated with any discussion of the 'functions of money' is that it tends to ignore the issue of the *forms of money*. The forms of money are not co-terminous with the discussion of its functions, and cannot be directly generated from this. Indeed, it is these forms – particularly with respect to the differences between commodity money and credit money – which render those 'hierarchy of functions' meaningful and with a significance, as the immediately prior paragraphs testify.

Interest-Bearing Money

The final and most important point about the functions of money from the point of view of this chapter, concerns the significance of the growth of interest-bearing money. With financial deregulation, greater competition, financial innovation and other developments, *all* money is increasingly earning an interest (except cash in hand, of course). This is particularly noticeable in the United Kingdom and the United States. The problem for orthodox monetary theory under these circumstances is that it upsets the traditional way in which demand for money functions have been routinely estimated. Demand for money functions rely upon the choice between non-interest-bearing money and a range of financial assets. It is the interest rate that makes that choice effective, but if 'money' becomes just another asset earning an interest, these distinctions break down.[4]

Suhr (1989) has analysed in forceful terms the general consequences of interest-bearing money for monetary theory, and its effects on the 'non-neutrality' argument. He argues that it has very significant (and detrimental) effects on the real economy. In his terms, interest on money provides 'financial capital' with a kind of double advantage compared to 'productive capital' – holders of financial capital get the advantage of liquidity and an additional return in the form of interest. To 'even out' the positions of financial and productive capital (to equalize the marginal utilities of deploying both) requires a 'tax' on money to increase its cost, not the attraction of an added benefit in the form of interest. The consequence of the double advantage in favour of financial capital and money is a macroeconomic distortion and a detrimental effect on the real economy, he suggests.

Without wishing to endorse all of Suhr's eclectic analysis, we can pursue an implication from it in terms of the functions of money referred to above. Let us put aside for a moment any objections to the idea of the (psychological) 'motives' for holding money, and concentrate upon the impact of interest-bearing money on the various forms of demand for money. The point here is that as the range of interest-bearing money expands, and as financial innovation and deregulation take hold, the relative importance of the different forms of demand changes. Put simply, the *speculative motive* begins to dominate all the other motives for holding money. Increasingly, money is subject to speculative activity, where this applies equally well to the retail market for money as well as the more traditional home of speculative activity, the wholesale market. Private individuals are now becoming increasingly 'financially sophisticated' and 'speculatively sensitive' in the context of interest rate changes. In a moment we elaborate on the possible consequences of this for the evolving European monetary union. Before that we look at the macroeconomics of the process in the light of the analysis so far.

SOME MACROECONOMICS OF EUROPEAN MONETARY UNION

The discussion of European monetary union is saturated by concerns with its possible inflationary consequences, and nowhere more so than in the United Kingdom. Whilst one might want to be sceptical about the reasons for this almost pathological and single-minded concern and propose an alternative, more sensible, package of issues that could form the content of the debate, one is forced to engage in that debate largely on its own terms, at least in the first instance. This course is followed in this section.

The possible consequences of ERM membership and moves towards EMU for small, open, economies of the UK type can be analysed in the context of Figure 5.1. This lays out the basis of a simple asset market approach to integration (Artis, 1991). Figure 5.1 shows the three main variables that have become the object of economic policy in the 1980s: the interest rate, the exchange rate and the inflation rate. The problem is one of setting the interest rate (i) and the exchange rate (e) to achieve zero (or near zero) inflation (p). The two axes show the nominal interest rate and the nominal exchange rate. Through the origin is drawn a zero inflation ray ($p=0$). Below this is an inflationary area ($p>0$). It is inflationary because it signals low interest rates and a depreciating currency. The idea is that aggregate demand is stimulated by low interest rates, and internal cost inflation is accommo-

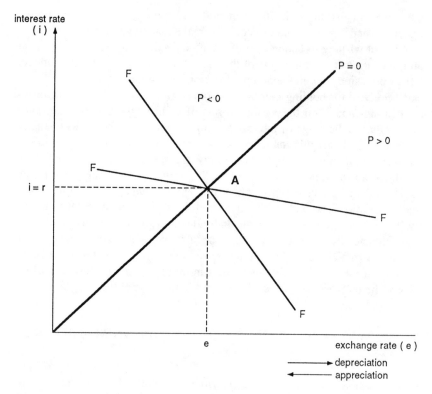

Figure 5.1   Exchange rate and interest rate equilibrium

dated by a depreciation of the currency. Above $p=0$, on the contrary, is a deflationary area ($p<0$), involving high interest rates and an appreciating currency. This indicates a tightening of domestic demand, a choking-off of exports, and deflationary consequences as a result.

Also shown in the diagram is the line FF which represents the equilibrium demand for (and supply of) foreign bonds. For any given balance on the current account, this shows the combination of the interest rate and the exchange rate required to raise finance on the capital account to balance the payments overall. Thus, it might also be termed a 'credible balance-of-payments constrained optimal policy trade-off schedule between i and e'. Given any balance-of-payments position, this curve shows the credible foreign exchange position in terms of the sustainable exchange rate and interest rate.

The shape of FF depends upon the state of integration of the (in this case) European capital markets. The more integrated these become, the flatter the FF schedule, indicating an increasing unresponsiveness of domestic interest rates to exchange rate fluctuations. With total integration the FF line becomes horizontal (there is a single European-wide interest rate), and the analysis developed below would collapse. Thus what is said here pertains only to the transition process towards full monetary union.

The equilibrium interest rate and exchange rate are given by the intersection of FF with the zero-price line at point A. At this point, because there is zero inflation, these are also the real interest rate and real exchange rate.

Clearly, Figure 5.1 embodies a good many assumptions and implicit theoretical considerations that not all would happily accept, but in light of the theoretical pragmatism argued for in the Introduction we can use it to illustrate something both about recent United Kingdom economic policy and a strong argument coming for the UK about fixed exchange rate systems being 'half-baked'.[5] Whilst directed at the particular UK case here, many of these arguments pertain to any small(ish) open economy that sets about joining the ERM in the run-up to EMU.

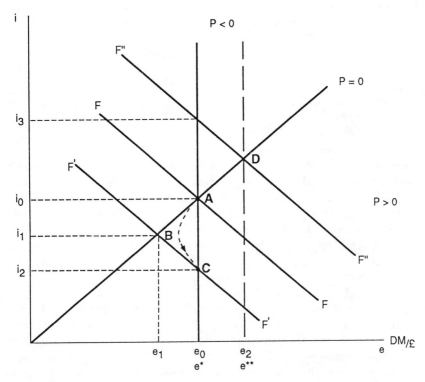

Figure 5.2   Dynamics of adjustment

The complicated-looking Figure 5.2 presents the basic analysis. We begin in equilibrium at point A on FF where $p=0$. The exchange rate is e_0 and the interest rate i_0. Supposing the government now decides to enter the ERM at this exchange rate against the Deutschmark. Although there was some allowable variation of the pound to the DM exchange rate under ERM, we can take this as a surrogate fixed exchange rate mechanism for the purposes of this analysis. This fixed exchange rate is designated e^*.

But the mere fact of fixing the exchange rate (or even semi-fixing it, as under the actual conditions of the ERM) increases the credibility and reputation of the UK authorities (see Chapter 1). The markets now expect that there will be time consistency in policy-making, that domestic inflation will be curbed and so on, so that policy credibility increases (indeed, this is exactly the reason the UK authorities gave for their decision to join the ERM in the first place). However, this credibility/reputation factor alters expectations and moves the foreign exchange line to F'F' – the market would now be prepared to finance the current account at a combination of lower domestic interest rates and higher exchange rates. (In fact, lots of different events could alter the position of FF, including unexpected exogenous shocks.) Under the circumstances outlined, a new equilibrium would be established at B on $p=0$, with the new interest rate at i_1 and exchange rate at e_1.

Given the new fixed exchange rate, however, this is now impossible. If this exchange rate target is credible and held to (thereby maintaining the enhanced reputation of the government), it would be impossible to move to the new higher implied exchange rate e_1, and the pressure would be on for interest rates to fall even further, to i_2 at point C. (In effect point C represents a position of 'excess credibility'.)

A further effect is for inflation to appear – C lying below $p=0$. Interest rates are 'too low' (stimulating domestic inflation), and this is accommodated by a now (relatively) low exchange rate, still at e_0/e^* Herein lies the source of some economists' hostility to the ERM and EMU – there is an inflationary bias written into systems of this type, it is argued. Alan Walters is the best known British exponent of this position (Walters, 1986 and 1990). The substance of his criticism is that the ERM is a nominal exchange rate targeting system. If nominal exchange rates are targeted, this implies the equalization of nominal interest rates across Europe as well. An inflationary bias arises in the UK case, he argues, because (nominal) interest rates are much lower in the rest of Europe, towards which the UK rate will have to move (that is, towards i_2 in Figure 5.2). But with a higher inflation rate in the UK than in the rest of Europe, the required policy move would be to increase real interest rates by increasing the nominal rate. Thus, the ERM route leads to the exact opposite of the required correct policy mix. As a consequence of lower real interest rates, inflationary pressures will grow.

Leaving this particular argument to one side for a moment, what happens at point C? Because of higher domestic inflation, the government's newly found enhanced credibility begins to falter. If it falters entirely, the effect could be to shift the FF schedule out to position F''F'', say. Here, nominal interest rates are increased dramatically to try to head off the domestic inflation. But if the government is constrained to maintain the fixed exchange rate, full equilibrium is not thereby restored. Interest rates move to i_3, which initiates a *de*flationary phase ($p<0$). Clearly, pressure is likely to grow for exchange rate realignment under these circumstances, but this would just go to undermine credibility and reputation even further. Supposing, however, there *was* a realignment – the exchange rate was devalued to e_2 and a new fix initiated there (at e^{**}). This would not solve the problem in a fundamental sense, since it could just reactivate the whole sequence all over again.

From this analysis there is a tendency for the economy to swing wildly from an inflationary position to a deflationary one, and back. Given a constrained exchange rate, the interest rate is the only policy variable under government control, and it moves erratically.

We can now put some added empirical flesh onto these analytical bones by tracing what might have happened to the UK economy in the context of the ERM during the late 1980s, before it actually entered the system. In terms of Figure 5.2, supposing FF is taken as showing the position at the end of 1987. Chancellor Lawson then tried to shadow the Deutschmark at 3.00 DM to the pound, thus 'fixing' the target at e^*. Meanwhile, partly as a consequence, his credibility rose, so that F'F' became the new operative foreign exchange line. To start with, things went reasonably well through the early part of 1988 as the pound shadowed the DM at 3.00. But soon inflation accelerated as the economy moved towards point C. The Chancellor was forced to keep interest rates down in the first instance to maintain the exchange rate target as credible. However, very soon the domestic consequences of all this emerged, inflation increased, and the Chancellor was forced to abandon the exchange rate target, allowing the rate to float up against the DM to 3.20 (approximately its value at the end of 1988/beginning of 1989). The pressure to keep the interest rate down was now off and, indeed, for domestic reasons it was marked up. But the abandonment of the exchange rate target and the higher interest rate policy undermined the Chancellor's reputation and credibility. The FF curve tended to move outwards as a result to F''F'' say, as interest rates moved sharply up (towards i_3) and the exchange rate depreciated towards e_2 at approximately 2.80 DM mid-way through 1989 (marking the effective end of the period of attempted targeting). The government's hope, presumably, was that inflation would move towards D under these circumstances.

This kind of analysis could be extended to other periods and other set-tings, though for the time being the UK economy has slipped into a period of sustained deep recession. (This would probably best be indicated in Figure 5.2 by a position where e_1 hits the schedule FF directly above point B, that is, a tendency towards deflation with high interest rates and an overvalued pound.) But when it eventually emerges from this recession, the above analysis could become pertinent once again; it could operate to haunt it in the future (see also the analysis of the events in September 1992 below). What is more, a similar problem could confront other 'smallish' and weaker open economies on the periphery of Europe (Italy, Greece, Spain, Portugal – even Belgium, Denmark and Sweden?). As a result these countries could find themselves effectively bumping along around the bottom of the busi-ness cycle, experiencing quick bouts of inflation followed by deflation, with wildly oscillating interest rates. They would be in a position of 'permanent recession'.[6]

The Walters solution is to avoid getting enmeshed in anything like the ERM or EMU (an argument echoed by Minford, 1992). What are we to make of this Walters-type critique (which is by no means new or original)? In its own terms its logic clearly stands. In addition, most recent analyses point to the shortcomings of nominal exchange rate manipulation in affect-ing the real exchange rate or in terms of real adjustments. The emphasis is shifting to real exchange rate targeting. But this critique pertains only to a *transitional* stage or system. Indeed, Walters himself is much less antagonis-tic towards any already established European monetary union – though this is highly dependent on its precise character (Walters, 1990, Chapter 7).[7] If inflation rates are stabilized and converge, real and nominal interest rates and exchange rates also converge, so the problem disappears (other than for unanticipated, unaccountable and unaccommodatable shocks to the system as a whole). Under the circumstances of convergence and stability – which are the anticipated outcomes from the point of view of those committed to the ERM and EMU – the difference between the exchange rate and the interest rate disappears as an alternative policy instrument, so any analysis in terms of Figure 5.2 no longer holds.

It is in the transitional period that problems of adjustment arise. One might agree that this period will indeed be a very unstable one, highlighted by the September 1992 events. The objective should then be to get through it as quickly as possible, precisely the opposite to the UK government's posi-tion as outlined in its responses to the Delors Report. To those committed to the 'bicycle theory' – that the EMS will topple unless it pushes on to the next stage – like the French, the issue is clear. The French and their allies argue that the move towards further monetary union and the creation of the European Central Bank (Euro-Fed) will enable them to *regain* some of their sovereignty, rather than to lose it. They prefer the 'pooled sovereignty' of a Euro-Fed to the continued and increasing domination of the *Bundesbank*. As the remaining formal French, Italian and Spanish exchange controls were eliminated in the early 1990s, these nations came increasingly under the sway of decisions made in Germany, as did the United Kingdom whilst it was still a member of the ERM. This is likely to become increasingly politically unacceptable (and increasingly *in*credible to the markets, one might add), hence the determination to press on with Stages two and three of the Delors Report as soon as possible. More on this later.

Another response to the 'inflationary bias' possibility highlighted by Figure 5.2's analysis of the transitional period would be to open up other policy options. Why should only the three variables included here comprise the *exclusive* object of government policy (Artis, 1989)? For instance, fiscal policy could be brought to bear on the inflationary potential highlighted at point C. Equally, incomes policy might also be brought into play, particularly if cost–push were the immediate cause of the inflationary pressures. It is a political constraint in the United Kingdom and other parts of Europe at present that prevents these options being fully discussed.

Fiscal policy is a short-term measure. There may be very good reasons for introducing such measures in the circumstances of European integration (see Chapter 3). But longer-term and more structural solutions also need to be sought if the European-wide recessionary potential indicated by the above analysis is to be avoided. The mention of incomes policies hints at one possible avenue. But this is where we can introduce the more general analysis of neo-corporatist arrangements, and their impact on the wage bargaining process and, as a result, on inflation. The point here is to recognize that the zero-inflation ray ($p=0$) drawn in Figures 5.1 and 5.2 is dependent upon a particular institutional mix of bargaining over wages and other economic variables. If that institutional mix were altered, so would be the position of the $p=0$ schedule. Institutional reform could push the schedule down to $p^*=0$ in Figure 5.3, thereby eliminating the inflationary potential at point C.

The manner in which this argument works is illustrated by Figure 5.4. This is based on the 'new Keynesian' analysis of the labour market in neo-corporatist settings (discussed in Carlin and Soskice, 1989; Henley and Tsakalotos, 1991; Layard, Nickell and Jackman, 1991; and Soskice, 1991, amongst others). It shows the real wage rate on the vertical axis (w/p) and the unemployment rate on the horizontal axis (u). The two sets of schedules drawn on this diagram represent the feasible real wage (FRW) and the bargained real wage (BRW), respectively. The FRW is drawn on the basis of oligopolistic market conditions in which the firm is assumed to face constant labour productivity, a price inelastic demand for its output, and to set its price on a simple mark-up on cost basis. Under these circumstances the

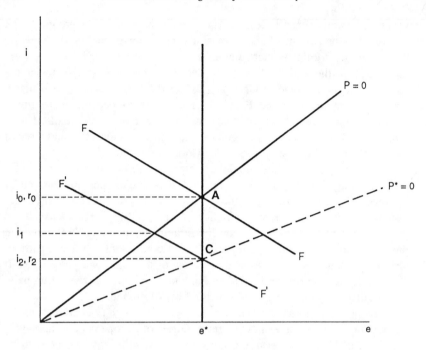

Figure 5.3   Institutional reform and inflation

FRW is constant; it represents the firm's claim on resources given the conditions specified. As against the FRW there is a BRW (sometimes designated a 'target real wage') to which workers will aspire at any given rate of unemployment. The target will be higher the lower is unemployment, because workers will feel able to extract wage increases from employers the tighter the labour market. What is more, this analysis assumes some collective bargaining so that trade unions can exercise that power.

However, the exact manner in which this works is a crucial element of this type of analysis. Given the parameters of the relationship, there will be one level of unemployment at which the BRW is compatible with the FRW. This is known as the NAIRU (Non-Accelerating Inflation Rate of Unemployment). But different institutional conditions pervading the labour market produce quite different outcomes for this NAIRU. This can be illustrated with respect to the position and slope of the BRW schedule shown in Figure 5.4.

Broadly speaking, *decentralized* bargaining produces a flatter BRW *and* one further out to the right. With decentralized bargaining, the level of (un)employment is more sensitive to the real wage, but it also produces higher levels of overall unemployment. On the other hand, while *centralized*

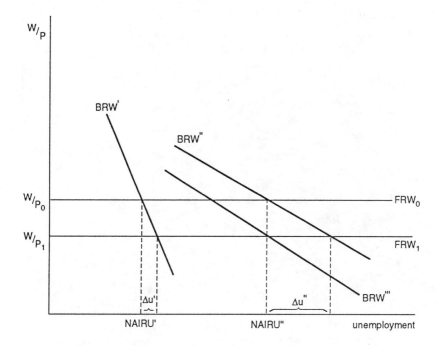

Figure 5.4   Labour market analysis

bargaining produces a less sensitive response of (un)employment to the level
of the real wage, it tends to produce *lower* levels of overall unemployment
(Henley and Tsakalotos, 1991, pp. 433–9; Layard *et al.*, 1991, pp. 129–39;
Soskice, 1991, pp. 37–58). The lower levels of unemployment are illustrated
in Figure 5.5, adapted from Soskice, 1991. Here, the horizontal axis measures an index of centralized union *and* employer bargaining over wages,
those economies closer to the origin with more centralized bargaining arrangements showing lower levels of unemployment than those to the right
with more decentralized arrangements. In addition, there are a number of
other positive economic performative consequences that arise in the context
of more centralized bargaining arrangements, that have to do with the better
investment, profitability and growth records of those countries typified by
such centralized institutional features (Henley and Tsakalotos, 1991, Table
1, p. 427, Table 3, p. 441 and Table 4, p. 442 summarizes the evidence).[8]
   The outcome can be illustrated with reference to Figure 5.4. The centralized (neo-corporatist) BRW is shown as BRW'. Where this cuts FRW_0 gives
the NAIRU' compatible with that particular institutional mix. On the other
hand, the decentralized (non neo-corporatist) pattern of wage bargaining
produces a BRW like BRW", which cuts FRW_0 at the higher NAIRU".

Unemployment

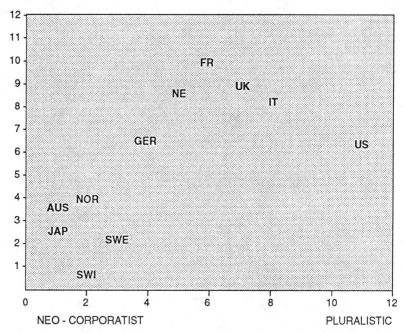

Note: Unemployment is averaged over 1985 and 1989. Italian unemployment refers to north and central Italy.

Source: Soskice, 1991, p. 40.

Figure 5.5   Centralized and decentralized bargaining outcomes

Figure 5.4 also illustrates what happens if an unanticipated shock hits the system. This has the effect of reducing the feasible real wage from w/p_0 to w/p_1. Under these conditions the neo-corporatist institutional configuration is better able to cope with this shock than is the decentralized one; the change in unemployment is $\Delta u'$ compared to $\Delta u''$.

Returning to Figure 5.3, if $p=0$ is that zero-inflation ray compatible with BRW″ in Figure 5.4, then the move to $p^*=0$ would require a radical change in the institutional labour market bargaining configuration associated with BRW′. This represents a structural reform of the labour market and other features of the economic mechanism, with great economic significance. Those economies typified by neo-corporatist arrangements seem better suited to both out-perform their rivals under normal circumstances and to cope better with exogenous shocks. Economies like that of the UK, which have gone furthest down the route to decentralization and which are the most hostile to neo-corporatist forms of interest group governance, particularly in the context of labour market coordination, could thus exhibit the worst of both these worlds.

The advantage of neo-corporatism is that it enables *real* economic variables to be targeted by governments (employment, investment, output, training, and so on), not just monetary ones. It provides a context in which explicit macroeconomic bargaining between the 'social partners' on a wide range of economic matters can, in principle, take place. Of course it does not solve every problem, nor is it (or has it been) always successful. But historically it has a proven record of greater achievement, at least in the European context. As discussed in Chapter 3 the contemporary problem is whether it is now being so undermined by the new neo-liberal onslaught that these positive performative outcomes are about to disappear. As the European economy integrates further, the specific role of the *individual* economies, whether they be neo-corporatist or not, will tend to lessen in the face of whatever new central mechanisms of regulation emerge at the European-wide level. Thus the question is whether these new central institutional mechanisms can reduplicate those neo-corporatisms that might be slowly disintegrating at the national level. Can a transnational European-wide neo-corporatism be constructed that replaces the purely national ones? In addition, is it likely that those countries with little corporatist tradition can in the meantime transform their own domestic institutional structures in a way compatible with the wider advantages attributable to existing neo-corporatist mechanisms? Further, what about the candidate EC member countries to the east and north? How do they fit into this emergent complex structure? Although already discussed in a preliminary way in Chapter 3, these points are developed further in Chapter 7 and the concluding chapter.

One other important implication of the analysis conducted around Figures 5.2, 5.3 and 5.4 concerns the issue of devaluation. In the run-up to EMU it is tempting to suggest that there will be a generalized devaluation of most EC currencies against the German Deutschmark. This has certainly been advocated by many British commentators for the pound (Muelbauer, 1991; Wren-Lewis, 1992), and one suspects this was on the secret agenda for a wider range of central bank governors (Grahl and Thompson, 1992). The events of September 1992 confirmed that the tensions in the existing system threatened to overwhelm it and produce just such a generalized devaluation. After EMU, which is proposed to be introduced sometime between 1997 and the end of this century, there would never be another opportunity to devalue.

The problem here, however, is a well-known one. The reason the British government gave for joining the ERM in October 1990 was to prevent further devaluations. The traditional way the British economy has maintained its competitiveness in the past has been via just this mechanism. But, it was argued, this only accommodated that inflation. It did not strengthen the resolve of British manufacturers to resist inflationary wage claims, for instance, or to enhance their determination to raise productivity and control internal costs in line with their main international competitors. The resort to a devaluation strategy continually let those manufacturers 'off the hook', so to speak. By tying the hands of the UK economy to the strongest in Europe via the ERM – Germany until just recently had the best inflation record – British firms would be forced to swim with the competitive tide, or they would sink. The government would no longer 'bail them out' with a devaluation of the currency.

In many ways this argument is a compelling one. It *has* been a weakness of the UK economy that devaluation substituted for strong pressure to remain internationally competitive via means of productivity growth, marketing skill, and a general attention to business strategy and cost-cutting. Although it would be wrong to exaggerate the lack-of-resistance-to-inflationary-wage-rises line as though this were the only, or main, reason for British uncompetitiveness, the resort to further devaluations *without at the same time introducing other policies as well* could just signal a return to some rather bad old ways for what remains of the British manufacturing sector. The key phrase here is that italicized. Thus one might not wish to advocate devaluation except in the context of some other very firmly established policies. Here, the formal analysis conducted above becomes important once again. In the context of Figure 5.2, devaluation to e_2/e^{**} could serve only to restart the cycle of interest rate fluctuation once again and would solve nothing in the long run. What is needed, by contrast, is to focus attention on the institutional reform discussion associated with Figures 5.3 and 5.4. Thus devaluation *with* institutional reform could provide the basis for a longer-term sustained attack on the structural weaknesses of the economy and reasons for British uncompetitiveness, though, of course, it cannot guarantee the success of this. However, a devaluation without at the same time a determined commitment to some other long-term policy changes is unlikely to solve anything. An interim measure might be the introduction of an incomes policy, of course, which would have the effect of shifting the BRW″ curve downwards to BRW‴, (Figure 5.4), under normal circumstances also reducing the NAIRU. During mid-1992 there were intense pressures on the UK to devalue; the problem was that to accede to these pressures would have been a classic 'panic' measure. Absolutely no preparation, either domestically or internationally, had been made to negotiate the move or to reform institutional structures along with it. As we shall see in a moment, these comments proved only too telling in September 1992.

THE UK'S NEGOTIATING POSITION

Perhaps not surprisingly, then, the UK government set quite a different agenda for itself in the EMU context. Instead of attending to its own structural problems it began with a negotiating position that stressed various proposals for versions of the 'competing currency' option as an 'evolutionary' alternative to the Delors Report approach. An early version of this envisaged complete competition between all Community currencies, while a later version resurrected the idea of a parallel competing currency based upon a 'hard' ECU (a similar option to one already discussed in the context of the Delors Report and dismissed by it). The original United Kingdom version, based upon official currency competition, was not quite the competing currency approach favoured by Hayek and his supporters (Vaubel, 1977). This envisaged a totally free monetary system where any agent could, in principle, issue money. Under these circumstances money constitutes the liabilities of those agents the public shows a confidence in by being willing to hold and use such liabilities. In principle, then, there could be as many competing monies, issued by private sector institutions, as the public was willing to use.

By contrast, in its final form the United Kingdom's approach would have implied the establishment of 12 legal tenders issued by the central banks in the various countries of the Community, so that prices would have been expressed in 12 currencies and consumers would have been free to choose in which of those currencies they undertook their transactions.

The later and more serious suggestion emanating from the United Kingdom envisaged the creation of a 'hard ECU' to parallel individual domestic currencies. The idea here was that this might eventually 'out compete' those other EC currencies. The existing ECU suffered from its composite character, it was argued, reflecting only the *average* performance of its constituent national currencies. The hardness of the new ECU would be guaranteed by the requirement that it could not be devalued against any Community currency – each participating central bank would be *obliged* to maintain the ECU value of the European Monetary Institute's holdings of its currency by agreeing to repurchase those holdings against hard ECUs or some other currency. Thus any national central bank that issued an excess money supply of its own currency, relative to the strongest national currency at the time and hence relative to the hard ECU itself, would be obliged to redeem that excess against hard currency. The EMI would be the only institution able to issue hard ECUs and would manage them against the surrender of holdings of national currencies at an exchange rate set at an intervention margin against parity. The EMI would attract assets in the form of deposits denominated in EC national currencies, and it would issue interest-bearing liabilities in hard ECUs.

The technical problem with this idea, whatever other merits or shortcomings it might have had, is exactly who sets the rate on the hard ECU and how. Would this be set by the EMI or the market? The rate on the EMI's hard ECU liabilities would not be entirely of its own choosing. The private sector would look at these in relation to their options of holding other ERM currencies. Supposing they did not know which of these other currencies would change value, but they knew they could exchange them against the hard ECU at par. The risks associated with holding other currencies under these circumstances might be expected to lead to an interest rate on them at premium to the hard ECU. Thus the hard ECU's market rate would likely be lower than domestic national interest rates. Private economic agents would arrange their currency portfolios accordingly, but they would always have the option of selling zero-yielding national currencies for ECUs at a pegged exchange rate if they wished. Thus, in effect, the participating central banks would be giving private agents a riskless, open-ended currency call option which they could call to their advantage any time some ERM currencies were appreciating. Why would central banks do this when their losses would be potentially open-ended?

This point is analogous to another way of raising an oft-quoted objection to all competing currency suggestions – Gresham's Law effects can take hold at times of considerable financial uncertainty and add to monetary problems. Take the United Kingdom's original suggestion for totally competing currencies. The idea was that 'good money' would drive out 'bad money'. But supposing someone has the option of trading in Deutschmarks or Greek drachma, and the Deutschmark's value is stable while the drachma's value is depreciating. Given that they are both legal tender and the seller cannot refuse a currency of trade, which currency will be the one chosen to trade in? Clearly it will be to the purchaser's advantage to 'hoard' (relatively) appreciating Deutschmarks and 'off-load' depreciating drachma. This will only go to *increase* inflationary pressures as bad money drives out good.

Now, there are many good reservations about this simple Gresham's Law example for modern financially sophisticated economies (Vaubel, 1974, lists the objections), but it still represents a compelling and robust critique of competing currency approaches that has never quite been silenced (the *Bundesbank* President at the time, Karl Otto Pöhl, explicitly raised it in the Delors Report as his main objection to the parallel currency suggestion).

In fact, neither the competing currency nor 'hard' ECU idea attracted support within the EC negotiations over EMU. Rather, a different variant of the latter emerged at the Inter-governmental Conference as something of a compromise to smooth the waters leading up to the Maastricht conference. Proposed by Germany and Spain, this 'hard*er*' ECU looks as though it will eventually replace all other currencies, if and when monetary union takes place towards the end of this decade. This version of the ECU would be 'hardened' by being more closely linked to the DM.

Thus, more or less everyone is agreed that some form of ECU will evolve as the common currency of Europe (if there is to be a common currency for Europe – see Association for the Monetary Union of Europe, 1990). The burden of the above remarks about the hard ECU is that problems always arise when this is thought of as a composite currency of some kind, rather than as a totally independent currency in its own right issued separately by a central bank and not dependent upon any direct link to other currencies. This is the plan as it stands in the middle of 1992, with the creation of a genuine Central Bank for Europe as discussed earlier in this chapter.

One interesting feature of the ECU is that it already plays an important function within the international monetary system. The official ECU acts as a unit of account for the EC and as something of a measure of (exchange rate) prices within the EMS. On the other hand, the private ECU is now a well-developed financing instrument. By the end of 1989 ECU business was the sixth most important in the London banking market; it had also grown in importance as an official reserve asset (3 per cent of global reserves in 1989). Even the British Treasury has issued ECU-denominated bonds. The private ECU's development as a financial asset has been spectacular (Guglielmotto and Passatore, 1987), and by all accounts is set for further significant increases. The question is, what are the consequences of this growth for monetary union if the ECU becomes the European currency of the future?

One problem is that as yet the ECU does not fulfil a transactions function. It is not really a means of payment or a measure of prices. But this is exactly what is required if it is to assume the mantle of a real currency. Indeed, it was argued above that the means of payment function was the central articulating characteristic of money. However, the ECU has grown up as a financing instrument, but in the context of international monetary dealings only. This will, and has, made it particularly vulnerable to speculative activity. If anything the present ECU is only a 'store of value' within the international financial system, but it was argued above that this function is the most ambiguous because of the sign/representation problem. The implication of this analysis is that the ECU could become even more vulnerable and further dominated by the speculative motive for 'holding' it, just as it is assuming its new mantle as a retail transactions money. The argument above was that *all* money is becoming subject to the speculative motive anyway. It could be argued, therefore, that this represents the single most important challenge facing the development of the ECU and of EMU, and it looks as though it will be an unavoidable one. In addition, under such circumstances the need for a clear and coherent regulatory framework for the European financial system becomes even more pressing, though from the earlier analysis this remains a neglected area.

We can illustrate this a little more by looking at the conditions needed for a successful policy of controlling the money supply. In the past 'successful' monetary unifications have taken place where there was already a *de facto* single transactions-based currency, along with considerable economic unification. Contrast Germany – the *Zollverein* – where a successful unification was quickly achieved in the 19th century, with Italy, where it took over half a century or more (see Holtfrerich 1989 and Sannucci, 1989; see also Chapter 7 on the contemporary German unification discussed in these terms). Under the present, wider European conditions almost the exact opposite is the case.

What is more, the case of West German monetary control is revealing. The greater success of Germany in fighting inflation is fundamentally attributed to the constitution of the *Bundesbank;* its independence from political control and the statutes that require it to control inflation as its major objective. As we saw above, in the run-up to the founding of the Euro-Fed this German 'model' transfixed policy-makers. But it is worth asking what other conditions have enabled the *Bundesbank* to be relatively more successful at controlling the German money supply than other European countries have been. Here we could point to the (until recently) relative lack of importance of 'off-shore' DM holdings. Only in recent years has the Deutschmark become an important currency in international trade and finance. German manufacturing business is also very domestically oriented, with relatively few overseas production facilities (though admittedly these are now growing more rapidly within Europe). This is one of the reasons for the slow build-up of overseas DM holdings. Domestic currency deposits are still dominant. The structure of the German banking and finance system has supported this (German insurance companies, which control as much as 70 per cent of long-term savings, are not allowed to buy non-Deutschmark-denominated assets, and they must have a complete currency match for their obligations). Until 1986, short-term bank bonds were also subject to discriminatory domestic currency reserve requirements.

It is these (and other) features of the German economy that have enabled the authorities to control effectively their money supply just as much as, if not more so than, the constitution of the *Bundesbank*. And as these features are changing, so difficulties are beginning to emerge. The *Bundesbank* has had to change its traditional emphasis from M1 targeting to M3 targeting plus sterilization as a response to the increase in off-shore DM holdings (mainly in the UK and Holland) and the potential disturbances this has engendered. With 'forced' financial deregulation and innovation, partly at the behest of the EC move to the single market, these pressures on the German authorities will multiply.

The general point here is to drive home the difficulties of controlling the European-wide money supply as the new ECU takes over – not only the existing ECU-denominated external debt, but all that 'converted' into it, which is at present denominated in existing ERM currencies. It is less the constitution of the Euro-Fed and more this problem that should be at the forefront of policy-makers' minds. One has only to recall the history of the US dollar in the post-war period to recognize the potential seriousness of this problem for the EC (see also Chapter 3's analysis).

A PARTIAL BREAK-UP OF THE ERM? THE EVENTS OF SEPTEMBER 1992

Many of the post-Maastricht tensions alluded to above became manifest in mid- to late 1992. First the Danish electorate voted by a narrow margin against the Treaty on 2 June, then the Irish voted for it. This was followed by a very narrow margin in favour by the French in their referendum on 20 September. In the run-up to these political events, stresses appeared in the money and capital markets. A month earlier, in August, the dollar came under a sustained attack, which despite support buying by 18 central banks continued to fall against the Deutschmark. In early September the weakest currency aligned to the Deutschmark, the Italian lira, came under fire and was first devalued by 7 per cent within the ERM as the Germans decreased their interest rate (Lombard rate) by a quarter of a per cent. Something of the order of £15 billion worth of lira was used in the attempt to hold off this devaluation. However, this failed to ease the pressures, and attention switched to sterling. On Wednesday 16, after massive intervention that cost upwards of £30 billion, UK interest rates were first raised by 5 per cent to 15 per cent and then the pound was floated free of the ERM, along with the lira. Subsequently, on the same day, UK interest rates were brought down to their previous level and the next day by a further 1 per cent. A week later the pound had devalued by nearly 15 per cent against its previous Deutschmark central rate. After the French referendum, a speculative attack against the French franc developed but was beaten off with the sustained assistance of the German *Bundesbank*.

The British government was the loudest in its complaints. It condemned the ERM mechanism in general and the *Bundesbank* and 'speculators' in particular. But this condemnation presumed that its long-term economic strategy was both correct and viable. The difficulty with this argument arises over the valuation of the pound within the ERM mechanism. The British government insisted that its currency was not overvalued, and thus not vulnerable in relation to the 'fundamentals' of the economy. But most sensible commentators, including the German authorities, recognized that the conditions for the maintenance of the exchange rate at DM2.95 to the pound were just not there if any pressure were to mount against sterling. The British argument forgets that the UK joined the ERM in October 1990 at what the officials then involved recognized as a very ambitious rate. It did not consult with its partners on either the timing of its entry or the rate at which it should enter, presenting them with a *fait accompli* by letting them know only an hour before the close of trading what it intended to do. The government then set about talking the rate up, at one time even suggesting that the pound would usurp the Deutschmark as the central stable currency of the ERM. It failed to look to the conditions in the real economy, where the most serious recession since the 1930s had taken hold and where the balance of trade continued to deteriorate; it failed to raise enough taxes to keep its budget deficit within acceptable bounds; and it failed to raise interest rates at the appropriate time. Thus the UK government was hardly blameless.

In fact the German government offered the UK a depreciation within the ERM as much as ten days before 'Black Wednesday' (at the EC finance ministers' meeting in Bath), which the UK refused. For all these reasons the *Bundesbank* was understandably reluctant to support the pound indefinitely and unconditionally when the pressure mounted. Why should the German government have to use all its own reserves or resort to printing Deutschmarks to try to support the unsupportable? Initially, pressure on the pound did not come from speculators but from quite sensible and blameless company secretaries and finance directors who saw the writing on the wall for sterling and wished to protect their liquidity positions by getting out of the pound. Only later did genuinely speculative moves begin.

The *Bundesbank* certainly did act differently in the case of the French franc. But there were good reasons for this. The attack was a genuinely speculative one from the start. The 'fundamentals' of the French economy were basically sound, it having lower inflation and similar interest rates as Germany at the time, and, although in recession, not such deep long-term difficulties as the British economy. The French had also displayed a 'co-operative' attitude towards Europe in general and the ERM in particular. If the franc had been devalued, or forced out of the ERM altogether, the Germans realized that the Maastricht Treaty was truly dead.

The result for the UK is uncomfortable to say the least, but it is a position rather of its own making. Inflation looks set to rise as a result of the devaluation, since the UK government now has no sensible policy to deal with domestically generated inflationary pressures. The fundamentals of the real economy have not been altered. Its diplomatic efforts in Europe seem to have completely failed, it having squandered what little political capital it still had within the EC. In an attempt to get the whole ERM suspended, and the 'fault lines' in the mechanism mended, the UK isolated itself. The long-term result for the Maastricht Treaty and EMU beyond still hangs in the balance, however, for reasons outlined earlier in this chapter and elsewhere in the book. Although the events of September 1992 did not help this process, they should not be viewed as the central reasons for its difficulties. What these events have probably hastened, if they do prove to have any long-term effects, is a real move towards a 'two-tiered' Europe. The inner core of Germany, France, Benelux and Holland (along with Denmark possibly, and Austria and Switzerland) could more easily move to monetary union around the DM, while the rest tag along very much behind in a rag-bag second-tier formation.

CONCLUSION

Returning for a moment to the main analytical and policy substance of this chapter, there is no pretence of having an answer to how the European money supply will be effectively controlled if the ECU becomes the single European currency. Nor is it the claim that inflation is singularly a consequence of money supply growth. However, allowing the money supply to get out of control can at times, under certain circumstances, lead to inflation and uncompetitiveness. Thus any responsible authority must have a policy of controlling the money supply in some form or another. The analysis above has been directed to highlighting the issues that must be faced in the run-up to EMU if monetary conditions are not to get out of hand.

In addition, this chapter has focused upon the convergence criteria that emerged from the Maastricht negotiation, and the difficulties likely to be encountered by the present members of the EC in collectively moving towards meeting these criteria. The overall theme was the deflationary bias this will engender for the European economy as a whole. The EC should go about constructing new institutions to manage EMU with great care, particularly the Central Bank. As it stands, the way this will operate on the basis of the Maastricht Treaty provisions is either very unclear or completely inadequate. Thus the macroeconomic outlook for further European integration looked bleak even before the events of September 1992. Unless some serious rethinking is done by the Commission and the EC member governments, the process of EMU could come apart at any time. The realistic prospects for this are pursued in the final chapter.

NOTES

1. There are fewer problems with these criteria for the main EFTA candidate members. But those from Eastern Europe present another matter, see Chapter 7.
2   '[...] the primary objective of the ESCB shall be to maintain price stability' (Chapter II, Article 2).
3. On monetary policy (its main task) three models began to emerge during 1992 in the detailed negotiations between the members of the EC's Committee of Central Bank Governors: a French proposal for a very decentralized Central Bank, where the operation of monetary policy would be kept as far as possible among the existing national central banks, working in cooperation with the ECB as part of the ESCB; a German proposal for a *Bundesbank*-type of arrangement in which monetary operations are conducted through national central banks in much the same way that the state central banks in Germany are used to assemble and process bids for central bank funds in Germany; and finally a British-style system of centralized decision-making in one location, setting interest rates and providing funds through a set of attendant institutions. Though this system has not been pushed hard by the British, they have argued for a decentralized system allowing them to keep some of their unique monetary institutions.
4. Johnson (1984) documents the shrinking non-interest-bearing money base in the United Kingdom; Arestis, Hadjimatheou and Zis (1992) test for its analytical significance on demand for money functions. Clearly, behind a good deal of this analysis lies the Keynesian LM–IS-type approach, which also relies upon the distinction between (non-interest-bearing) money and interest-earning assets.
5. Walters (1986 and 1990) is the best known exponent of this view.
6. This analysis represents a variation on the discussion in Chapter 1 involving the two levels of policy-making, the international and the domestic (Figure 1.2). The problem it poses is the construction of a 'win set' under the circumstances of an international monetary regime (the ERM) and a domestic policy constraint/objective of zero inflation. The argument here is that a 'win set' cannot be successfully constructed, or at least not without the introduction of additional policy variables – see the analysis in the main text.
7. It would have to be a monetary union backed by gold or a bundle of commodities to tether the monetary unit to some 'real' variable.
8. Henley and Tsakalotos sum up thus: 'The first theme is the high growth and employment performance of those economies with a high degree of corporatism, such as the Scandinavian economies, the Netherlands and Austria. This has been noted by many other authors.... It also emerges ... that income and employment growth in corporatist economies have been relatively stable' (p. 426). '... we can clearly see on average the superior growth and investment performance of the strongly corporatist economies during the 1973–75 recession' (p. 440). 'The results show ... that investment in the strong corporatism group is on average the least sensitive to short-run fluctuations in [corporate] income' (p. 442).

6. Management and Industrial Policy in Europe

INTRODUCTION

As the European Community moves towards closer economic and monetary union, the rapidity of the transformation in the industrial bases of the 12 states is likely to gather momentum. This is so even as they are coincidentally passing through probably the most fundamental restructuring of their economies since the end of the Second World War, occasioned by the worldwide recession of the late 1970s and early 1980s.

This chapter concentrates on an aspect of this double restructuring that is less well researched and less widely discussed than other features. The spatial incidence of this restructuring, its effects on labour, the systemic forces driving it, the broad macroeconomic strategies to cope with it, the economic rationale for the single market and the like, form the usual focus. By contrast, the emphasis here is upon managerial strategies and the internal company calculations that firms are adopting in the face of a transformation in their production process technologies, and upon how the official European economic management bodies are, or should be, reacting to this. The central analytical concept in the discussion is 'forms of economic calculation'; what this means is elaborated upon below. The chapter takes a deliberately narrow focus to highlight the impact of such managerial calculation and decision-making on the process of transformation in the manufacturing sector that is already partly under way in Europe. But the main point is to drive home the need to adopt a more radical approach – to push for a wider embrace of the trends discussed here, both from the point of view of management and in terms of public policy.

However, the intention is not to become complacent about the new calculative regime emerging around the management of complex production processes, but rather to suggest ways this might be used to press for a more dynamic objective overall. The discussion below develops a critical relationship with the trends identified. If the European economy is to maintain its competitiveness, and hopefully enhance it, it is argued that close attention must be paid to the issues discussed in this chapter.

Elsewhere, the impressive record of United States writers on these matters has been thoroughly documented (Thompson, 1987, reprinted in Thompson 1989a). This chapter partly reinforces and extends the contribution these authors have made to our understanding of the new managerial practices. In one of the most depressing, but also most fascinating, books to have emerged from that genre of American writings dealing with the decline of corporate America, Holland (1989) provides a scrupulous and scholarly account of the decline of a US machine tool company (Burg Tool), which speaks for the machine tool industry as a whole and for much of the US manufacturing sector beyond. The book charts the systematic undermining of managerial practices associated with the support of what Wheelwright has called 'the manufacturing function' in American businesses (Wheelwright, 1985), and its replacement by a regime of short-term financial calculations designed to generate as much liquidity as possible. The exemplary virtue of this book is that it coolly dissects the implications of this change in managerial style. Holland's analysis points to the fact that this change is not something re- cently arising in the USA (and elsewhere one might add); it is an endemic feature of US business practice. The book charts the devastating conse- quences of such changes on the viability of the manufacturing sector, and it suggests an alternative reconstitution of calculative practices that could help place the management of complex production processes back at the centre of concern in the USA. This chapter shares a similar concern for the evolution of European management techniques and its possible consequences, and it draws heavily on contemporary American business school writing.

The main reason for taking these American business school authors as the point of departure for this analysis, is that they represent an advanced contri- bution to the reformulation of managerial calculations needed to meet the challenge of industrial restructuring under contemporary conditions. No par- allel body of literature of such quality has emerged as yet in the United Kingdom or elsewhere in Europe. Of course, this is not to say the US writings referred to are beyond reproach. The need is to engage critically with them, as developed below. The chapter also has something to say about the forms of economic calculation current amongst continental European business, particularly in Germany.

WHY EMPHASIZE MANUFACTURING?

Why does manufacturing matter? It is important to provide a strong rationale for a concern with the fate of European manufacturing capability that is not just sentimental (see, in particular, Cohen and Zysman, 1987; and Williams *et al.*, 1990 for the UK). The romantic idea of a 'post-industrial society' is strongly etched into contemporary debate about economic development, as is the connected argument about the (unproblematic) trend towards a service-based economy. Here, a number of interrelated matters arise.

In the first place, there are consequences of these trends for jobs and household incomes. The decline in manufacturing has been accompanied by a decline in that 'intermediate' category of manual semi-skilled jobs, traditionally filled by male heads of households. In addition, it has been the manufacturing sector that has produced the highest paid jobs for a wide section of the ordinary working population. Service sector jobs are traditionally lower paid 'secondary' jobs filled by women employees. The reason why manufacturing has produced higher paid jobs has to do with the traditional high value-added in this sector and its higher productivity.

Without wishing to endorse all the undesirable consequences arising from a heavily gendered division of jobs, there is a significant consequence for household incomes as the manufacturing sector declines. Basically, this involves the substitution of higher paid jobs for lower paid, often part-time, jobs, and it means a reduction in the standard of living with all its knock-on implications. The reconstruction or consolidation of manufacturing thus crucially affects future economic prospects.

Secondly, the output from the service sector is not as readily internationally traded as is the output from manufacturing. For instance, although the manufacturing sector only represents some 22 per cent of UK total national output (GDP), it still accounts for approximately 62 per cent of its international trade (exports). In addition, although difficult to measure precisely, international trade in services has not been growing at a faster pace than trade in manufactured goods. What is more, for instance, until just recently the UK economy was losing world share of export trade in services at a rate comparable to that of its loss of share in manufacturing trade *(Bank of England Quarterly Review, 1987* – the UK's share of world trade in manufacturing has recently risen slightly, however).

Thus there are likely to be some major balance-of-payments implications of the decline in manufacturing in any economy; something clearly emerging in the case of the UK and the USA over the past decade, and a possibility for Europe as a whole in the future if the analysis of Chapters 3, 4 and 5 proves correct. Those countries with a robust manufacturing sector are able to manage their balance of payments more effectively than those countries where manufacturing has declined, and particularly where the traded goods account has gone rapidly into the red. A positive traded goods account also enables countries to manage more easily their exchange rate, since it secures an added credibility for policy pronouncements (for example, Germany and Japan).

Finally, we should point to the interdependence between manufacturing and services. The issue should not be posed in terms of services *or* manufacturing. Rather, it is increasingly clear that these are closely interlinked; an effective service sector implies an effective and efficient manufacturing one. If either of these sectors declines, so can the other. Indeed, we might still recognize the leading edge of manufacturing in stimulating a range of new and improved services, where the trade in the one is accompanied by trade in the other. Thus a balanced growth in both of these sectors is necessary to maintain a successful economy.

For all these reasons manufacturing is important, and the reconstruction, restructuring or consolidation of manufacturing a central concern for public policy.

EUROPEAN RESTRUCTURING

As has been analysed at length in previous chapters, the debate about European restructuring has been dominated by the 1992 single market programme, with possible full economic and monetary union to follow by the end of the century. This debate is proceeding under a very orthodox set of economic arguments associated with the gains from freer trade and economies of scale (Chapter 4).

As we have seen, the dominant form of analysis driving the official justification for the 1992 programme is a neo-liberal one. The European economic system needs to be purged of the continuing obstacles to freer competition. The impurities to be swept aside include the remaining non-tariff barriers to trade, the obstacles to minimum efficient scale operation on the part of firms, and any other impediments to market competition. The implication is that once these inefficiencies have been eliminated by the 1992 liberalization programme, the newly competitive European economy can be left to itself to generate the welfare benefits.

One result of the analysis conducted in Chapter 4 was that the 1992 programme is unlikely to have very much impact on European industry in terms of EOS benefits. This is where the American literature becomes important, since it was the first to challenge systematically a future involving the production of standardized goods via mass production techniques to reap internal economy of scale advantages. The Commission's image of the European future, embodied in its basic approach to quantifying the benefits of 1992, is one of increased size of firm generated by European-wide mega-mergers. Of course, this sits rather uneasily with the basic neo-liberal programme of more competition.

It is worth reiterating an early critique of EOS from the American business school community (Hayes and Wheelwright, 1984). These Harvard Business School authors stressed that it was an over-reliance on size and EOS, along with the deployment of discounted cash flow techniques, that had been one of the main reasons for the decline of the American manufacturing sector. As part of their critique, the authors highlighted various forms of *dis*economies of scale (which were fully analysed in Chapter 4). Against the emphasis on larger size, these authors introduced the idea of a 'minimum economic-sized plant'; one that is the smallest size possible commensurate with competitive and operational viability, and that has a highly focused manufacturing function.

This kind of a critique of the calculative practices of American businesses has an equal weight when directed at European, and particularly British, management, which share many of the features of US practice. But it is also part of a more developed attack against, amongst other things, the predominant notions of Anglo-Saxon management education. Currently, these are embodied in the MBA programmes that have swept through the UK and which are now increasingly being adopted within the countries of mainland Europe.

As traditionally set up, MBAs have concentrated on three core areas: organization and control theory, financial and portfolio management, and marketing. These tend to be taught in terms of their analytical rigour and strategic elegance. A detached stance is adopted, stressing the formal and universal character of managerial techniques, which suits the idea that management exists as a 'tool' to be deployed in any situation. What it downplays is how to decide on appropriate process technologies; the management of complex production processes; the 'hands on' experience of well-managed line operations; the relationship between research and development, design, technical innovation, and so on; that is, just those elements crucial to a robust 'manufacturing function'. These are the neglected elements in business school education, and within MBAs in particular. It is interesting to note that the most successful European economy, namely Germany, does not have a single business school teaching an MBA or equivalent programme (according to Lane, 1989, p. 93). It does however, have 'business education' of a particular type within its lower-level education structures, which is becoming increasingly popular as a subject to study. More on this below.

CHANGES IN PRODUCTION PROCESSES

Many of the more astute American business school writers have been quick to spot the importance of Japanese production process technology for the restructuring of US manufacturing industries. They have been instrumental in popularizing the character of best-practice Japanese techniques. However, it is possible to clarify the importance of these further and to note their limitations, as well as to point to some of the shortcomings of the most advanced American analysis. We do this here with the future of post-integration European industry very much in mind. The adoption of best-practice Japanese techniques is something that European industry has itself become very much aware of.

Let us begin with some clarification. Figure 6.1 is drawn from one of the best accounts of the problem facing American managerial practice. In their book, Hayes, Wheelwright and Clark (1988) suggest that a thorough reform of managerial calculation is necessary in order to develop a dynamic and

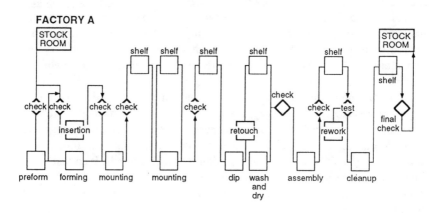

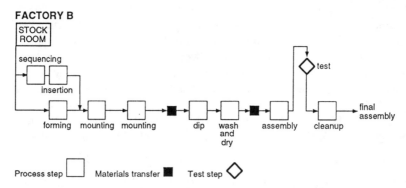

Source: R.H. Hayes *et al.*, *Dynamic Manufacturing* (1988), Figure 7–2, p. 199.

Figure 6.1   Shop-floor manufacturing configurations

robust manufacturing organization fit to compete in the contemporary economic order. At the heart of their analysis lies the question of the design of the shop floor. The two basic manufacturing architectures shown in Figure 6.1 refer to two different factories producing much the same product, utilizing similar machines and processes and having comparable computer software, but with significantly different hardware management systems. The basic structures of the production process flows are quite differently configurated.

In Factory A, batches of product move through various conversion processes – forming, mounting, connecting, dipping, washing and so on. At each of these stages the products are inspected ('checked') and then stored as work-in-progress before moving on to a subsequent process. In Factory B, essentially the same equipment has been arranged to permit a process flow where checkpoints and in-process storage have been eliminated and work-in-progress inventory has been cut dramatically.

> The whole process is more integrated and streamlined. Far fewer transactions are required to manage it, and fewer material handlers are needed to move material through the process and in and out of storage areas. The result is a much faster (three days versus four weeks) and more efficient production cycle (Hayes, Wheelwright and Clark, 1988, p. 199).

This analysis of two actual factory configurations is indicative of many general features. Commentators returning to the USA and Europe from Japan often note the 'untidiness' of US and European factories compared to Japanese ones. Stocks and work-in-progress litter the factory floor, and a generally disorganized impression reigns in US and UK factories in particular. In addition, Hayes *et al.* note that Factory A-type conditions tend to generate a greater degree of centralization of decision-making, while in type B conditions both responsibility and authority are consistently pushed down to lower levels. They also noted the different supplier network conditions in the two actual cases they studied to generate Figure 6.1. Firm B had 250 suppliers, many small to medium-sized, locally-based and personally known to the managers in Factory B. Factory A, by contrast, had over 1000 suppliers, a more anonymous relationship to them, and one based predominantly on price considerations.

All these features should be familiar to those cognizant with the literature on flexible specialization discussed in Chapter 4. But Hayes *et al.,* while clearly familiar with this literature and sympathetic to it, are not committed to its systemic/general character or implications. They do not see it as necessarily the embodiment of a new paradigm of industrial organization but just as one form among many of the 'manufacturing functions' of the future. This is much the same position as that taken by the MIT Commission on

Industrial Productivity in its main report (Dertouzos, Lester and Solow, 1989). In this case, again, the analytical stance is one that sees flexible specialization as just one element, though an important element, in the problem facing the US manufacturing sector as it struggles to regain its international competitive edge. Neither of these two approaches exaggerate the importance or novelty of flexible specialization or places it necessarily at the centre of a strategy for industrial regeneration.

However, more recently a new variant of the flexible specialization argument has arisen, and gained considerable credence amongst business personnel in particular. This is the idea of 'lean production', advanced in its most developed form so far by Womack, Jones and Roos (1990). This book claims a detailed study of the new Japanese production techniques (mainly in the car industry, however), which it sums up under the title 'lean production', and which is then contrasted to mass production. Such lean production is technically defined in terms of the absence of a large indirect set of 'supervisory' and maintenance workers, low levels of stocks, and the presence of reskilled, multi-tasked workers using flexible equipment for small batch, just-in-time production with rapid changeover. Rework is kept to a minimum by an emphasis on total quality production. Component supply is flexibly organized, as is the lean distribution system. All in all, it is argued, this combination delivers variety at lower cost than mass production, and hence its success.

But there are a number of problems with this broad characterization of the reasons for the superiority of Japanese car manufactures as compared to those in the USA (Williams *et al.*, 1992). In particular, it exaggerates the importance of stock differences (which are not as great as the lean production enthusiasts suggest); it misunderstands the advantages of the Japanese ability to take labour cost out of *any* production process, attributing this to the conditions of the 'lean' factory only; it underestimates the importance of different macroeconomic demand conditions to the sustaining of continuous flow working and capacity utilization in factories, and the importance of the home market demand conditions in both cases (US home market saturated, Japanese home market expanding); finally it also misunderstands differences in 'manufacturability' of cars in both cases (their manufacturing design characteristics), and underemphasizes the importance of lower wages and tighter working conditions in giving the Japanese a competitive advantage.

We can examine some of these claims and counter-claims further by referring to Figure 6.2. One important point not discussed in the literature reviewed above but pursued here, is the consequences of the different 'styles' of manufacturing for the forms of internal economic calculation conducted by the firm. As we shall see, this is important from the point of view of the nature of financial calculation in relation to the technical organization of

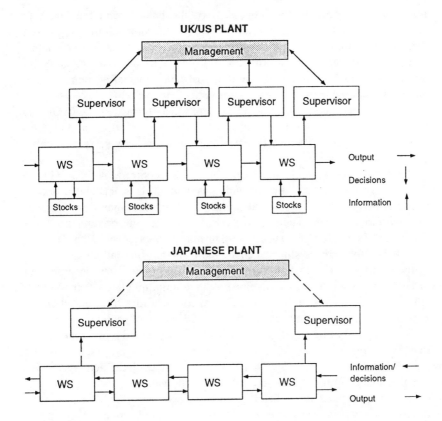

Figure 6.2   Stylized 'US/UK' and 'Japanese' plants compared

production. Figure 6.2 represents a generalization of the elements contained in Figure 6.1 and some of the comments made about the technical form of 'lean production' above. The typical 'US/UK' plant in Figure 6.2 roughly corresponds to the type A factory in Figure 6.1, while the type B factory roughly corresponds to the typical 'Japanese' plant (in a moment we come on to the typical 'European' plant). For the purposes of this discussion, these different factory forms represent 'ideal types', which help to clarify conceptually the implications of differences in production technique and financial calculation. They are not meant to be accurate descriptions of actually existing plants and factories, which would demonstrate considerable variation and hybrid arrangements.

Taking the top part of Figure 6.2 first, here we have a very 'complicated' and 'untidy' production system (which should not be confused with a complex one). At each of the workstations (WS), a stock and inventory are held.

Information concerning the processing of the batches and the levels of stocks is passed up to the supervisory level for decisions on the progress of the output through the factory and to keep a check on costs, faults, quality, and so on. Management information and decisions are also regularly involved – production targets monitored, cost and financial accounting conducted, orders fed back into the control system, and so on.

Thus, in this case, while output in a physical form flows *horizontally* through the factory – if in an interrupted fashion – information and decisions, a good many of which take a 'financial' form, flow *vertically* within the organization.

If we take the typical 'Japanese' factory by contrast, with a JIT and 'kanban' system in operation – and thus with little stock and work-in-progress inventory – both output *and* information/decisions flow *horizontally* within the firm. There is little need to refer information up for a decision to be made at the supervisory or management level. What is more, the information and decisions taken are more about 'physical' characteristics of the process than monetary ones. The 'kanban' – which can be simply an order form placed in a vinyl envelope or an aluminium plate attached to the side of a components bin – plays the dual role of order form and delivery notice. It specifies the amount and timing of delivery of each type of part or in-process good to be supplied, and is usually dispatched a few times a day to each upstream shop or WS. As the order is completed, the 'kanban' is sent back to the downstream WS with the goods/parts specified. Each WS receiving a 'kanban' from a downstream WS, in turn dispatches its own 'kanban' to each WS located immediately upstream, and these chains of bilateral order–delivery links can be extended as far as outside suppliers.

The JIT/'kanban' system is also known as a 'zero inventory' method, and this represents one of the key elements in how a firm's internal financial calculations must be reformed if it is to reap the proper benefits of this system. Here we introduce Kaplan and Johnson's (1987) well-known analysis of the deficiencies of traditional cost accounting though, as we shall see in a moment, they formulate their solution to this identified deficiency rather inadequately.

Kaplan and Johnson's original point was that traditional management (cost) accounting concentrates too closely on direct labour cost, particularly in terms of overhead allocation. As the importance of direct labour costs in the production process diminished and the importance of overheads increased, the allocation of overheads to products or cost centres on the basis of the direct labour they involved would produce a growing distortion in the information available to management. It meant, for instance, that performance indication on a cost-centre-by-cost-centre basis, or pricing and profit calculation on a product-by-product basis, became increasingly divorced from the 'true' costs involved in these operation and production areas (Cooper and Kaplan, 1987).

The remedy suggested by Kaplan, Johnson and Cooper is for a more elaborate cost monitoring and control system, particularly with respect to overheads. However, the form of these systems also needed to change, they suggested. As well as financial reporting, firms need to develop more *physical* measures of performance – and not just in terms of direct machine hours (as a surrogate alternative measure of labour hours for overhead allocation) – or direct material cost systems. What are increasingly relevant for competitive advantage, they argue, are dimensions such as throughput times, quality measures, yield measures and customer satisfaction – all of which require different sorts of internal performance measurement. Thus, just a single cost system is not enough (Kaplan, 1988; see also Patell, 1987).

What is required is an analysis designed to track costs in their multifarious dimensions; first to uncover the allocable nature of what have traditionally been regarded as overhead costs – to make fixed costs variable – and then to match these costs to particular products more accurately.

The problem with this remedy is that it essentially calls for more of the same. If it is the case that traditional standard cost systems in manufacturing were designed to value inventory and not to measure product cost, what should be done when the objective is to have zero inventory? An elaboration of the system, even to make it more accurate in the tracking of product costs, seems at odds with the change in the whole philosophy of manufacturing represented by the lower part of Figure 6.2. Indeed, this would seem to indicate the necessity to think about measures designed to reduce the total costs of the organization as a whole, at least in the first instance. The 'Japanese' model is designed to eliminate or decrease the number of internal divisions within the plant – to reduce the number of 'cost pools' – not to reinforce them by more correctly allocating 'true' costs to them (Foster and Horngren, 1987). Kaplan's 'Kantian' project – to press correctly the conceptual map onto the real – is, anyway, bound to fail.

While recognizing that JIT makes the direct traceability of some costs easier, the crucial emphasis is upon total plant performance rather than on the performance of each individual cell, and upon the general reduction in the amount and extent of 'overhead' costs. This latter point is a direct implication of the 'kanban' system with its elimination of extensive 'vertical' reporting and decision-taking.

Another implication of the system is to emphasize process costing at the expense of orthodox job costing, with a reduction in the number of cost trigger points within the plant and the establishment of 'backflush' costing on the basis of these. At its extreme, such a backflush system may only need one or two trigger points near the end of the process (at the finished product or point of sale stage), combined with a component entry audit at the begin-ning. The overriding objective, then, is to reduce drastically the complexity of the costing system as the product flow itself becomes more streamlined (not to make it more complex *à la* Kaplan *et al.*) and to increase the incen-tives for plant-wide economies rather than to concentrate on individual subunit efficiencies.

The attempted elimination of stocks is also important for another reason. It provides the incentive to improve continually the design of the production process overall (Williams *et al.,* 1989b). Any build-up of stocks highlights the appearance of an inefficient link in the production chain. Traditional standard costing systems are designed to monitor stocks and work-in-progress inventory via analysis of variance methods. They build in acceptable levels of stocks/waste, when the objective consistent with JIT/'kanban' methods is to eliminate stocks/waste altogether. Thus cutting stocks cuts costs *and* waste.

However, we also need to be critical of the full implications of the Japa-nese model, even as we sing its praises. Fundamentally, it represents an authoritarian approach to the production process, demanding a level of effort and work commitment from employees that can amount to outright coercion at times. It probably demands a level of work intensity and effort too high to be acceptable in most European or American contexts, though by all ac-counts the speed and intensity of work in Japanese transplants in the UK is as onerous as it is in mainland Japanese plants. One problem is that *any* form of factory and work process is going to demand a level of high tempo effort and boring, routineized intensity from its workers that cannot be avoided. The idea that somewhere there is a nice, comfortable, low intensity, interest-ing and non-routineized factory working environment is a romantic myth.

However, having made these remarks, it is worth exploring other alterna-tives which could combine both efficiency savings and competitive advan-tages with a more acceptable working regime and more engaging working environment. One such approach is illustrated in Figure 6.3. This shows a schematic representation of a Swedish car factory operated by Volvo in southern Sweden (Berggren, 1989; Alvstam and Ellegard, 1990; Hammarstrom and Lansbury, 1991). The architecture of this factory involves a series of horseshoe-type production bays in which production teams work on a vari-ety of machines to construct complete cars. The factory has been described as looking like a giant garage. It is designed to have a throughput of 40,000 cars a year. One thing it seems to involve is the break-up of a strictly 'linear' output and information/decision-making structure typified by the other two examples discussed so far. A less hierarchical, more cooperative, informal and 'partnership'-type structure operates in terms of its working environ-ment and control arrangements, which is represented in circular form in

"EUROPEAN" PLANT

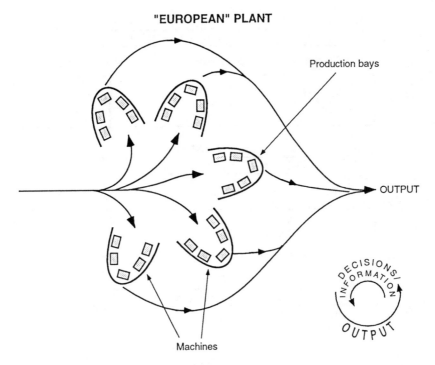

Figure 6.3   Stylized 'European' plant

Figure 6.3. In contrast to the other two types, it is a non-assembly line, but still high volume production process. The managerial accounting/control system in these types of plant is also quite different to that in more traditional plants (Jonsson and Gronlund, 1988). A more decentralized system that has to build a flexible 'learning' mechanism into the generation of its operational statistics is called for.

This particular example might be used as a model for the 'European' plant of the future, in contrast to either the 'US/UK' or 'Japanese' models just discussed. If the analysis of Chapter 4 proves correct; that the European economy of the future will move towards a more flexible production environment, then the model of typical plant configuration also needs to change to meet that new production environment, and with it the nature of the work process and the management accounting regime. A possible hybrid between the 'Japanese' and the 'European' configuration may actually be emerging already, and this of itself requires consideration of the points made above about the approach to management accounting in the Japanese-style production environment.

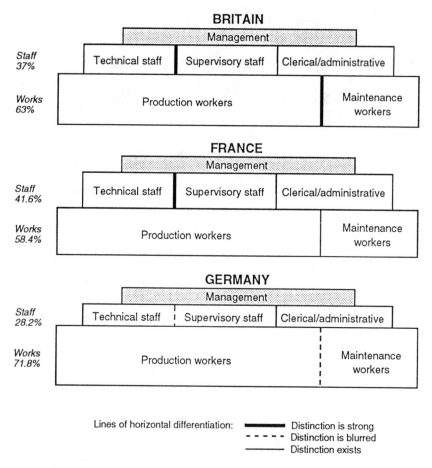

Source: C. Lane, *Management and Labour in Europe* (1989), Figure 2.2., p. 47.

Figure 6.4   National organizational configurations

Finally in this section, it will be useful to point to the variety of typical European industrial organizational forms so as not to give the impression of a single monolithic model. One way of doing this is shown in Figure 6.4 (Lane, 1989), where the comparative national organizational configurations of the UK, France and Germany are sketched. Note that Britain seems to have the most 'demarcated' system, France the most 'hierarchical' and Germany the least differentiated. In many ways the German system is closest to the Japanese model so far described in this book. The emphasis is clearly on production (reinforced in Lane's excellent analysis), with only a loose differentiation between the various functional areas and levels shown.

In his discussion of the historical development of German management, Locke (1985; see also Locke, 1984 and 1989) points to the strictly academic nature of German 'business economics', as taught in the university sector. Most management education in the usual sense of the term goes on 'in-house' and recruits from those with technical expertise (Lane, 1989, Chapters 4 and 5). Those with law degrees are also important in management.

Locke stresses the centrality of accounting education in the training of German managers, particularly cost accounting. But that cost accounting is closely related to engineering and production concerns. Germany would seem to have highly developed technically-based cost accounting systems in place which are designed to control costs in sophisticated high technology industries. But while management accounting in this form is strongly represented, financial accounting is underplayed and underdeveloped, quite the opposite to US and UK practice. (In the UK the single most important employment for graduates is accountancy.) The contemporary German system still owes much to the legacy of Schmalenbach, the founder of German 'business economics' (Forrester, 1977; see also Schoenfeld, 1972 and Kern, 1975).

EXTERNAL REPORTING AND THE NEW PRODUCTION PROCESSES

Mention of the traditional importance of financial accounting in the USA and the UK raises the issue of the implications of the changes in internal firm calculation for external reporting and assessment. This section reviews some changes in emphasis that may be needed to cope properly with a renewed interest in the 'manufacturing function' and the management of complex production systems.

The main point is to challenge the almost exclusive emphasis on the profit and loss account and balance sheet that typifies the existing financial assessment of companies in much of Europe. The argument is that there is a need to develop an alternative battery of techniques and processes that will speak to a more 'productionist' objective and that will link to the kinds of changes going on in the within-the-firm realm of calculation just described. Clearly, the institutional obstacles to the implementation of any of the suggestions developed below are likely to be formidable, something explained in a moment. In addition, the kinds of calculations discussed below should be seen as *supplementing* the profit and loss account, not as completely replacing it. That would be neither totally desirable nor institutionally feasible, though one might agree that the traditional emphasis should be pushed into a secondary position as far as possible.

In the face of the rearrangement of the internal character of firms and in their relationships to their suppliers, Johnson and Lawrence (1989) suggest the image of the new extended form of industrial organization could be summed up as a 'value-adding partnership', or kind of network structure (see Thompson, 1992a, 1992b and 1993). It is this suggestion of generating chains of value-added measures that we take up first in this section.

Value added (VA) is a concept that has more purchase in Japan and Germany, where it already forms part of the normal presentation in company accounts (Gallizo and McLeay, 1988). There are two basic ways of calculating value added (Wood, 1978):

1. The cost subtraction method: sales revenue – (bought in components + bought in materials + energy + services) = VA.
2. The appropriation method: (wages + taxes + retained profits + distributed profits + depreciation + interest) = VA.

In principle these two methods should produce the same results.

We can rearrange the appropriation method to show a measure of the value added available for distribution (VAD):

$$VAD = VA - (depreciation + retained\ profits).$$

VAD is that amount available to be distributed to the owners, the creditors, the workers and the government.

Secondly, we could compute a measure of the resources available for distribution to only one factor of production, such as labour (VADL):

$$VADL = VA - (depreciation + taxes + profits + interest).$$

There are a number of important advantages of this VA-type approach.

In the first place the costs of labour are a part of VA, the opposite to the traditional approach. With traditional accounting methods, wages are treated as a cost and profit as a residual surplus (to capital). In the VA case wages are a residual 'surplus' after the 'costs' of depreciation, finance and profits have been subtracted. This can have important ideological and operational consequences, since it implies that increasing labour productivity via training and skill can increase VA, and it lessens the 'hire and fire' reaction of companies as they face fluctuations in their business fortunes. With the profit and loss account treating labour as a cost, there is a continued incentive to 'cut labour out' to reduce costs.

Secondly, the objective of maximizing VA is equivalent to maximizing GNP and growth. On the other hand, there is no clear or obvious relationship between maximizing profits and GNP or growth. Profits can increase while growth or GNP declines. Thus a VA measure more easily links company position with the condition of the national economy than does a profit measure. Since there is also a close link between marginal VA and employment, VA links a reduction in output to a reduction in employment. It also enables the import content of output to be highlighted via indicating the importance of imported semi-manufactured goods in domestic production. Similarly, the 'deindustrialization' argument is better discussed in terms of VA than profits, since the share of the latter can quite easily increase in an economy while the manufacturing sector and VA declines.

Thirdly, as emphasized by Johnson and Lawrence, VA speaks to the image of a company or economy as being a kind of 'partnership' between all the elements involved in production. It emphasizes the collective nature of production and shows what the 'team effort' is doing to raise gross national value added. It is thus more acceptable to labour than profit, with all the latter's exploitative overtones. In this way it is also more conducive to a neo-corporatist form of social organization, where the social partners play a collective leading role in determining economic outcomes.

Thus VA would seem to have much more informational content than profit calculations. It has its problems however.

Supposing we were to set the objective of maximizing VA and in some way comparing it to capital employed (C) – hence generating the ratio VA/C. This is obviously problematical in that it might encourage low labour productivity. Maximizing the ratio encourages an increase in VA and a reduction in C – leading to 'Stone Age economics'. One way round this could be to compare VA to labour employed (L), thereby maximizing the ratio VA/L. Clearly, whichever of these were chosen it would be worthwhile generating the other. No single ratio or criterion is going to be sufficient for an adequate assessment.

Another problem with VA arises when comparisons of company positions are made over time. If a company 'subcontracts' part of its production, its VA falls. Thus, in a period when subcontracting is growing rapidly, as contemporarily (Chapter 4), and firms are breaking up their operations into autonomous or semi-autonomous parts, VA calculations must be treated with caution. Of course, this problem does not arise at the aggregate level. That is why it is important to look at value-added chains in interlinked production environments that may form branches or sectors of production.

One possible response to some of these issues is to tackle the problem from a different angle. Another way of redressing the imbalance against labour found in traditional financial accounting would be to promote the idea of a firm's 'wage fund' in an analogous way to how the 'capital fund' is at present treated in conventional accounting. Firms are legally obliged to keep their capital intact. Capital here constitutes a fund which can be augmented and depreciated (formally it constitutes the 'equity base' of a company). Why should there not be an equivalent 'labour fund' that is treated in the same basic way? Thus it would be legally binding for the company to maintain the level of the fund used to reimburse labour. This could also be augmented at times and depreciated either as the company sees fit or by some formula tied to the increase in wages (adjusted for the effects of inflation). But it would require the firm to find alternative ways of using the labour it had, rather than to off-load this onto the labour market during difficult periods. This would mean the firm would have to begin a different type of planning; to upgrade and diversify its output as demand changed and to prepare for difficult times without simply sacking labour.

Another alternative is to look to the total factor productivity (TFP) measure favoured by Hayes, Wheelwright and Clark (1988, Appendix B). This is a variant of the VA approach discussed above. It describes a measure of overall performance in transforming a variety of inputs into products (either at the factory, department or other unit level). Total factor productivity is calculated as follows:

$$\text{TFP} = \frac{\text{output of product}}{\text{sum of the resource inputs}}$$

The sum of the resource inputs could include labour-hours, machine-hours, components, energy, capital employed and so on. The obvious difficulties arise in: (a) calculating the inputs used *just* in the production of one or in a number of products; (b) calculating items such as 'capital employed' which have no obvious physical form; and (c) calculating 'output' itself – exactly how is this to be consistently valued?

The advantage of TFP measures is that they are 'physical' measures in the first instance and not 'financial' measures (though they need to be translated into a monetary form). Secondly, they are 'economic' measures rather than 'accounting' measures. Thus they should not be confused with the efficiency ratios calculated on the basis of accounting information, assuming pre-established variance standards or utilization ratios.

THE FINANCIAL SYSTEM, EURO-MERGERS AND SHORT TERMISM

Discussion of the nature of these possible changes in the financial reporting mechanisms of the future European business environment raises the general issue of the differential financial systems in Europe and the implications these will have for European integration and merger activity. This is often thought to be an area for the sole prerogative of private managerial decision-making, but it is likely to become increasingly an object of public policy, if nothing else because of the financial systems' central importance in the funding and regulation of manufacturing industry. In this way it is fundamentally implicated in both competition policy and industrial policy.

Broadly speaking, there are two types of financial system current within Europe. On the one hand there is the 'Anglo-American' model typified by the UK (and USA) where the stock market and a decentralized market-based approach predominates; on the other is the 'continental' model typified in the popular imagination by Germany (and Japan), and to a lesser extent in Europe by France and Spain, where the banks and a more centralized, administrative approach prevail. This distinction is most marked in terms of corporate control, but it also invades the general business of financial intermediation.

Of course, as soon as one draws such a stark distinction between two models it becomes clear that the actual practice of financial systems involves many common features and similar arrangements. In addition there is the view that these distinctions, while they might have been important in the past, are now dissolving in the face of the deregulationist neo-liberal policy programme of individual governments aided by the Commission's own competition policy.

Given that this chapter is mainly about the future regulatory structure of industrial activity, we concentrate here on the nature of corporate control. The characteristics of the two different models can be summed up under the title of 'insider' and 'outsider' systems, the typical properties of which are shown in Table 6.1 (Corbett and Mayer, 1991).

The close involvement of banks in corporate control in the insider system takes a number of forms. In the first place, banks own equity in the industrial sector; some on their own account and some as custodians for private investors. Secondly, banks have representatives on the boards of these firms, often in the position of chairman of the Supervisory Board in German firms (Edwards and Fischer, 1991). This is not the case in the outsider system. Thirdly, the banks can influence corporate activity more directly as a result of the previous two points. Sometimes this takes the form of leading in the rescue or restructuring of firms (for example, in France and Spain). Fourthly,

Table 6.1   Properties of insider and outsider systems of corporate control

Insider systems	Outsider systems
Concentrated ownership and control	Dispersed ownership
Association of ownership with control	Separation of ownership and control
Control by interested parties (banks, related firms and employees)	Little incentive for outside investors to participate in corporate control
Absence of hostile takeovers	Hostile takeovers that are costly and antagonistic
Other stakeholders are represented	Interests of other stakeholders are not represented
Intervention by outside investors limited to periods of clear financial failure	Low commitment of outside investors to long-term strategies of firms
Insider systems may encourage collusion	Takeovers may create monopolies

Source: Corbett and Mayer (1991), Table 4, p. 65.

banks often provide large amounts of corporate finance in the form of loans to their client firms, though contrary to popular belief this is not the case in Germany, where internally generated funds are the most important source (Edwards and Fischer, 1991). However, in insider systems banks do tend to provide the bulk of any external finance, and on a long-term loan basis, contrary to the stock-market based outsider systems (Mayer and Alexander, 1990). Fifthly, even where bank ownership may be modest in insider systems, there is a greater reliance on the cross-holdings of equity stakes between related companies. Finally, shareholding is concentrated in insider systems whereas it is dispersed widely in outsider systems, and there is a much smaller number of quoted companies in insider than there are in outsider systems. All in all, it is important to note that the Anglo-American market-based outsider systems are the exception rather than the rule in Europe, and in the world as a whole.

The question these differences raise is what are the consequences of the insider and outsider systems in terms of economic performance? As might be expected, this is the subject of fierce controversy (Centre for Business Strategy, 1990; Franks and Mayer, 1990; Marsh, 1990; Corbett and Mayer, 1991; Pitt-Watson, 1991). In principle, the competitive market-based system would seem to offer the most efficient and attractive method of corporate control – self-regulation on the basis of the pursuit of interest. But it has increasingly come under attack. In the first place, the mode of gaining control tends to be highly antagonistic and conflictual. Contested takeovers are the order of the day in outsider systems, whereas they are rare in insider ones. This is costly and distractive, leading to all manner of pre-defensive strategies by managements. Secondly, the form of corporate control only represents shareholder interests. The interests of other stakeholders (employees, customers, suppliers, the local community, the 'national interest', even) tend to be ignored. Thirdly, and probably most importantly, it is accused of leading to 'short termism', that is the inability of management to develop a long-term investment strategy, to devote enough resources to R&D and training, to think in terms of organic internal growth rather than external growth through merger or acquisition, and to take any long-term decisions. It leads to a great emphasis on competition for corporate control and consequently neglects competition in product markets.

To support these accusations those criticizing the emphasis on 'financial engineering' indicate the disappointing relative economic performance of the outsider system countries. As suggested in Chapter 4, previous rounds of merger activity in a country such as the UK have shown little sign that this has led to a better company performance overall. The policy problem this poses for European integration is the likely nature of the unified financial system as it matures with monetary and economic union. Will liberalization and deregulation lead to the dominance of the Anglo-American over the continental model, even though the former has proved to be less effective and efficient in the long run than the latter?

The late 1980s saw an international boom in merger activity within Europe, to a large extent fuelled by expectations associated with the unified single market. The USA remained the most acquisitive nation in European merger and acquisition (M&A) activity, with Japan also heavily involved. Although national mergers dominated in this activity in the 1980s, they have been growing at a slower rate than European cross-border M&As in the more recent period. There was a massive four-fold rise in cross-border mergers within the EC between 1985 and 1989, while national mergers over the same period rose by only 60 per cent. By 1990 Community mergers were as likely as national ones (Nicolaides and Thomsen, 1991).

On the face of it, this looks like a rational response by European business to all the economy of scale arguments discussed in Chapter 4. Greater integration will bring into being a unified market of some 320 million consumers, and firms have been developing market expansion strategies as a response. The matching of strong sectors in one company with those of another, increasingly in another European country, are attempts to reap latent production and marketing synergies. The non-European companies in volved in M&A activity are attempting to pre-empt the possibility of a 'fortress Europe' by having some production base within the EC.

But the European merger boom, such that it is, is quite unevenly distributed amongst the Community members, and as between sectors. The UK has been by far the most active Community member involved in both domestic and cross-border mergers (Centre for Business Strategy, 1990; Tsoukalis, 1991). In 1988, 85 per cent of mergers involved UK firms, with France running second with only 5 per cent. This position was reversed in 1990, with France becoming the most important intra-European investor followed by Sweden, while Britain was pushed into third place (OECD, 1991a, Table 28, p. 109). Just four sectors – food, chemicals, electrical engineering and mechanical engineering – accounted for 60 per cent of European mergers between 1983 and 1987 (Centre for Business Strategy, 1990). The EC service sector has proved very resilient to M&A activity, particularly intra-EC mergers. Even though the UK remained the most active EC M&A country, nearly 70 per cent of its international activity was outside the Community in 1987/88.

To a considerable extent the EC national differences in the importance of M&A activity are due to domestic financial systems and general M&A policy. The UK has the most open system. Germany has the toughest anti-takeover defences in Europe, with restricted voting arrangements and large family shareholdings. This means that perhaps less than 10 per cent of German quoted companies are vulnerable to outside bids, and antagonistic bids are very rare. Family shareholding is also a feature of the Italian system, with few listed companies and very low public holdings of shares in these. While France has become a big spender on cross-border acquisitions, it maintains strong defences against foreign takeovers of its indigenous industries, aided by the formal relationships and informal loyalties between the state bureaucracy, civil servants and the captains of its industry (Chapter 3).

It has been suggested that Europe as a whole is moving more towards an Anglo-American style of system, (with relaxed regulation and opportunistic adventures in acquisitions), which in the long run will tend to create a unified approach based upon the City of London (Parker, 1991). The European Commission, meanwhile, has installed its own scrutiny procedure. The Commission's criteria cover mergers involving companies with joint turnover exceeding ECU 5 billion (expected to be reduced to ECU 2 billion by 1994), and with each having a turnover within the EC in excess of ECU 250 million. Thus this covers only very large mergers. But if one of the companies already does more than two-thirds of its business in one Community country, the merger is exempt. The criteria the Commission uses to judge mergers are also ambiguous. Although competition is supposed to be the main criterion, there are exceptions where 'the development of technical and economic progress is concerned'. In addition, how far the Commission can intervene in mergers involving Community companies and outside EC companies is not clear.

The problem with the unified approach argument is that national institutional differences still remain, despite some definite moves towards the liberalization and deregulation of EC financial markets *(Bank of England Quarterly Bulletin,* November 1989, Table J, p. 522). Secondly, it is not clear that even national mergers are effective, let alone cross-border ones. UK conglomerates in particular have found massive difficulties in buying businesses they know nothing about, and are increasingly faced with the 'unbundling' of their diversification strategies as profits and growth fail to appear. Even the expansion-by-buying strategies in the USA have presented considerable financial, managerial and operational strain, with ruinous effects on many British companies. Cross-border European liaisons have been plagued by dissension, trying to blend different business cultures and differing attitudes, and facing continued 'political chauvinism'. Only rarely have large cross-European mergers in the same industry married partners with truly complementary strengths, most being marriages that combine different corporate cultures with similar industrial weaknesses. In addition, there is the problem of the continued antagonism within the EC between the dictates of its competition policy and the remnants of an industrial policy. Tensions remain between the ambition to strengthen European indigenous manufacturing capability and an M&A policy that takes a hands-off approach. The French in particular have been keen to veto certain potential mergers when these have either threatened French interests directly or undermined the possibility of creating Euro-champions. The French continue to favour subsidization of some industrial sectors and a continued strong state involvement in industrial affairs (even as they have embarked upon their own privatization programme). Finally, while Germany has so far been instrumental in keeping 'industrial policy' considerations out of EC merger policy (after all, German industry is the strongest and most dynamic in Europe and faces few acquisition possibilities), that does not necessarily imply that it will allow its well-established and proven financial system to be totally undermined by a rather poorly functioning Anglo-American one.

Many of these points are also pertinent to other collaborative strategies that the Commission expects to be encouraged by the 1992 programme. These include joint venturing. Joint venturing has grown as a corporate strategy in recent years, mainly as industrial projects seem to have become too big to be handled by any single firm. The argument is that barriers to trade inhibited this desirable and worthwhile strategy, so that a successful 1992 programme will redress the balance. But Kay (1991) argues that this misunderstands the nature of collaborative joint venturing. It is a strategy of 'last resort' for firms:

> ...cooperative arrangements such as joint ventures are often costly and cumbersome to set up and administer, dissipate profit streams and, most crucially, may erode the firm's competitive advantage by giving potential rivals access to valuable technological knowledge (Kay, 1991, p. 351).

Under these circumstances, the more open market outcome of the 1992 programme will reduce the incentive for collaboration via joint ventures, since it will allow firms to trade more easily across borders (though at the same time, on this analysis, it does not discourage other collaborative strategies such as mergers).

But in general terms, there are strong reasons to believe that institutional differences will remain within Europe after the completion of the internal market. Indeed, these may be enhanced as the implications of the analysis contained in this and other chapters of this book unfold. If smaller scale and more flexible manufacturing processes take hold, if these are to be conducted in a new regionalized or localized framework as European integration takes place, then the financial systems of a more differentiated Europe will themselves be forced to adapt to a more decentralized framework. If they do not, European economic performance itself might be further compromised.

CONCLUSION

It is clear from the above analysis that an interventionist industrial policy as traditionally understood is not developing at the European level. The ideological tide has moved against this, and there remains a question over whether such an industrial policy would be sensible for the Europe of the future, even if it were politically possible. We come back to this in a moment. But nor is it clear that that which is standing in for such an industrial policy at the European level, notably 'competition policy' of a neo-liberal form, is an adequate substitute. For one thing it does not address the issues of corporate management highlighted earlier in this chapter.

In the rest of this concluding section we look at the issue of redefining industrial policy to match the contemporary transformative circumstances of industrial structure and financial control.

First, an important point is that any political entity in the contemporary world will be forced to develop some kind of an industrial policy. This is impossible to avoid. The issue thus becomes the *form* of that policy, not whether one should be formulated or not. The form of industrial policy comprises two main connected dimensions. The first of these – what might be termed its *primary level* – addresses issues of appropriate business and investment strategies, the choice of production process technologies, and market assessment and consolidation techniques. The other dimension to industrial policy – which might be termed its *secondary level* – concerns the way the primary dimension or level just outlined is linked to other areas of economic policy-making. For instance, traditionally the primary level of industrial policy has been linked to employment policy, understood in terms of the attempt to preserve employment in particular sectors or geographical areas. In recent years it has also been linked to defence policy, to regional policy and to tax policy (particularly corporate tax policy). But this does not exhaust the strategic links between the primary level and other policy areas. It can be linked to social welfare policy, to competition policy, to environmental policy, to financial policy, to education and training policy, to technology policy, and so on. Thus 'industrial policy' understood in these terms comprises a complex interlinking of the features indicated at the first level, with *some* of those features indicated at the secondary level.

The strategic decision for any industrial policy that is not to emerge simply by default or *ex post*, is to decide with which of the other areas of policy-making the primary level is to be most closely linked. Historically this has determined the kinds of decisions that can be, or will be, made by both private firms and public bodies about strategic investments, the process technologies that embody that investment, and the market characteristics the outputs will be called upon to meet, that is, about primary level considerations.

Under present circumstances it would be undesirable to (re)link the primary level very closely, or solely, to traditional employment preservation objectives or to defence policy objectives. Both of these have strongly informed the industrial policies of the Community members in the past, and have largely been a failure. At present it is the relationship between competition policy and trade policy, and the primary level, that is tending to inform the implicit industrial policy emerging at the Community level. However, under contemporary conditions it is important to re-examine this relationship, and to rethink explicit links between the primary level and technology policy, environmental policy, education and training policy, and social welfare policy. It is these strategic links that will inform a progressive industrial policy of the future. The reasons for this are because of the changes consequent upon the post-1992 economic situation in Europe.

The economic effects of the post-1992 process are likely to be complex, uncertain and uneven. However, some general trends can be discerned. In the first place, initially at least, it will be the core efficient industrial regions of Germany, France and Italy that will benefit the most from the enlargement of the market, while the less efficient peripheral regions will suffer. This could even lead to a structural 'virtuous spiral of growth' at the core of Europe, with a 'vicious spiral of decline' around its edges (a kind of industrial 'two-speed' Europe – see Chapter 5). Without a significant and sustained redistribution of economic resources to the periphery, such a structural pattern could easily emerge and consolidate. Given that there is 'excess potential demand' at the periphery, and 'excess output capacity' at the core, such a redistribution would be in the direct long-term interests of both parts of Europe. This point relates to the need to think about industrial policy in terms of the linkages between social policy, environmental policy, regional policy and the primary level, as described above. ·

Secondly, and again initially, it is likely that the large oligopolistic firms in the dynamic sectors of the European economies will be the ones most able to readapt to the post-1992 situation quickly and effectively, and these will thus benefit. Not all of these companies necessarily have their home-base in the core regions, so the benefits here are likely to be more dispersed.

Thirdly, and probably most importantly, these two trends are likely to be cross-cut by the newly emerging dynamic industrial districts and regional economies that are springing up in various parts of the EC (Chapters 4 and 8). In the longer term, these districts and regions are likely to out-perform many of the existing established core regions (though there is some geographical overlap between them), and the smaller to medium-sized businesses that inhabit these new regions will tend to undermine the position of the large oligopolistic conglomerates that initially benefit from the 1992 programme.

This point relates to how a more decentralized internal market may develop as a result of integration, and the implications this has for industrial policy. There are still distinctive and subtle differences in the forms of demand in each of the Community countries (and within these countries themselves), even for what look to be quite standardized commodities and services, which will endure well after the 1992 programme is completed. What is more, these are likely to grow and develop in importance as we enter a world of increased differentiation and niche-oriented production. Market impulses are likely to take increasingly the form of non-standardized, specialist, low volume, rapidly changing demands that existing mass producers and conglomerates are ill-equipped to supply. It will be the flexible and robust, smaller-scale companies making up the new industrial districts and regional economies that will be best placed to meet this transformation in the character of market demand that is already partly upon Europe. Firms will have to *expect* uncertainty in their demand patterns and must learn to provide a flexible response if they are to survive. Those regional economies and industrial districts with extensive integrated subcontracting and supply networks, where the crucial relationship between competition and cooperation is a managed one, and where firms embody flexibly specialized production process technologies and support a highly focused R&D and design capability, are the ones most likely to prosper in this economic atmosphere. This is not to suggest that the large-scale focused manufacturing firm is completely dead. But it does suggest that for it to survive it will also have to engage with the need for flexibility and uncertainty in a way not the case with the standardized mass production technologies of the past. Nor is this to suggest that the working life in all these newly configured factories will be to the liking of either those directly involved or those arguing for a more humane working environment.

Thus to remain competitive at the European and world level, a quite different business strategy is required. Outlooks and attitudes need to change radically. This relates to the way in which the primary level of industrial policy as outlined above is conceived, and the way it must in turn be strategically related to technology policy, to education and training policy and to competition policy. To remain competitive in this kind of environment requires, above all, flexibility. In turn, this requires a highly trained and skilled workforce, but also a set of managers able to perceive the importance of a focused manufacturing environment, to be able to manage complex manufacturing systems, to know how to manage the design and innovation processes and to integrate them with production. None of these skills will develop spontaneously, and nor are they well taught at present. In addition, competitiveness requires a competition policy that is sensitive to the demands of the de-merging and unbundling strategies of companies, rather than one geared simply to supervising more mergers and takeovers.

The burden of these remarks should be seen as arguing very much for a decentralized industrial policy that provides support for the information networks that might be established at the local level; that relies upon initiatives to be taken to strengthen local and regional economies in terms of complementarities between the firms operating in these localities; that helps to facilitate closely integrated supply networks, and the like. It is not to argue for another high profile, centrally directed, highly interventionary and expensive industrial policy, this time organized at the European level. Thus this represents an explicit argument against the notion of a new 'strategic' trade or industrial policy of the Krugman/NTT type for Europe.

The emphasis on value-added calculation in the above analysis should be viewed as complementary to this idea of an industrial policy. Each of the measures discussed offers a different assessment of company (and economy) performance to the profit and loss account. Each has the general advantage of referring more to the 'physical' processes of transformation going on in the firm than to the financial ones. In this sense the measures 'mirror' more closely the actual changes in the production processes discussed earlier in the chapter, and they help to refocus the conditions for a viable and robust manufacturing function.

These measures enable us to secure a certain distance from the terms in which the argument about 'short-termism' has been predominantly discussed, centred as the latter is on the financial ratios used in company assessment by financial institutions and managements. Clearly, no sensible person who is concerned about the decline of the manufacturing capability of countries such as the UK and in certain places on the European mainland would want to deny the importance of financial ratios and the practices of investment institutions in adding to these difficulties. But the real point is to focus on the internal calculative practices of firms and the management accounting systems they deploy. Firms can think 'long term', but make quite the wrong decisions. Also, most firms *do* think long term already – they have strategic plans. But these are governed by a particular deal-driven philosophy involving acquisitions and takeovers, rather than a strategy of internal organic growth. The kinds of considerations discussed in this chapter work towards a different philosophy, one more consistent with a 'growth through internal development' position.

7. Eastern Europe and the Ex-Soviet Union

INTRODUCTION

As the express train of events in the countries to the east of the EC gathers ever-greater momentum, is is difficult to know exactly where to begin an analysis of these events, or how sensible that analysis will seem even in a few months' time. This chapter investigates the consequences of the disappearance of the planned economies of Eastern Europe and the Soviet Union for the process of European integration. The issues raised by these events would require a book of their own, thus this chapter is inevitably selective.

The chapter begins by laying out the conventional manner in which these events have been analysed. The approach here is a formal one, abstracting from the detail of the specific events, and concentrating on the underlying theoretical and practical issues at stake. It partly exaggerates the points made in order to highlight them. Much of this conventional analysis is sensible, and it raises issues that must be grappled with by those countries presently in transition. But it also acts to disguise important processes and possibilities. Thus, in combination with the conventional approach, a critical assessment is conducted which tries to bring out some neglected features of the transition process in these economies.

The usual way of approaching the reforms of Eastern Europe and the ex-Soviet Union is to emphasize the following features (Fischer, 1991):

1. Price liberalization and the marketization of the economy.
2. Privatization and the construction of property rights.
3. Macroeconomic stabilization.
4. Current account convertibility/capital account liberalization.

The first two features focus on the microeconomics of the process of adjustment, while the second two focus on the macroeconomics of the process. There are clearly strong overlaps between all four areas. In general, the overall process is seen as one of establishing a fully-fledged market economy.

Another preliminary issue posed by conventional analysis is whether the process of forming the capitalist economy should be considered in terms of a single 'big bang', or whether it should be phased in sequentially over a period of time. Broadly speaking, the argument for the big-bang approach (or 'comprehensive systemic reform', as it is often termed) is that the Soviet-type systems in decay are true systems that cannot be reformed piecemeal (Boycko, 1991; Ericson, 1991, pp. 25–6). The interdependencies within the economies under transformation require an all-or-nothing approach. The lessons from the partial reforms adopted by a number of the Eastern European economies in the late 1960s and in the 1970s, demonstrated that these could not bolster the system or produce the required flexibility in economic decision-making. This failure was at least in part responsible for the total collapse of the systems in the late 1980s and early 1990s. Thus the radical reformers are right in seeking the total destruction of the traditional system and its replacement by a capitalist-type market economy as quickly as possible.

On the other hand, the argument for a longer period of transition and the careful sequencing of reforms rests upon the difficulty and disruption that a 'big bang' might bring. The timing and scope of reform need to proceed flexibly, rather than as a rapid once-and-for-all process. At its simplest, the sequencing could be a two-stage affair; first stabilization and then structural adjustment (Rybczynski, 1991). This might be seen as a macroeconomic adjustment followed by a microeconomic one. A rather more extended version of this sequencing would be to suggest first monetary stabilization, followed by real stabilization, then institutional change, and finally structural change. Alternatively, a sequence based upon the order of the reform process sketched above might be instituted, with microeconomic 'marketization' and 'privatization' reforms proceeding first, followed by the macroeconomic stabilization and convertibility processes.

The problem is perhaps best thought of as one of introducing packages of complementary policy reforms around the areas mentioned above. The scale of reform is massive, and not exhausted just by the heading already mentioned. For instance, take the general issue of price and market reforms indicated by the first two features listed above. The liberalization of the distribution of goods and services implies not only price reform, but the demonopolization and privatization of the means of production as well as the means of distribution proper, the removal of quantitative restrictions, the adjustment of external tariffs and quotas, the reorganization of the labour market to allow hiring and firing of labour and the liberalization of wage bargaining, and the introduction of a properly functioning finance and banking system. Similarly with the issue of institution-building and structural reform. Here, legal reform is the most pressing; this redefines the whole nature of the state. There is a need to introduce a tax structure and budgetary and regulatory institutions to administer this. Unemployment insurance and other elements of a social welfare system are also implied and pressingly required.

Various countries have pursued variations on a number of these themes and suggestions. It is generally thought that countries such as Poland and (East) Germany demonstrate adoption of the big-bang approach, while Czechoslovakia and (initially) the Soviet Union tended towards the more leisurely sequencing process (the '500 Days' Shatalin Plan in the Soviet Union, for instance). As the Soviet Union broke up, however, so did any sequencing that might have first been proposed, and a more rapid big-bang approach seems to be under way in the ex-Soviet Union economies (such that any serious reform can be said to be actually under way in many of these emergent countries).

In this chapter we are less concerned with the details of each of these countries' reform processes. Rather, the general issues they raise and the implications these have for the European integration process are focused upon. The rest of the chapter proceeds as follows. In the next section we look closely at the overall components of the reform process as sketched above. We also discuss the problems that have emerged with respect to the experiences of the Eastern European countries and the ex-Soviet Union as they have embarked upon their own reform processes. We then proceed to discuss the case of German reunification as a separate issue, since it raises important implications for the whole of the European integration process. After that we consider some of the more 'political' implications of the existing conjuncture in the relationship between the evolving Eastern economies and the EC. This includes an analysis of the issue of migration, or potential migration, from the East to the West. Finally, the chapter goes on to review certain policy issues that arise from the analysis with respect to the future of the Eastern European countries and the ex-Soviet Union for the process of European integration in general. In this case we discuss the possibilities of the widening of the Community to include the Eastern European economies.

THE REFORM PROCESS OVERALL

Price Liberalization and Marketization

Perhaps the first issue encountered when discussing economic reforms is the essential nature of price liberalization and the marketization of economic activity. The existence of administered prices is thought to indicate suppressed disequilibria in all markets (Jackson, 1991, pp. 18–19). It is this that results in the misallocation of resources in these economies. This is manifest in all the well-known ills of their economic systems: the neglect of infrastructure capital investment; the increasing technological gap between them and the West; the relative (and sometimes absolute) decline in their growth rates; the increasing bottle-necks in the supply of goods and services (indeed, the relative lack of such supplies); the relative growth of the secondary economy and the corruption involved therein; an increasing 'monetary over-hang' in the form of cash issued to households and credit lines extended to enterprises and the state that cannot be absorbed by real productive activity or purchases (thus resulting in 'suppressed inflation'); a general and increasing discordance between the officially sanctioned plans and norms of the rule-making bodies, and the actual conduct of economic activity by agents in the economy.

An obvious response when confronted by these problems is the resort to a thorough price liberalization and the marketization of the economy. This means loosening the administrative controls of central planning and the decentralization of decision-making, thereby strengthening the forces of competition. Under these circumstances, however, it is often suggested that economic and political decentralization must go hand in hand. Whilst the model of economic decentralization is relatively well developed by conventional economic analysis, the issue of the complementary political decentralization is less easy for economic analysis to deal with. But even economic decentralization is not unproblematic in the context of the rapid transformation of Soviet-type economies. Indeed, Murrell (1991) has suggested that neoclassical economics, for instance, does not offer an effective theory of economic reform, mainly because it cannot provide an acceptable explanation of the vast differences in performance between the capitalist and the socialist systems in the first place. The problem is to account for the progressive 'creative destruction' that embodies the dramatic transformations being undertaken in the ex-Soviet-type economies as they 'marketize' and, he suggests, no equilibrium model of the neoclassical type meets this challenge, even in the context of microeconomic reforms.

It is well recognized, even by those supportive of a rapid movement to the wholesale marketization of economic activity, that price liberalization presents a high risk of hyper-inflation. If firms (or the economy generally) remain somehow under 'worker influence', as prices increase (which is the expected outcome of price reform), wages will in all probability also rise, and a fairly standard hyper-inflationary spiral could result. The orthodox remedy here is to institute monetary and fiscal discipline at the same time as introducing price liberalization. In particular, state and enterprise financing needs reforming to eliminate subsidies and to introduce or tighten the budget constraint.

One problem with price reform is the sheer number of prices that need to be changed. In the old Soviet Union alone, there were in the region of 25 million different administered prices (Fischer and Gelb, 1991, p. 96). What principles should guide the re-formation of prices? One possibility is to use world prices. But this assumes the simultaneous opening of the domestic economy to foreign trade. What is more, without a general opening of the economy, domestic interest rates and asset prices will continue to diverge from world levels. But in addition, world price levels only offer a 'rational' price reform for traded goods. Added to this is the fact that about half the Eastern European economies' trade was traditionally conducted with other Comecon or CMEA countries, which was thus also trade in administered prices.

The rapid collapse in intra-Comecon/CMEA trade in the early 1990s (for instance, Soviet trade with Eastern Europe diminished by 25 per cent in 1990 and by an even greater amount in 1991 – Shleifer and Vishny, 1991, p. 342), and the lack of its quick replacement by Western trade, is one of the major factors in the decline of GDP and the advent of recession in the Comecon/CMEA countries. It is only Poland, Hungary and, to a lesser extent Czechoslovakia (ignoring the special circumstances of the GDR), that have so far been able to substitute significant volumes of trade from the West for that lost in the East.

This brief discussion of some of the implications of 'decentralizing' economic decision-making brings us back to the issue of political decentralization. Whether we like it or not, the break-up of the Soviet system has led not only to the unhinging of the Comecon/CMEA system, but also to the break-up of many of the previously 'unified' states that comprised the elements of that system. The obvious example of this is the Soviet Union itself, but there are strong centrifugal tendencies in a number of the other countries of the system, notably in the Balkan area but also including Czechoslovakia (which in June 1992 decided to split into separate Czech and Slovak nations). The general question this raises is whether the redefinition of political boundaries has any implications, positive or negative, for the reform process and its possible success. Clearly, this also has implications for the EC, since it is the reverse process there – the construction of a new, partly political integration – that is well under way.

The immediate context of the Eastern European/ex-Soviet Union debate centres on the consequences of the break-up of previous political unities for the process of economic reform. Is this enhanced or hindered by such break-ups? The larger question posed by this process is whether country boundaries matter for economic activity (Hogan, 1991; Nordhaus, Peck and Richardson, 1991; Shleifer and Vishny, 1991). The ex-Soviet Union countries, for instance, seem to be becoming more economically independent, increasingly developing their own currencies and possibly trade restrictions, and experimenting with import-substitution policies.

In the case of the ex-Soviet Union, Shleifer and Vishny (1991) argue strongly that '[t]o promote faster market reform, the West should aid the republics rather than the centre' (p. 358). In part, this argument has to do with the political legitimacy of local leaders and the tailoring of any assistance to local needs, but it is also an argument about the West gaining added leverage over the whole reform process (p. 359). The risk of trade wars between the republics is recognized, but thought not to be a serious one. Curiously, however, after making a very strong case for 'marketization through political decentralization', the two authors conclude by suggesting: '[T]here is no guarantee that economic reform at the republican level will be strictly better than reform originating from the centre' (p. 360).

Hogan (1991), on the other hand, feels that the devolution of power to the individual sovereign states will very much complicate the transitional process (p. 307). The substantial interregional division of labour within the old Comecon and Soviet Union areas is likely to unravel quickly, though without the means to create a new trade-based specialization between the now independent countries. The trade collapse will inevitably hurt all the states concerned, particularly in the absence of hard currency substitutes.

It is Nordhaus, Peck and Richardson (1991) who tackle the problem head on. They comment that from the perspective of mainstream neoclassical theory, the exact political boundaries between nations are intrinsically unimportant, at least for long-run economic performance. They go on to suggest that it is the dissolution of the Austro-Hungarian empire after 1919 that best represents the prospects in the case of the Soviet Union today. In the case of central-southern Europe in the 1920s, tariffs, exchange controls and separate currencies were soon in place. What was crucial was the break-up of a large free-trade area with an effective political regulation, rather than of an 'empire' as such. The economic consequences in the 1920s were major inflation and a stagnation of growth in the countries concerned during much of the inter-war period, though not all of this can necessarily be attributed to just the dissolution of the Austro-Hungarian Empire.

Borders matter in the ex-Soviet Union because of the extraordinary degree of political and economic centralization, the monopolization of the productive structure, natural resource specificities, and the significant interregional and interrepublic trade. Similar comments, though less dramatic, could be made about the Eastern European economies as well. Thus the problem once again is not so much the break-up of another 'empire', but the form of the economic and political regulation that will evolve in the post-Soviet Union era within and between these countries. This reiterates the issue of political regulation that has arisen in the case of the EC (discussed elsewhere in this book). Economic activity is usually one of the first casualties when any interrepublican or inter-ethnic strife breaks out in the wake of the undermining of effective political governance between nationalistic entities.

The general implication of this discussion of liberalization and marketization, whether given an exclusive economic or wider political gloss, is that it is just not sufficient to 'loosen all the constraints' and then sit back and expect the virtues of the market and competition to spontaneously emerge. Explicit and positive efforts are required to *construct* an adequate and effective market system. Difficult choices must be made about the creation of the institutions of effective market governance and regulation. The problem is not simply one of allocative efficiency. We take these crucial issues up in the next section and further below.

Privatization and the Construction of Property Rights

The discussion under this heading has obvious overlaps with that just undertaken. But here we concentrate upon the privatization issue explicitly, and connect it to the legal framework in which the reformed economies are increasingly having to work.

A number of different 'models' of privatization have either been proposed for the transition in the ex-Soviet-type economies or implemented during it. Broadly speaking they are as follows (Sadowski, 1991, pp. 50–51):

1. The restoration of the private rights over property for the previous owners of that property, or their descendants – sometimes known as reprivatization.
2. The wholesale and direct disposal of the firm and its effects to private individuals.
3. The sale of stocks and shares to private persons representing property claims in the enterprise.
4. The transfer and distribution of property rights to private persons free of charge, via some kind of voucher system.

Instances of the first form of privatization can be found in Germany and Czechoslovakia, of the second in these two countries and in Poland, of the third in all three countries and, although less well developed, instances of the fourth form also occur in all these countries. The Russian Republic also intends to deploy a combination of vouchers and more conventional sell-off mechanisms in its privatization programme. Thus a variety of methods have actually been, or are about to be, introduced.

It is perhaps the second and third methods that are the most widespread. The second has tended to be deployed in connection with small and medium-sized businesses, where family control can often be established relatively easily and quickly, no great problems with capital generation arising. The third (and fourth) methods are those tending to be employed where large-scale firms are concerned. These rely upon the generation of (or distribution of) relatively large tranches of capital.

The Eastern European economies and the Soviet Union displayed one of the most highly concentrated productive structures in the world, with huge enterprises. One of the tasks set for the privatization programme was there-fore to break up these enterprises to avoid any undesirable private monopoly outcomes. At the end of the 1990s in the Soviet Union, for instance, indus-trial enterprises with more than 1,000 employees accounted for 73 per cent of total employment, while those with less than 100 employees accounted for only 2 per cent of employment. Between 30 per cent and 40 per cent of Soviet output was produced on single sites (Boycko, 1991, p. 40; see also Hogan, 1991, Figure 3, p. 316). Thus in some instances the process of privatization has taken a three-phased form; first the *corporatization* of the enterprises into autonomous firms still owned by the state, then their *restruc-turing* to attempt to eliminate potential monopoly distortions, followed by their *privatization proper.*

Rather as in the case of price reform, a problem for the big-bang approach is the sheer number of large state enterprises involved. At the beginning of the 1990s, Hungary had about 2,000 large state enterprises primed for priva-tization, and Poland 7,500 (Fischer and Gelb, 1991, p. 99). In the Ukraine alone, Hogan estimates that there were upwards of 30,000 state enterprises, including perhaps 15,000 employing over 1,000 people, and 1,000 enter-prises employing over 3,000 people (Hogan, 1991, p. 316). As Kornai (1990) has noted, these numbers put a massive constraint on the speed of privatiza-tion and should point to a gradualist approach. Thus the objective might become the progressive reduction of state ownership and the fostering of the growth of private activity, but with no necessary objective of the rapid and total elimination of the state sector. The private sector thus eventually makes up the dominant share in national output, but a 'mixed economy' outcome is expected and accepted (Sadowski, 1991, p. 47). In fact this is the pattern emerging in the early privatization starters such as Hungary and Poland; a rapid growth in the private sector, but one still relatively small in relation to total activity (Wolf, 1991, p. 52). The unresolved question remains, how-ever, the legitimate extent of the public sector that is to remain and its exact constitutional form.

Another often quoted form of privatization, but not one included in the list above despite the fact that it seems to have been widespread in practice, is so-called 'wild' or *'nomenklatura'* privatization. This involves the bureau-crats in the ministries, and managers of state enterprises, illegally or surrep-titiously converting public property into private property for themselves.

Thus not all the ownership reform in these economies follows the dictates of the economist's rational model of marketization. The creation of the market can also display corrupting elements.

Accompanying all this privatization activity has gone the construction of a viable legal framework. Property rights, or economic legality (Litwack, 1991), implies the progressive displacement of discretion (by 'bureaucrats') with the rule of law in matters economic. The kinds of law involved here would be contract, tax and bankruptcy laws, amongst others. Classic Soviet-type planning relied upon the institution of a system of material balances between the centre and the enterprises, which in the subsequent administrative allocation of resources relied upon an extensive system of discretionary bargaining within and between the bureaucracies involved. These continual discretionary adjustments to the plan embodied the very feasibility of the planning mechanism. They relied upon the existence of an elaborate network of personal contacts and 'fixers', employed by every enterprise and ministry, which exercised those adjustments. In this universe, the pecuniary reward system played a very subordinate role in the overall incentive mechanism, and where it did operate it also worked in the context of a discretionary manner, involving personal superior/subordinate-type relationships. By all accounts, sometimes major (but more often petty) corruption was rife.

The image of the system designed to replace this is one of a 'contract-rich' market system. Discretion is eliminated, replaced by a system of 'rational–legal' contractual orders. The reputation effects of personal relationships are dissolved by a system that facilitates impersonal trade. At its extreme, the attempt can be made to render the whole of economic existence as reducible to a set of fully specified contracts, by investing near enough everything with property rights. Clearly, one does not need to go this far to recognize that there is a requirement for the rule of law and a sensible contract system in the ex-Soviet-type economies, and it is this more flexible attitude that hopefully will gain the upper hand.

The reason for making this point is to insist that all complex contracts are unavoidably incomplete, even in an advanced and well-functioning market system. Indeed, in the most successful market systems there is increasing space for some 'discretion' to be built back into economic relationships, as we have seen in the case of the 'flexible specialization' arguments reviewed in Chapters 4 and 6. Given bounded rationality and the possibility of opportunism, any contract-as-promise unsupported by credibility notions and commitments (which create the space for 'discretion') is difficult to envisage. Thus reputation effects cannot be avoided. It is precisely the commitment to a long-term relationship, which often cannot be reduced to a balance sheet or profit and loss item, that requires the institution of networks of personal contacts to lubricate the conduct of economic relationships within the mar-

ket system. There is a danger, then, that in their enthusiasm to dispense with
a discredited and corrupt system of economic management, the ex-Soviet-
type economies will go too far towards the other extreme. The advocates of
a fully contractualized economic universe, with only arms-length and impersonal competitive economic interactions allowed to characterize the system,
are speaking to an outmoded vision of competitive capitalism, and one, it
might be added, which is strictly speaking impossible anyway.

This critique of a certain type of economic analysis that has been imported
into the debate about the introduction of property rights in the ex-Soviet-
type economies allows us to conduct a rather more general critical assessment of the orthodox ideas of privatization and marketization expressed so
far in this chapter.

An interesting problem here is exactly what is to be 'privatized' to create
a market system. To analyse this properly, we must remember what the
system of resource allocation and distribution amounted to under central
planning. This comprised an administrative system of incredible hierarchical
complexity. It was designed to gather information, disseminate instructions,
coordinate interactions, manage change, and monitor and enforce command
performance. Typically, at its apex stood a Council of Ministers, with a vast
array of central planning and control agencies below responsible for trans-
lating plans' objectives and policies first into implementable assignments
and instructions, and then into actual deployments of resources, goods and
services (Ericson, 1991). In the Soviet Union these central agencies comprised over 20 state committees, functional bodies and other ministries dealing with economic matters. These included *Gosplan* (planning), *Gosnab*
(materials and equipment supply), *Gosstroi* (construction), *Goskomtsen*
(prices), *Goskomtrud* (labour issues), GKNT (science and technology),
Sel'khoztekhnika (agricultural equipment), *Gosbank* (the State Bank), CSU
(the Central Statistical Administration), the Ministry of Finance, the Committee of People's Control, and others. Below these agencies stood over 50
branch ministries, all actively involved in the planning process (five food
and agricultural ministries; ten ministries of fuels, raw materials and chemicals; nine ministries for different kinds of construction work; 11 ministries
for different kinds of civil machine building; and nine ministries primarily
producing for the military). Each of these ministries was further subdivided
into departments (*glavki*) by region, branch and output category. This minis-
try/departmental structure was duplicated within each of the 15 Soviet republics ('Union-Republic Ministries'). Finally, at the base of this elaborate
system, were the organizations that carried out the actual production, construction, transportation, distribution and trading activities in the economy.
In 1986 there were 46,000 industrial enterprises, 23,000 state farms, 27,000
collective farms, 17,500 inter-farm and associated enterprises, 1,000 agro-

industrial associations, 17,000 construction organizations, and almost one million wholesale and retail trading organizations (Narkhoz, 1987; quoted in Ericson, 1991, p. 14). What is more, alongside this incredible organizational pyramid were a large number of parallel monitoring and control hierarchies, exercising important powers of investigation and intervention to ensure that the intentions of the state planners were followed. Although less elaborate, this kind of structure could be found duplicated in all the Eastern European economies.

The reason for describing this hierarchical structure in some detail is to bring home the point that privatizing the bottom rung of this ladder, however difficult that may be because of the number of establishments involved, is not of itself sufficient to create 'the market system'. Primary emphasis has been given to this task, however, with a relative neglect of what is to replace all the other elaborate institutionalized management mechanisms that made up the previous system. Thus, in a way, what was needed was to privatize this elaborate administrative system itself. This is what comprised the mechanism which the market was to replace. If the market was to substitute for this, it needed to 'mirror' it in some way. But clearly, no one would be willing to 'purchase' the administrative and managerial elements of this system; it could not be 'privatized', however necessary that might have been. But this does not mean that privatizing those tangible productive elements that could be corporatized, restructured and then sold off, amounts to a marketization of productive activity. Indeed, in some senses this was of lesser importance for the task of marketization than the creation of an alternative institutionalized managerial structure to replace all the activity of those now defunct ministries and departments. They performed that massive coordination task akin to the market, however inefficiently. This reinforces, then, the argument that the market system has to be deliberately constructed and created on the basis of definite choices about the forms of contracts; the types of institutions and the conditions of their operation; the forms and levels of public intervention and involvement, and the like. In most cases the work here still remains to be done in the economies of transition.

However, some things have been done. The installation of a legal order and civil code is, of necessity, under way in these economies. But interestingly, although the Eastern European countries have expressed a strong interest in becoming associated with the European Community, the legal orders they have adopted are in no way compatible with those of the main EC countries, nor with the 1992 European Community framework (Svejnar, 1991, p. 132). In the main, the creation of an entire legal system from nothing in these countries has resulted in an incomplete and at times inconsistent set of economic laws.

Some countries have, however, begun to adopt an organizational configuration for their labour market negotiations similar to that of Germany and
Austria. Thus, before its break-up Czechoslovakia had moved towards a
nationwide wage settlement system, bargained between the government and
the trade unions (with some involvement of the new private sector), that
could be supplemented by plant-level collective agreements (Brada, 1991,
pp. 173–4). Although in its infancy, this model demonstrates strong proto
neo-corporatist elements as discussed in Chapters 3 and 5. It is a tripartite
set-up, reflecting mainstream European practice, which does not throw the
settlement of wages totally onto individual enterprises. Similar systems seem
to be developing in Hungary, Poland, Romania and elsewhere.

Another set of problems arises with the decision to restructure, but also
often to liquidate, state-run firms. Such decisions have arisen as these organizations have been primed for privatization. Behind this lies the idea that
once exposed to an asset valuation based upon proper market-determined
(often international) prices, the organizations concerned exhibit a negative
financial net present worth. In addition, a good many of the previous state-
run enterprises have been drastically restructured to suit currently acceptable
Western notions of business success. This has meant breaking up what were
often quite viable *productive* combinations of assets and people in the face
of financial pressures of a purely balance-sheet type. Not all of the state-run
enterprises were, therefore, necessarily productively inefficient in their potential, though many of them proved unviable financial entities. Little was
done to address this problem in the rush to privatize as much as possible as
quickly as possible. A good many opportunities were therefore lost to preserve technologically and organizationally modest (but quite productively
viable in the medium term) manufacturing enterprises in branches such as
construction, bakery, shoe manufacturing (and even some consumer-durable
production), that were geared up mainly for domestic supply.

Another important area where the institutional conditions for the operation of the market involve definite choices concerns the financial system.
This concerns the creation or reform of the retail and wholesale banking
sector, the nature of the central bank and the general mechanisms of corporate finance and control. The latter is particularly important given the analysis of the differences in this regard conducted in Chapter 6. In many of the
economies in transition the existence of inter-enterprise credit has become
one of the main ways of sustaining output and circumventing otherwise
'outsider' forms of control. It is accused of erecting informational obstacles
to a proper 'market rules'-based assessment of individual firm real credit
worthiness (Calvo and Frenkel, 1991, p. 140). Balance sheets need to be
'cleansed' of these extraneous credit relationships before an effective scrutiny of efficient and inefficient borrowers can be conducted.

But this begs the question of the form of the institutional arrangement best suited to such an effective scrutiny of the worthy and the unworthy. As analysed above, the privatization programmes embarked upon by the economies in transition have promoted the widespread dispersion of share ownership. But is the dispersion of share ownership – the creation of a 'share-owning democracy' – necessarily the best way of securing effective control and scrutiny of the newly privatized enterprises? The problem is that there may be little incentive for small and dispersed shareholders to participate in the control and restructuring of such firms (Corbett and Mayer, 1991). They will want to develop an extensive and liquid secondary market, offering a low risk and low cost means of exchanging their rights to ownership. As was suggested in Chapter 6, the existence of highly sophisticated stock markets is not necessarily a good sign of effective corporate control.

The fact is, however, that the advisers and advice being received by these countries have tended to come from the USA and the UK, which have the most developed of the 'outsider' systems. But the choice needs to be posed. The crucial relationship between reform of the private banking system and corporate activity needs to be more closely focused ('insider systems') before the countries in transition effectively opt for the 'wrong' model of corporate funding and control.

Macroeconomic Stabilization

The traditional process of macroeconomic stabilization takes the form of fiscal and monetary reform designed to bring state and enterprise finances under control and to prevent inflation. In practice this has meant the introduction of a deflationary package for the economies in transition. Monetary and fiscal orthodoxy is the order of the day. During the late 1980s there was a massive increase in the money supply in the USSR (Ellman, 1991, Tables 1 and 2, pp. 486–7). In 1991 there was open inflation in the Russian Republic exceeding 100 per cent; repressed inflation also continued, incomes were rising at a faster rate than output, and there was a flight from the rouble (though to a limited extent – Nordhaus *et al.*, 1991, p. 338 – see below for the reasons for this).

In many cases the governments in these countries have virtually no monetary liabilities outstanding to their private sectors, thus monetary control must take the form of substantial reductions in the budget deficit, rather than open market operations. This makes the actual control of the money supply no easy task when the government deficit is so large – in the Soviet Union it reached upwards of 20 per cent of GNP just before the break-up. In this environment a further problem arose because some of the republics were clamouring for the development of their own individual currencies. In that many of them have no foreign exchange reserves, but will inherit substantial foreign debt, the confidence necessary to establish monetary stability will be difficult to achieve.

The role of interest rates is also hard to predict, and it relies upon the existence of a functioning financial system. Supposing interest rates can be raised, the response from the household sector could be to increase savings. But the response in the firm sector depends upon whether there is a coincidental tight budget constraint. Without this firms could just refinance their growing interest charges, and the reform would be undermined.

In addition, the monetary overhang effects mentioned above can be important in the fight against inflation. The issue here is how to neutralize these effects. Such financial balances could just be confiscated or frozen of course, but this is likely to be politically very unpopular. One thing that the raising of interest rates does is to make the voluntary holding of these balances possible (in the form of financial assets), though the problem here is to generate positive real interest rates in a period of often high inflation. The sale of state property can also absorb the overhang. Finally, the balances can be 'bid away' by a deliberate policy of inflation, though this is a high risk strategy because of inflation's other unexpected and undesirable effects.

The two major institutional changes which need to be considered in association with macroeconomic stabilization are the reform of the central banking mechanism and the creation of an efficient tax gathering system (McKinnon, 1991). If the state and firms can simply continue to borrow from the state bank at below market rates, the build-up of bank credit simply adds to inflationary pressures. Without the generation of positive real interest rates, agents will prefer to hold physical assets rather than financial ones. Nor can fiscal deficits of the state be financed successfully by the issue of government bonds to the non-bank public when negative real interest rates apply, unless serious 'money illusion' prevails.

On the issue of fiscal policy, seizing the cash surpluses from profitable enterprises can no longer suffice as the main 'tax gathering' method for government finances. Rather, a system of VAT, excise taxes, customs levies and income taxes needs to be introduced, along with a corporation tax system for the liberalized corporate sector. As yet, however, the construction of a system of tax laws and tax institutions in these economies has progressed very little. At best, the tax regimes remain 'disorganized', though the more advanced countries such as Hungary did install a fairly comprehensive tax reform package as far back as 1988.

One problem, however, is that even countries such as Czechoslovakia and Hungary, which either had no government budget deficit and virtually no growth in the money supply in the early 1990s or only a small deficit and low money supply growth, still experienced significant inflations (Brada,

1991, p. 176; Hare, 1991, p. 196). Poland, another inflator, also had a small budget surplus in 1990 (though by 1992 its budget was in deficit). This makes the point that inflation is not just a monetary phenomenon. It can emerge for a number of reasons. The elimination of subsidies is an obvious stimulus to inflation, as is a devaluation of the currency (which had been an important source of inflation in Poland). But there are other sources, like that produced by wage increases above productivity improvement levels. The main problem in the transition has been the precipitous decline in productive activity overall and a dramatic fall in output, which even in the absence of a budget deficit and growth in the money supply can be inflationary. Indeed, this is probably the most serious cause of inflation, but one that is the least recognized by orthodox economic opinion (which emphasizes the monetarist approach to inflation). Its particular policy prescriptions centre on the orthodox remedies of deflation; monetary and fiscal retrenchment. But these policies could end up making the economic situation worse.

This can be illustrated with reference to Figure 7.1. Here, the vertical axes measure aggregate demand (AD) and aggregate supply (AS), while the horizontal axes measure credit availability (M). The diagram shows two different economic configurations, (A) and (B). The two schedules show the elasticity of aggregate supply and demand with respect to credit availability. As shown, the initial credit availability is the same in both cases (OM), as is the position of actual demand and supply, OQ_d and OQ_s. Thus the level of excess demand is the same in both cases, shown as X_d. This demonstrates the classic situation of a supply-constrained, excess demand economy of the Soviet type.

However, depending upon the precise position and slope of the schedules, the orthodox prescription of a monetary contraction could make things worse. In case A, the orthodox policy does work. Restricting the availability of credit moves the economy towards the lower level of output and credit equilibrium at Q_e and M_e. But in case B things are made worse by the same policy. A restriction on credit and a deflationary policy only serves to *increase* excess demand. The correct policy here would be to expand credit and reflate so as to attain higher output and credit equilibrium. In many ways the situation depicted by case B corresponds better to the ex-Soviet-type economies than does situation A. The fundamental problem is not one of restricting output, but one of expanding the supply to meet demand. Command-type economies are geared to emphasize supply, rather than to meet demand, which is indicated by the slopes of the schedules shown in B. In the longer run, however, the objective might be to substitute the usual pressure from supply for one based upon the stimulus of demand, better indicated by the schedules in A.

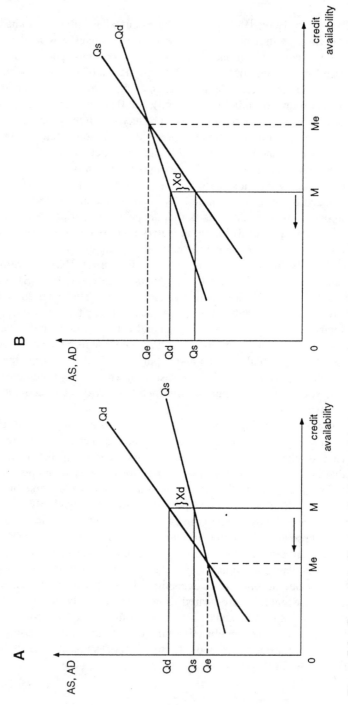

Figure 7.1 Economic adjustment in the transition

174

Orthodox opinion tends to neglect the need for a broader look at the particular causes of inflation under very particular and different conditions, and the tailoring of advice for its control or remedy to those specific conditions. The need to prevent an output collapse could thus be a high priority, which implies a sequencing of reforms over a longish period. We return to this argument in a moment.

Current Account Convertibility/Liberalization of the Capital Account

As part of the preparation for the full marketization of economic activity, the call for convertibility quickly arises. This is seen as part of the internationalization of the domestic economy, subjecting it to the rigours of international competition, reforming domestic prices, subjecting the currency to market disciplines, opening up the capital account to international financial and real investment flows, and so on. A whole sequencing arrangement in its own right can be involved here, with various types of convertibility gradually being introduced.

First, as part of a domestic monetary stabilization package, *internal convertibility* might be introduced, as happened in Poland after January 1990 and in Czechoslovakia a year later. Internal convertibility means residents have a legal right to acquire and maintain *domestic* holdings of certain assets (such as currency and bank deposits) denominated in foreign currencies. The manner and form of these holdings can vary considerably: they might be restricted to a small number of assets; there may be restrictions on the class of person who can hold them; the rate of exchange may be fixed or floating; there may be a single exchange rate or multiple rates. The Polish reform – which took the form of a comprehensive fixed (adjustable peg) rate system with a single exchange rate – was accompanied by a devaluation of the zloty. But the internally convertible currency thereby created did not have any international functions, since the export and import of zlotys was forbidden and there was no use for the domestic zloty in international trade (Lipton and Sachs, 1990).

However, internal convertibility can be extended to include the right of some individuals or organizations to undertake limited trade in foreign exchange, as happened in the Baltic states and in the remaining Soviet Union in 1991 (Ellman, 1991). Internal convertibility of this kind is usually seen as a first step towards the *full convertibility* of the current account. This means that all residents can freely transact in all currencies and can hold assets abroad as well as at home, and foreign nationals can hold assets in the domestic currency as well.

The advantage of internal convertibility is that it hardens the domestic currency by linking it to the foreign exchange market, providing a nominal anchor for price reform and thereby introducing residents in a gentle way to the workings of the international economy. It allows the exchange rate to serve as a monetary target. Developed along with a liberalization of foreign trade, it can stimulate exports and imports by opening the economy to foreign competition, thus increasing the efficiency of these. It can make foreign investment more attractive, facilitate capital repatriation, and so on. Hungary, which phased in trade liberalization *before* convertibility and over an extended period of time, benefited from this process. But as Ellman (1991) points out, all these virtues rely upon a very favourable political and institutional climate, as well as an economic one. The rapid rise in the money supply in the Soviet Union/Russian Republic, and the (linked) issue of inflation, would make the maintenance of internal convertibility at a stable exchange rate very difficult in this case. The government budget position as outlined above adds to these problems. Successful internal convertibility requires the installation of hard budget constraints on both the government and the state enterprises.

Under these circumstances, and as the currencies of the economies in transition have proceeded towards full convertibility, the issue of Western aid to create stabilization funds has arisen. Poland negotiated a stabilization fund of one billion US dollars to support its internal convertibility. As the Russian rouble approached various forms of external convertibility beginning in January 1992, it was promised a six billion dollar stabilization fund from April of that year. These stabilization funds provide foreign reserves that can be used to intervene to defend the value of the zloty and the multiple values of the rouble, as this became convertible or partially (externally) convertible during 1992 (Nuti and Pisani-Ferry, 1992). (The Czech government was provided with standby resources from the IMF, the EC and the Group of 24. However, Bulgaria, which made the leva convertible in February 1991, did not receive such support mechanisms and has little foreign exchange reserves.)

A key issue in the convertibility debate is with which foreign currencies should the exchange rate be linked and at what rate of exchange. Of course, the currency might be linked to a commodity like gold, or a 'basket' of commodities, rather than to another currency. But the Eastern European and the ex-Soviet Union countries have converted against currencies rather than commodities (though one of the Russian rouble rates was fixed in terms of the price of oil). They have gone for fixed, semi-fixed or floating-peg systems. Poland initially pegged against the US dollar, though it then devalued several times and moved to a basket currency system, one that Hungary and Czechoslovakia also adopted. Given that most of these countries see themselves as naturally allied to the EC, the ECU or the Deutschmark might have been a better choice, particularly as their trade patterns are likely to develop strongly in this direction (Davenport, 1992). Psychological factors partly motivated the decision it seems; the dollar, being the dominant black market currency in the countries involved with an already widespread public acceptance, was given the largest weight in the Polish basket (though the DM occupies this position in the Czech basket).

As far as the level of the exchange rate is concerned, the decisions involved similar concerns. In the Russian Republic the initial tourist rate was 117 roubles to the US dollar in early 1992, which was generally thought to be a significant undervaluation. But the multiple rates then in existence varied from 5.4 to 230 roubles to the US dollar (Nuti and Pisani-Ferry, 1992, p. 6). The benchmark indicator emerging during early 1992 for the fixed unified rate the country hoped to introduce as the Western stabilization package became operative, was 20–30 roubles to the dollar. This was in line with academic advice and world price conversions in interrepublican trade.

Any serious undervaluation would constitute a stimulus to inflation, as Russian prices would be encouraged to catch up with world prices. Thus the recommendations for an appropriate exchange rate rested upon purchasing power parity (PPP) considerations. An appreciation of the currency thus looked likely in the first instance (that is, fewer roubles for each dollar), unless some other unforeseen events intervened. To allow this to happen would require an increase in the supply of dollars; this is what a stabilization fund delivers without any necessary increase in inflation. A too low a rate, however, might risk the danger of a flight out of the rouble into dollars (as rouble-holders sold their roubles under unexpectedly favourable terms), and lead to a quick exhaustion of the stabilization fund. The general argument has been that PPP is the appropriate exchange rate to aim at, and Poland and Czechoslovakia are thought to have fixed their exchange rates more or less at this level after some initial adjustments (Brada, 1991, p. 175).

As far as the liberalization of the capital account is concerned, here the governments have been more cautious. All have expressed the wish for some foreign ownership of their industries and capital. This has mainly proceeded in the form of the foreign purchase of the potentially profitable parts of the privatized state sector. In addition there has been some joint venturing and 'green field' FDI. But there has yet to be a full and open capital account liberalization.

Discussion of the stabilization fund for the Russian Republic mentioned above raises the more general role of Western aid as a whole to the economies in transition. The particular fund mentioned was part of a wider US\$ 24 billion aid package negotiated between the G-7 countries and Boris Yeltsin's government. One point to remember here is that this aid package was made up of loans, not gifts, though most of the technical terms for the loans were 'soft' ones. In addition, the package is predicated upon the recipient meeting required terms for the reform process. These push it along a very orthodox route towards a fully marketized economy.

This is not the only instance of Western aid and assistance being directed towards the Eastern European economies and the ex-Soviet Union, but it is difficult to estimate exactly how much this aid amounts to. The World Bank has agreed a US\$ 30 million fund for technical assistance. There has been a good deal of humanitarian aid and other technical assistance, though this has tended to be organized on an emergency *ad hoc* basis. Large-scale financial aid needs coordination and expansion, however.

One way to view the extent of such assistance is to compare it to the Marshall Aid programme directed at Western Europe after the Second World War. As discussed in Chapter 2, Marshall Aid amounted to about 3 per cent of US GDP in the early 1950s. An equivalent amount in 1992 would have been US\$ 180 billion, and this for a single year only. Of course, the USA is in a different economic position in 1992 than it was in the early 1950s, so it might be fairer to think in terms of a shared burden of aid from the three leading economies; the USA, the EC-12 and Japan. Three per cent of their joint GDP in 1992 would have amounted to US \$480 billion, so that only 1 per cent would still have amounted to US \$160 billion. Compared to the amounts actually granted, this shows the limited extent of the aid actually being considered in the present period. We return to the possible implications of this below.

The issue of a 'big bang' versus the sequencing of reforms outlined at the beginning of this chapter is not the only way the mechanism of the transition might have been posed. One thing it does not take into account is whether it would have been more sensible to have taken a *sectoral* approach to the reform process from the outset. Thus instead of going for a comprehensive and quick all-or-nothing approach on the one hand, or a sequencing of comprehensive stages on the other, an alternative would have been to have looked for key economic sectors within which to begin the process of marketization. In some senses this is what the Chinese have done in the case of agriculture, where a dynamic, liberalized ownership and operating sector has been created, but set within an overall economic structure – and above all a political structure – that has not been radically reformed.

Without wishing to defend the continued existence of an authoritarian political structure, many of the Eastern European and ex-Soviet Union countries might have learned something from the Chinese economic reform. Two key sectors stood out in these countries as ripe for an 'experiment' in reform: the agricultural sector and the construction sector. In both cases the countries concerned were particularly inept at organizing these areas, which were also at the heart of much of the popular resentment with respect to those regimes as a whole. The indifferent quality and continual poor supply of food and housing undermined the legitimacy of the regimes and fostered discontent.

One interesting feature of both sectors is the kind of real interdependency they display with other sectors, and in connection to the international constraint on the economy. Broadly speaking, both agriculture and housing are 'labour-intensive' sectors; they do not require vast amounts of capital equipment as a *necessary* feature of their production processes, and they *can* rely upon an unskilled/semi-skilled labour-force. In addition, the construction and agricultural industries traditionally display high 'local' economic multipliers. The demands they make for inputs, for instance, can usually be supplied domestically; they are also extensive and are locally 'dense'. This creates an extensive supplier network which has the potential for quite rapid, though modest, efficiency and performance gains if the originating sector is itself reorganized properly and efficiently. Thus the marketization of these two sectors could have had a beneficial effect, not only with respect to that immediate sector and its supplier network, but also as a demonstration effect on other non-directly involved sectors.

An added corollary and advantage is that the import content of each of these sectors tends, as a result, to be (potentially at least) lower than the average for the economy as a whole. This can be of great benefit in relation to the problems identified above concerning the international constraints on the economy. Thus a concentration on one or two key sectors like this, with an eye to their initial demonstration effects and their particular circumstances and potentially favourable real economic outcomes, might have added a different dimension to the reform process overall. The economies would have gained experience with limited 'sectoral privatization' before embarking on a more thorough-going reform.

However, whilst possibly attractive in its own right, this argument becomes difficult when measured against the enormous problems actually faced by these countries in the early stages as they began their political and economic transformations. Indeed, this comment applies to a good deal of the other remarks and forms of analysis outlined above. The problem was that a 'rational' analysis and judgement emerged as a luxury which the political momentum of events just swept aside. Whilst there might have been good intentions and good ideas as to how the reform process could unfold, the political dynamic of actual events pushed for a rapid and fundamental change in a way almost out of the control of any centre of political organization or any group, let alone any single person.

This raises the final point for this section. Despite what has been argued above about the need to phase in a properly sequenced reform programme and to extend the timescale for the transition, once the process is under way in a relatively uncontrolled fashion, as seems to be the actual case in the ex-

Soviet Union countries and in much of central-southern Europe for instance, then the case for an even more thorough-going 'chaotic' transition becomes stronger. In some ways, then, these economies need *greater* 'chaos', otherwise the reforms threaten to be still-born and only introduced as half measures. For a serious and successful transformation to a fully-fledged market economy, the old system somehow needs to be completely destroyed. This allows the easier formation of the new institutions that are necessary to articulate a totally different system. If the process cannot be ordered and controlled 'rationally', so that the period of transition becomes elongated and subject to a sequence of stages that has some rationale, it might be 'better' in the long run if chaos reigned and a complete collapse ensued.

This is not to *advocate* such an outcome. It is rather to recognize the logic of the existing situation. For those involved, the potential human misery and degradation should not be underestimated. But any process of transition so deep and momentous as that being experienced in these countries cannot be completed without very significant hardship and sacrifice. There will inevitably be a massive increase in inequality, for instance, whether one likes it or not (McAuley, 1991). All previous economic and political transformations of this significance have led to some becoming very wealthy, while others have lost out relatively. There seems no reason to believe that this transition will be any different. In a moment we return to some of the possible amelioratory policies that might be considered at the level of Europe as a whole. But before that, in the next section, we look at the experience of the unification of Germany to assess the impact of this on the process of European integration as a whole.

GERMAN UNIFICATION CONSIDERED

The German Democratic Republic (GDR, or East Germany) was widely regarded as the most advanced of the old command economies, but it quickly succumbed to the advances of the Federal German Republic (FGR, or West Germany) when its internal political and economic structure collapsed during 1989 and 1990. The Berlin Wall 'fell' on 9 November, 1989 and just over a year later, on 2 December 1990, the united Germany's 60 million voters went to the polls in the first all-German free elections since November 1932. As a prelude to this, the Economic and Monetary Treaty between the two Germanies was signed on 18 May 1990; this initiated a complete currency union under two months later on 2 July. This signalled the demise of the GDR as an independent economic unit. The formal dissolution of the GDR took place in October as it was effectively absorbed into the FGR (a modern-day *Anschluss*). These momentous events took place at such a breath-taking speed that it is still difficult to judge their full significance.

Whether *economic* unification took place quite so quickly as political union is another matter. These events can be considered under the twin headings of the micro and macro aspects of the process. In the German case, many of the problems already discussed in connection with the other ex-command-type economies arise again, so we will not duplicate that discussion. Rather we concentrate upon the novel features specific to the German case.

Property right uncertainty was not a feature of the ex-GDR situation, since the east simply adopted (or had imposed) all the legal framework of the FRG. Thus the institutional mechanisms of a market economy were instantly on hand, but in their specific German form. In principle this should give the ex-GDR a major advantage compared to other similar economies in transition. In addition, the ex-GDR has had all the advantages of the massive economic assistance that the West German economy could offer. The restitution of property to its former owners figured strongly in the early attempts to privatize the ex-GDR economy. But the process of assessing claims has proved long and laborious (Siebert, 1991, pp. 297–8). The portfolios of other firms created from the *Kombinate* (ex-GDR conglomerate enterprises) not subject to the restitution process have been invested in the *Treuhandanstalt*, a public body charged with the responsibility for selling these to private interests. In some senses, then, the *Treuhandanstalt* has acted in the manner of a substitute for the old planning system, if in an interim fashion. It meets the issue raised above about the need to find surrogate mechanisms for a fully operative central direction of economic resources before the market system proper can be installed (Tribe, 1992).

In the meantime, enterprises have closed in the ex-GDR, industrial output has collapsed, net migration has increased, unemployment has grown, exports have disappeared and imports have mushroomed, all despite unprecedented subsidies from the West (Akerlof *et al.,* 1991; Collier, 1991; Siebert, 1991, Tables A2 and A3, pp. 336–7, Figure 6, p. 317). The uncompetitiveness of many ex-GDR firms has partly to do with the general inefficiency and technical backwardness of the eastern economy relative to that in the west. But it also has to do with the way monetary union was handled. This brings us to the more macro aspects of the transition process.

Despite the warnings in February 1990 from the then President of the *Bundesbank*, Karl Otto Pöhl, that a quick monetary union was 'fantastical', and of the potentially disastrous consequences likely to arise from setting a too generous exchange rate for the Ostmark (Collier, 1991, pp. 180–81), the momentum of political events propelled the Kohl government into doing both of these. Under political pressure, the *Bundesbank* originally proposed a general exchange rate of 2:1, with each individual able to exchange 2,000 Ostmarks of savings at the rate of 1:1. This was greeted with a mixture of despair and outrage in the east, and was soon abandoned. The eventual compromise allowed much more generous 1:1 conversion totals for savings,[1] though it kept in place the general 2:1 conversion. In addition, wages, salaries, rental payments and other prices were converted at the 1:1 rate, a crucial change from the original proposals. Along with this went an extension of all the FRG's social welfare, health and labour market benefits to the east.

These terms have been regarded as politically clever but economically disastrous (Collier, 1991, pp. 182–3; Irving and Paterson, 1991, p. 358). Chancellor Kohl had wrong-footed both the *Bundesbank* and his political opponents. The economic consequences, however, were financially to undermine, if not destroy, most of east German industry. Akerlof *et al.* (1991), for instance, estimated that these terms would make 92 per cent of East German firms financially unviable in the sense that they could not cover their short-run variable costs from their sales revenue. In particular, the generous exchange rate, implying a significant overvaluation of the Ostmark, and the absence of a period of transition in which this itself might be adjusted, had thrown all the economic adjustment onto the labour market and the wage rate. A series of employment subsidies were extended to the east to try to ameliorate the effects. In addition, generous reconstruction funds have been set up for infrastructure investment, and to encourage indigenous and foreign firms to set up in the east ('German Unity Fund' – DM 22 billion in 1990, DM 35 billion in 1991; 'Reconstruction of East Germany' Fund – DM 21 billion in 1991). By all accounts the effects of these measures in the east have, as yet, been minimal. Infrastructure investment increased there, though it faltered during 1991. German firms operating in the east have tended to see it as an assembly or distribution locality, rather than a manufacturing one. Market-based supply-side responses of this type take a long time to bear fruit, if they do at all.

The impact on the German economy overall has been dramatic, and this is where the consequences for the rest of Europe become important. During the second half of the 1980s, the West German economy had been in good shape. It had been expanding continuously since 1983, with growth of GDP 3.3 per cent in 1989 and 4.7 per cent in 1990; inflation was less than 3 per cent in both years, well below the Community average of 5.5 per cent; foreign trade was expanding rapidly (8–9 per cent); and the current account was massively in surplus. The position for the post-unification early 1990s is summarized in Table 7.1.

The dramatic effect on the current balance can be seen from Table 7.1, though interestingly the trade balance has remained positive despite the

Table 7.1   German economic indicators

	1990	1991	1992*	1993**
Inflation rate (%)	2.7	3.4	4.0	na
Unemployment rate (%)	5.1	4.6	5.0	na
General govt financial deficit				
DM billion	–65	–103	–105	na
% of GNP	–2.5	–3.7	–3.5	–2.9
Current balance (US$ bn)	47.9	–21	–14	–12
Trade balance (US$ bn)	72.9	20	21	27
Growth rate (%)	4.5	3.1	1.3	2.3

Notes:
* estimate
** forecast
na = not available.

Source: OECD *Economic Outlook*, December, 1991.

increase in imports to meet the demands of the consumers in the east. The inflation rate climbed steeply, though the position on unemployment in the country as a whole has not deteriorated. Another significant effect can be seen in terms of the government's fiscal deficit, which in 1991 reached 3.7 per cent of GNP, above the Maastricht convergence guidelines (though this was forecast to fall in 1992). The growth rate also fell significantly.

The issue this raises is the spillover effects of German economic and monetary union (GEMU) on the other EC countries and the international economy beyond. So much here depends on how the German economy itself reacts to these developments. Will it result in upward pressure on world interest rates and pressures for a real appreciation of the DM? The best way to think of this is in terms of two counter-acting economic forces. On the one hand these developments will lead to an increase in the German demand for other European consumer, agricultural, and to a lesser extent, capital goods, which could stimulate the European economy (Germany as 'locomotive'). On the other hand, the increases in the government deficit/current account deficit and inflation could force German interest rates up, leading to a very tight fiscal and monetary position in Germany, and as a result dampening down the whole of the European economy (Germany as 'drag anchor'). In the initial stages there seems little doubt that the excess demand for west German products by the east led to inflationary pressures. This was followed by the deteriorating government financial position as fiscal transfers to the east mounted, which added to the inflationary impulse.

If the supply-side shock of unification leads to a massive increase in all German investment opportunities and rises in productivity – the economic integration itself providing dynamic external economies of the Baldwin and Romer type (Chapter 4) – then the long-run prospects for the German economy look good. It will become a 'New Frontier'. The tendency towards an appreciation of the currency could be averted by this, though it depends upon how that investment boom was financed. A resort to foreign debt financing would further push the rate upward, for instance.

It is through the current account, however, that Germany acts as locomotive. Imports expanded rapidly in 1989 and 1990, falling away in the first half of 1991 but then growing again. Exports stagnated in 1990 and for much of 1991 before picking up again in 1992 (OECD, 1991b, Chart N, p. 49). The growth of imports has been strongest from the smaller EC economies, though France, Italy and the Benelux countries also benefited (OECD, 1991b, Chart M, p. 48). It is estimated that in 1990 and 1991 these trade stimuli added a half a percentage point to the growth of EC GNP in each year (Siebert, 1991, p. 327; Commission of the European Communities, 1991, Table 1, p. 8). These real stimulus effects on the EC economy as a whole look modest. They must be weighed against the monetary destabilizing and recessionary drag effects. The limited additional tax financing sought by the German government to pay for GEMU has increased fears that its negative effects might be prolonged. If the east were to become Germany's *'Mezzogiornio'* instead of its 'New Frontier', thus leading to a permanent drain on the economic and financial resources of the West, this might jeopardize German commitment, not only to any additional redistributive transfers to the less developed 'southern' European economies, but also to the European integration process as a whole. The excessively high resources cost of GEMU might affect its attitude to European EMU (EEMU). This has already been demonstrated in connection to the speed of EEMU, Germany expressing doubts about whether the criteria and timing agreed at Maastricht are really feasible in a post-GEMU world. Germany could become preoccupied with *its* east, and beyond that with *the* East more generally. German firms could become introverted or direct their attention increasingly to the newly emerging ex-Soviet-type economies discussed in the previous sections, not necessarily as sites for increased FDI, but as the destination for their exports. It is towards problems of this kind that we turn in the next section.

POLITICAL PROBLEMS AND PROSPECTS FOR THE EAST

Can the European Community as a whole offer serious assistance in the transformations of the ex-command economies? The major political problem here is the absence of an incentive to do other than the minimum necessary to avert an outright degeneration of the social order. But supposing that social order were to completely collapse in the East? This remains a real possibility, and in some ways is already slowly happening in southern-central Europe. But the ex-Soviet Union remains the key. If this were un-locked, and the economies there totally collapsed under the weight of their restructuring problems, one response could be pressure for mass migration westwards (Chapter 3). The EC has a very porous border to its east, and also to its south. In this instance the Eastern European economies stand as an economic buffer-zone for the EC.

A number of commentators have argued that with the demise of the 'Cold War' and the military threat associated with it, the new security 'threat' comes from the potential for mass migration (Widgren, 1990; Heisbourg, 1991). While difficult to assess, and not wishing to exaggerate its likelihood or possible consequences, the question of migration *has already* been posed for the EC. Europe has been the destination of up to 20 million migrants since the end of the Second World War. In the light of the principle of 'subsidiarity' discussed in Chapter 2, the EC sees much of the policy re-sponse to issues of immigration being left to the competence of the indi-vidual Community governments. This is unlikely to change in the near future, though the influx of a new wave of migrants from the East might pose the issue afresh and in an acute manner. This would not be a question of the slow assimilation of relatively small numbers of people, but a migration that could threaten to overwhelm even the larger of the existing EC mem-bers.

Callous though it may seem, the perceived 'threat' (real or imagined) arising from mass migration *is* one that could motivate the political leaders of the EC into action on serious assistance to the East, if nothing else in an attempt to preserve their own political power-bases from ultra-right political forces. It is the ultra-right that threatens to seize the initiative on migration and race, were it to become a central object of political contest within Europe. In the concluding chapter we pursue this issue further, but here we look at its economic inflection from the point of view of the Eastern Euro-pean and ex-Soviet Union economies.

The problem is to provide a 'ladder' onto which candidate member coun-tries can climb as a means for full entry into the EC. If the EC is not to become an exclusive 'rich-nations club' on the one hand, or simply a larger 'free-trade area' on the other, but is to mature into a regulated economic space with a strong commitment to its successful enlargement, then it must provide significant aid and assistance in the restructuring of the candidate economies to the east. At present they are not in an economic (let alone a political) position to make a successful entry without destroying the existing EC in the process. Their economies are nowhere near strong enough to withstand the competitive pressures within the EC as it is presently consti- tuted, let alone as it develops further towards monetary and economic union by the end of this century.

As suggested above, at present there is little pressure or incentive for EC leaders to do much about this, other than in terms of rhetoric and gesture. But with a 'threat' of mass migration, this position could change. And even without it there are good economic reasons for: (a) developing a common EC policy on migration, and (b) providing massive assistance to the Eastern economies to aid their restructuring efforts.

On the common EC policy front, immigration has important labour mar- ket effects and wider social effects. Whether one likes it or not, this is a sensitive political as well as economic issue. As the EC becomes a more integrated bloc, the spillover labour market and social effects will increase. Immigration into one country will increasingly affect another. Thus a com- mon policy becomes more pressing. A common policy will also provide a counterweight to any nationally specific adverse reaction to immigration. The EC should clearly try to avoid building another barrier to the East just as the old one is being dismantled, but that will require a much stronger and united humanitarian, political and economic commitment to those less ad- vantaged, fledgling democracies now in transition.

The specifically economic concern with immigration is how effectively could any newly arrived labour-force be absorbed into the domestic EC labour market, and what effects it would have there. The EC already has historically high levels of unemployment. In addition, if American experi- ence is anything to go by, we might expect newer immigrants to have a lower educational achievement, lower skills and lower earnings potential than indigenous labour (Borjas, 1990 and 1991). However, this is not to say that the European dimension will repeat the US experience. Nor is the US experience unambiguous. The decline in real earnings of the least skilled US workers may have little to do with immigration (Butcher and Card, 1991), and its overall impact on the operation of the labour market may be minimal (LaLonde and Topel, 1991). However, large-scale immigration is unlikely to *encourage* high value-added, high productive activity either (Chapter 6). It is more likely to feed the sentiments of those looking for ways to decrease the real wages of all European employees. But what is seen as good by individual businesses may not be good for an economy overall.

The objective of any programme of assistance, however, should not be considered just in terms of preventing potential negative impacts on the existing EC economies, though it might be thought of as this in part. The dominant objective must be to assist those economies themselves to solve their own economic and social problems so that the incentive for their populations to move is removed. Providing money on its own will not necessarily help, though large amounts of financial resources will be needed. The problem is unlike that of the position after the Second World War with Marshall Aid and Western Europe – the Eastern economies are not already market economies. Thus they need a different kind of longer-term assistance, mainly in the form of infrastructure investment, technical aid and directed trade credits.

Such a package might be thought of in terms of a 'Euro-Keynesian' policy (Hirst and Thompson, 1992). The objective of this would be to provide the funds to the East so that its population can purchase the goods and services from the West; a pump-priming process that would benefit both halves of Europe. While it has become impossible for any single economy to pursue an independent 'national Keynesian' policy, the continental-wide nature of the EC/European economy allows it the scope to do things single governments cannot do; even strong and important ones like a united Germany. But, as is argued in Hirst and Thompson, such a policy package, even to appear credible let alone feasible, requires a 'deepening' of the EC first. This deepening would require the establishment of a viable, independent 'public sphere' around the Commission, with enough powers to exercise a progressive fiscal and monetary policy at the European-wide level involving significant commitments to genuine redistributive objectives. Thus from this perspective, rather paradoxically, the widening of the Community first requires its deepening. This important point is taken up in the concluding chapter, though it should already be clear that the likelihood of this happening is fast diminishing in the post-Danish referendum world of the mid-1990s. But such a programme was not part of the original Maastricht Treaty negotiations, so even if the ratification of this regains its momentum, the same point equally applies.

CONCLUSION

What are the trajectories within and between the Eastern European and the ex-Soviet economies, and what do these hold for the future of European integration more generally? These are the issues confronted in this chapter. At the risk of an oversimplification, and in the face of a very complicated and non-homogeneous situation amongst these countries, we might sum this process up around two contrasting images of their future.

One real possibility is for the intensification of the 'manic capitalist' elements that are already apparent as a characteristic of these economies. Such a manic capitalism embodies all the worst (and some of the best) features of capitalism rolled into a single, intense and uncontrollable dynamic of competitive corruption and mismanagement. The nearest equivalent would be the Latin American economies of the late 1970s and 1980s. It relies upon individual initiative run riot, a veritable orgy of 'destructive innovation' so beloved of the neo-Austrian tradition of economic analysis, but an uncomfortable outcome if one actually has to live through something like a version of its extreme form.

The other real possibility is for a 'populist economic nationalism' to emerge more strongly with respect to economic management. This could quite easily involve something of a *rapprochement* with the old 'socialist' forms of economic regulation, if in an attenuated and weaker form. Again, this tendency is not totally divorced from existing popular and official sentiments in a number of these economies. There is a certain nostalgia for the certainties and relative stability of the old order, however despised that might have been. Clearly, a stronger move along these lines would involve a much more directed set of policies, and one pushing towards the import-substitution/trade-war route in the context of international economic relations.

The political corollary of these economic configurations could be, on the one hand, an 'anarco-pluralistic', weak and ineffectual political order, and on the other a 'plutocratic authoritarianism' that reinstalls many of the features of the old political order, if in a disguised form. Each of these outcomes would attempt to manage the antagonistic social-pluralism they had inherited, though without much success.

Elements of the first of these political configurations can be found in Poland, where the parliament is caught in an ineffectual political stalemate, nothing of substance being decided between the myriad of political parties represented in the *Sejm*. Compromise on political differences is impossible, and inaction is the result. Elements of the latter typify the Russian Republic, where President Boris Yeltsin finds the rule by decree conducive to his particular style of leadership. Interestingly, elements of each can also be seen in the other. Lech Walesa is also prone to rule by decree, and the Russian parliament is hardly more effective in the face of Boris Yeltsin's dictates than the *Sejm* is in the face of Lech Walesa in Poland.

This leads one to speculate whether in fact the two economic scenarios sketched above are that different when it comes to the actual practice of economic governance. Perhaps these are better considered as complementary sides of a single proto-system; both present an image of an extreme Latin American solution.

But what of their impact on the European integration process? Clearly neither of these scenarios would be that conducive to the rest of Europe. This is why it is imperative that the EC and its allies in Europe take seriously the political problems in the East, as well as the economic ones. As has been suggested by the analysis in this chapter, however, and as is stressed again in the conclusion that follows, neither the existing character of the process of transformation in the Eastern economies nor the trajectory of European integration itself is conducive to a positive outcome on this issue. The united Germany is partly preoccupied with its own internal redistributive problems, while the EC as a whole looks likely to retreat from a strong commitment to the necessary independent institution-building of a pan-European type. In the next chapter we assess the overall conjuncture for Europe and the balance of its centrifugal and centripetal forces.

NOTE

1. For those between 14 and 58 years of age, 4,000 Ostmarks could be exchanged at the 1:1 rate; for those over 59 years it was 6,000. After shifts of savings into new accounts for children and the old had been completed, the average exchange rate was 1.8:1.

8. Conclusion

As we have seen in the previous chapters, the latest round of European integrationist moves has been justified on the basis of a linked process of liberalization, the internal market and growth. While the Treaty of Rome identified tariff barriers as the main impediment to the efficient operation of markets, the single market programme extended this to include non-tariff barriers. For these initiatives, the dominant public policy stance has become one of competition and commercial policy, stressing the virtues of a neo-liberal programme of eliminating restrictive practices and barriers to trade.

However, the actual way markets have operated to develop their own regulatory modes is not via the elimination of such restrictive practices, but in terms of fostering and developing them. Markets have created such regulatory devices as cartels, monopolies, barriers to trade and a range of other so-called restrictive practices. Thus there would seem to be a disjuncture between the officially sanctioned economists' policy programme and the actual way markets themselves organize for dynamic growth. Indeed, this is perhaps being recognized even at an official level in the form of the moves towards full economic and monetary union. To an extent the benefits of this initiative again refer to the presumed virtues of unrestrained competition, but they are actually being justified in terms of oligopolistic competition, economies of scale, concentration, mergers and rationalization. This image of integration is one at least partly at odds with that of the liberalization of competition, customs union theory, and the elimination of barriers to trade. Thus unless the European authorities recognize the way market regulation actually organizes for economic growth, they are in danger of setting the European economy on a wrong course for its increased competitiveness. The integrated European economy will require a new set of regulatory mechanisms commensurate with the transformed nature of economic organization and the current and emergent new forms of production process technologies. There is no reason to believe that the simple liberalization of competition and commercial policy will deliver dynamic growth benefits under these circumstances.

In addition, it is the political character of, and constraints upon, integration that needs to be foregrounded in this complex contemporary process. The political conditions of governance of the processes of integrative market and economic union is a key feature highlighted in the previous chapters. But the shape of the development of the European Community is difficult to gauge after the 1991 Maastricht Summit, at which limited progress towards economic and political union was made. This was so even before the Danish and French votes on the Treaty threw the whole process into further confusion after June 1992. Until the Maastricht Treaty, it appeared the Community was making real progress towards becoming an integrated and effectively regulated trade bloc. The 12 governments had all passed the Single European Act. If this measure succeeds in removing institutional barriers to trade between member states, then there will be a more integrated economic space in the EC than in the USA. In 1990 Britain joined the ERM, creating the possibility of eventual total monetary union between all EC members.

However, the problem is that the EC needed to make rapid progress towards integration in the early 1990s, or it would tend to go backwards under the pressure of emerging centrifugal forces. The events of September 1992 provided a telling indication of the possibilities. Prior to these events, pro-Europeans tended naïvely to assume that the process of economic integration was irreversible and that it would inevitably draw political integration in its wake. By the time of Maastricht, it became clear that major political and institutional changes in the structure of governance of the Community were essential if economic integration was to be pursued beyond the level of the single market, and that there were fundamental barriers to such developments.

The Community is currently poised between powerful centrifugal and centripetal forces, and is in large measure paralysed in its responses by the divergent politics and commitments of the different national leaderships. The centrifugal forces are new and powerful. They are the decline of political homogeneity, the faltering of prosperity and the collapse of a unifying adversary. The last is the most obvious, for, as analysed in Chapter 2, the EC was created in the shadow of the Soviet threat, and the cooperation on the part of the major European powers, France and Germany, was facilitated by that threat, along with the pressure from the USA. Now that the Soviet satellite regimes in east-central Europe and the USSR itself have collapsed, the EC is faced with a potentially fateful choice between those who seek to 'widen' the Community (to include as rapidly as possible as many European countries who want to join), and those who seek to 'deepen' the Community (to integrate further its mechanisms of economic regulation and to promote political union). The wideners know that the EC cannot at present integrate the Eastern economies unless it regresses to a loosely governed free-trade zone; expansion has therefore become the gospel of the 'anti-federalist' forces in the UK, for example. The upshot of this conflict is likely to be that rapid progress towards political union does not take place, and that the economies of the East are not integrated into the EC quickly, either *de jure* as full members or *de facto* as part of the new economic space. As was made clear by the analysis in Chapters 5 and 7, most of these countries simply cannot meet even the current conditions of EC membership, let alone those conditional on full EMU. And the most advanced of them, even given favourable outcomes for marketization and privatization, will not be able to do so for at least a decade.

Paradoxically, only rapid political union and the creation of strong citizen legitimacy for a centrally directed policy could allow the EC rapidly to reconstruct and integrate the Eastern states. Such a cohesive trade bloc could follow policies of large-scale aid and reconstruction that would simultane-ously promote development in the East and create full employment in the West by utilizing the East as a new source of effective demand through trade credits. Such a 'Euro-Keynesian' policy is conceivable, and the continental scale of the EC economy makes it possible in the way national Keynesian reflations are not, but it is inherently unlikely. At present, most European politicians are too risk-averse and too concerned with emergent nationalistic and regionalist forces to contemplate this policy. Moreover, it inevitably empowers Brussels at the expense of the national governments and will be resisted by the majority of national leaders for this reason.

The second of the centrifugal forces is the collapse of political homogene-ity. Since its inception in 1957, the Community has been dominated by a political spectrum from centre-right to centre-left. This is now breaking up, not towards the far left, but towards the ultra-right and, more importantly, towards populist, nationalist and regionalist parties. There are clear signs of political revolt against the established parties in several European countries and dissatisfaction with the nation state itself. This was most obvious in the 1992 Italian elections, with an across-the-board loss of support for the estab-lished parties and a strong showing by populist and federalist regional par-ties such as the *Lega Lombarda.* As the established national parties are challenged by right-wing nationalism, such as Le Pen's *Front Nationale,* or by regional secessionism, such as the Italian leagues, they will tend to retrench politically to defend the state, and will not, therefore, accept the ceding of power to the EC. Thus, perhaps paradoxically, the level of coop-eration achieved between the *states* of Europe in the period to the mid-1980s now threatens to hasten the break-up of those states into *nations* or *regions.*

The third of the centrifugal forces is the prospect that European economic growth will falter; that there will be a widespread and prolonged economic depression in continental Europe (Chapter 5). This has not occurred since the Treaty of Rome was signed. The integration of Europe has so far been achieved without serious costs, and all states have experienced generally rising output and real incomes (though with significant fluctuations). Were growth to falter, and this depends very much on the international environment and whether the USA recovers quickly from its recession, the pressures towards national protective measures could grow. These would not be for new tariff barriers within Europe, but towards reversing EC competition policy (which is to reduce state aid to industry), and towards greater independence in fiscal and monetary policy than the current EMS or the convergence criteria of the process of monetary union would allow. The EC could begin to dis-integrate as national states sought to protect their own economic bases, and this would be carried out by established politicians attempting to direct the threat of political competition from the far-right and regional political forces.

Europe is still at the point where a great deal of institutional work needs to be done to ensure that its effective economic integration is irreversible. At a primitive level – as a single market – integration is probably irreversible. The same does not hold for the development of the extended economic governance of this single economic space (for example, via a strengthened Social Chapter). For those committed to European union, the hope must be that there is no serious depression in the 1990s, that centrist politicians can contain the worst of the rightist pressures, that the issue of immigration does not become explosive and a gift to the right and, therefore, that the space is left for the centripetal forces to exert countervailing pressures towards integration.

There are indeed strong centripetal forces in Europe, as well as sources of strain and divergence. Crudely put, the Community's national states have lost the effective capacity to serve as regulators over certain vital dimensions of economic activity (for which regional governments are even less effective), and yet the central institutions of the Community have not acquired the political capacity to exercise those economic functions. This functional imbalance will put continuing pressure on both national policies and Community institutions. How such an imbalance can be resolved is another matter.

The issue is not just integration or the transfer of national regulatory functions to Community institutions, but the creation of new mechanisms, objectives and policies of economic governance appropriate to the Community level. The Community is not a nation state writ large, and so national economic and regulatory policies cannot simply be transferred and performed on a larger scale. The EC is a trade bloc of continental dimensions; therefore it can potentially do things European nation states cannot, and also it cannot perform certain functions that nation states have done. The question is one of a balance between Community, national and regional economic regulation; this is something to which we will return later in this discussion.

Monetary policy provides a striking example of this contradiction between the need for integration and the impossibility of merely scaling-up
national policies and institutions. The Maastricht Treaty supposes that the
outcome of EMU will be led by the European Federal Bank, a politically
independent central bank that would organize monetary policy and operate
without direct accountability to other economic policy-makers. It would be
the ideal image of the *Bundesbank* writ large (Chapter 5). It would also
pursue the same economic priorities as the *Bundesbank* – exchange rate
stability and an anti-inflationary policy. The problem is that a Community
central bank and a single currency can only exist after a period of 'convergence', which under present conditions will imply a deflationary shock to
most of the EC countries. But in the mid-1990s the last thing Europe will
need is a deflationary bout of Euro-monetarism in order to create a single
currency.

The problem is that although manufacturing has grown, in the 1980s in
particular under boom conditions, it is doubtful if much of French or Italian,
let alone British, industry could be competitive under a combined regime of
Euro-monetarism and relatively open trade with the world outside the EC.
Other countries' trade unions have not been so effective as Germany's at
controlling wage inflation. Italy, for example, traded higher growth for higher
inflation in the 1980s. To see what could happen, one only has to look at the
effects of monetarism in a country that had a large manufacturing sector –
the UK in 1979–81. An overvalued pound and high interest rates led to
devastating losses in manufacturing capacity (by about 25 per cent). It is
foolish to say that much of British industry was 'uncompetitive' *tout court*;
firms are only competitive in definite macroeconomic conditions, and if
these are sufficiently unfavourable then firms – good, bad and indifferent –
will go to the wall.

The implications of this are two-fold. First, the process of 'convergence'
must be slower, and its criteria looser, if it is to be less painful. Rapid
monetary integration as envisaged in the framework of the Maastricht Treaty
is, therefore, likely to be an unworkable policy for all 12 states and, in fact,
may damage European integration. The alternative is either a slower process
with looser targets and wider objectives, or a two-stage process with a fast
and slow stream. The danger with the latter process is that it will derail
convergence and create complex monetary obstacles to full economic integration – creating a first and second 'tier' of European countries.

Secondly, the idea of an 'independent' central bank at the European Community level is dangerous for the process of integration. Such a bank will
lack legitimacy and that lack will be reinforced by its divorce from wider
economic policy-making and by its tendency to set constraining conditions
for the latter. The effect of 'independence' would be to allow unaccountable

officials to dictate economic policy at a time when the central institutions of the Community would still lack legitimacy and citizen identification. The result could all too easily be a disaster for the process of building support for EC economic and political integration.

The wider policy dimensions of the regulation of the new European single economic space, and of Community-level economic and social policy, also raise serious questions about both the need for such common programmes and the difficulty of attaining them within existing institutions. How, for example, can Europe have a 'single market' unless it also has effective mechanisms to regulate that market's workings? Margaret Thatcher's vision of the single market was simple: a continent set free for economic liberalism. Goods and capital could move without being limited by national economic regulation. Such a market would put firms and capital markets beyond effective control, and they would thus be able to impose social costs and to avoid paying for them by allocating resources as they wished. Such a view is quite alien to most Community politicians. They operate on good Christian Democratic or Social Democratic principles and seek the highest measure of market liberalism consistent with long-run social efficiency. That means common European standards and regulation where they are necessary – in environmental protection, in company law and regulation of capital markets, and in social and in health and safety legislation. In such areas, existing Community institutions can probably perform such regulatory functions and enjoy legitimacy in doing so. The Community creates a common 'framework' legislation – a common structure of rights and regulations that enables all economic actors to operate with a measure of certainty throughout Europe. Sometimes this common framework takes the form of accepting national treatments.

The problems begin to arise at the point where programmes of harmonization in particular involve major spending; for example, on common standards of environmental protection or compatible social benefits. Not all nations and regions can afford to comply with the emerging 'first tier' conceptions of a healthy environment, nor can there really be a single labour market until there are common basic social benefits. The current 'Social Chapter' is a minimalist document for this very reason. A more ambitious social programme would imply serious redistribution of revenue within the EC, to bring economically weaker nations and regions up to common higher standards without a crippling fiscal burden. The Community's current approach is, on the contrary, to dilute common standards down to a minimum so that at least some agreement can actually be reached.

Similar difficulties will occur in other areas of policy. In particular there will be great resistance to any European regional policy that seeks to improve the efficiency of weaker regions by investment in infrastructure and in crucial supply-side factors such as education and training (Chapter 6). Policies to promote economic revitalization are essential on narrow economic grounds that are ultimately of benefit to the richer regions too. Widespread success and growth are needed to maintain a base of effective demand and social efficiency to sustain an extensive growing and productive advanced industrial sector. The idea of a Europe of 'tiers', where capital can profit by exploiting low wage zones is ultimately self-defeating. Such zones will be low demand, peripheral areas too, and thus limit the scope and competitiveness of the 'first tier' core of regions by restricting the growth of these markets. Moreover, no European Community region can compete in this respect with the vast low wage 'third tier' of countries that has opened up in Eastern Europe.

The drive to regional harmonization and social homogeneity makes sense in the long run, and from the perspective of the whole Community. The problem is that richer regions and states, like wealthier social groups within a nation state, will not be willing to spend on fiscal redistribution and social harmonization if they can avoid it. The question is one of both the legitimacy and the coherence of a European-scale policy. Europe can act differently from a nation state. It is a large enough economic entity to be able to maintain 'Keynesian' policies of maintenance of effective demand in the face of the international financial markets, had it the political coherence to do so.

The scale of the European economy makes possible policy options that no member national government can contemplate. The problem is that such options cannot be realized within the existing structures of governance of the EC. At the moment, for example, the national governments of the member states are strongly resisting Commission proposals to expand greatly the central EC budget, and to spend a sizeable chunk of that revenue on a large-scale aid programme for Eastern Europe. The EC is thus currently paralysed between the interests of the national governments and the central apparatus. The member states lack the scope for effective concerted action. They must, in major matters, proceed at the pace of the slowest, as Maastricht and its subsequent developments have shown. The central apparatus lacks the capacity to substitute itself for the state governments, it is a small bureaucracy capable only of 'framework' legislation and decision-making, and requires the cooperation of the national bureaucracies for implementation. It also lacks an independent source of legitimacy to reach over the heads of national governments to citizens in the member states.

Maastricht has resolved none of these issues of the balance of power between Community, national and regional levels of governance. The EC will never be a continent-wide single unified state. That option has been ruled out since the Second World War. Though there are things that unified states can do that looser configurations cannot, a federal state such as the USA has considerable advantages over the present EC arrangements. But it is unlikely that Europe can advance to even a proper federal status. Existing political forces are not in the mood to cede the necessary powers to Brussels. Any attempt to force this through would rapidly lead to the break-up of the EC. Rather, what is most likely is that some form of *con*federal arrangement will emerge. The EC will, at best, be a European 'public power', its capacities derived from treaties between the member states and from processes of decision-making in which those states will have a major part to play. If the EC is inescapably confederal in matters of both revenue and military power, the nation states will retain the power of decision, but they will make community-level policy by majority vote. This also means that the legal possibility of seceding from the Community remains for all nation states. The Community can never be a political entity exactly like the old national states.

It must develop, however, some mechanisms for securing citizen identification with, and political legitimacy for, Community institutions if it is not to forgo some of the main benefits of a continental-scale of organization. The construction of such an identity can in part only come with processes of integration, as indeed will legitimacy follow from the strengthening of central political institutions. That is why Maastricht was such a dismal failure at a time when Europe needed radical change. Most members of European élites accept that a single market requires a unit of regulation to match it. The main limits of possible policy in Europe are *political,* and concern the capacity of Brussels to mobilize citizen support for continental-scale policies involving major fiscal commitments and political risks.

The odds against rapid progress towards the 'federalist' objectives are high, particularly in the post-Danish and French referenda world of late 1992. But even if such progress were made, the Community as a political entity would still be a complex amalgam of overlapping powers and responsibilities. For the most ambitious economic policy goals to be realized, there would have to be a substantial measure of policy coordination at the Community, national and regional levels. Even if the central institutions of the Community were to gain considerably in citizen support and political legitimacy, they could not substitute central social coordination for the more complex processes of the orchestration of consensus and consent at national and regional levels. Nations and regions are the sites of social solidarity, and some of these entities have a far stronger capacity to coordinate the social interests than do others.

If one considers the sort of policies that could become possible, given the continental scale of the Community, the necessity and the difficulty of achieving this complex division of labour becomes obvious. Thus the Commission

– even with an expanded budget – is not in itself a large enough fiscal actor
to provide the stimulus for 'Euro-Keynesian' policies without coincident
fiscal and monetary policies in at least the majority of the member states.
Assuming that the Community could orchestrate such a policy on the demand side, then it is even more the case that its central institutions could not
create the complementary policies to contain money wage growth and prevent inflation. Such income restraint would fall to national governments:
some, like Germany, could deliver because of corporatist structures and a
relatively disciplined union movement, others, like France, would probably
be able to comply because unions are weak; but some countries are mani-
festly incapable of constraining wage growth without highly restrictive
macroeconomic policies, like Britain. A European expansionary policy would,
therefore, lead to patchy results, those states most able to restrain wages
growth would benefit, those unable to do so would lose out through accelerating unemployment or nationally imposed deflations.

It is difficult to see how this discrepancy between national experiences
and institutional legacies can be eliminated. There is little prospect, for
example, of a strong 'Euro-corporatism' that brings the social partners together to make binding agreements at Community level. Although there are
estimated to be upwards of 10,000 lobbyists on behalf of business regularly
operating in Brussels, business will not present itself at this level as a single
'social partner'. It remains divided by national and sectoral interests, and it
would prefer to lobby for those interests with the Directorates of the Commission on an issue-by-issue basis. Its national collective bodies are divergent in
their degree of organization, and in their objectives and their willingness to
enter into partnership with labour. German industry is highly organized on
the employers' side, with strong sectoral and peak employers' associations,
the member firms of which follow collective policy in a disciplined manner.
German employers retain strong commitments both to industry-wide bargaining on wages and working hours, and to the co-determination system of
consultation with labour at enterprise level. British employers' associations
are, by contrast, almost exclusively concerned with representing the most
general perceived interests of their members to government, and have few
powers to discipline their members or get them to take part in coordinated
consultation with labour. Wage bargaining has undergone massive decentralization in Britain since the 1970s, with very few industry-wide agreements. British employers are actively hostile to the idea of an extended
dialogue with organized labour to build consent for national policies – that is
'corporatism' and has no place in the modern British manager's lexicon.
This stark contrast shows that Europe will find it difficult to create institutionalized means of orchestrating consensus for macroeconomic policy at
Community level (Chapter 5).

European labour, through its federal-level organizations, may well wish to try to enter into a dialogue with the Commission about policy coordination and the orchestration of consent across the Community. It will have problems if it alone is interested and the employers refuse to play ball, but even greater problems on its own side too – for European-level consultations will not be able to deliver disciplined commitments by member unions in the nation states in such key areas as wages policy and wage restraint. In contrast to the employers' side, the European Trade Union Council has only ten full-time officials in Brussels. The European Metal Workers Federation, representing some eight million workers, had a General Secretary, plus one assistant and two typists working in Brussels in 1991.

This tells us that *some* nation states will remain the crucial actors in constructing a *political* basis of consent for the macroeconomic policies of the Community, and for their own fiscal, regulatory and industrial policies. Only at the national level can effective *distributional coalitions* be built, that is, framework agreements between the major parties and social actors about the conditions for, and the necessary costs of, economic success. Social Democrats and Christian Democrats in Germany both agree on a wide range of policies and institutions which sustain the economy, for example, but also enter into intense and open political competition. Such coalitions may be tacit or more orchestrated – what matters is that cooperation and competition between the major interests are in balance. In either case, it involves the commitment of social actors and the organized social interests representing them to a sustainable distribution of national income between consumption and investment, and to a pattern of expenditure that promotes manufacturing performance. For example, a critical mass of the German financial community accepts the priority of investing in German firms under terms and conditions that protect their competitiveness. Parties, organized labour and employers accept the need for public and private investments in education and training. In other countries such commitments and their orchestration would require explicit government action – the UK is the prime example, and Conservative governments over the last 13 years have seen this as no part of their task. It will be more difficult to extend such national coalitions to cover the costs of ensuring competitiveness at Community level. In future, social actors and their interest organizations will also have to take account of a 'European slice' of revenue, redistribution and policy commitments to further the working of pro-Community programmes.

Nation states will also remain crucial, in that it is they who provide the domestic constitutional framework and policy support for effective regional government. States differ massively in size, and the categories 'nation state' and 'region' have no ultimate coherence – Bavaria is a 'region' but could easily be a 'state'. Some nation states will remain strong political entities –

France and Germany are obvious examples. Others could well face strong disintegrating pressures, for example, Spain and Italy.

Regional governments are now key economic regulators, in that they are more able to assess the needs of industry. This is because they possess more localized and, therefore, more accurate information and because they are of a size that enables the key public and private actors to interact and cooperate successfully. Regions are small enough to possess 'intimate knowledge' and yet are sufficiently large enough to aid and regulate local economies through a significant revenue base. The regional provision of education and training, industrial finance and collective services for industry is gaining in importance; it is a vital component of the new 'supply-side' policies that promote industrial efficiency. As suggested in Chapter 6, if a new form of industrial policy is to arrive in Europe, it will best operate at this regional or lower level.

The most successful economies are those that have allowed the measure of local autonomy necessary for regional regulation and that have developed strong industrial districts. The UK has failed most conspicuously in this regard, and governments have centralized relentlessly since the 1960s. This has reduced local government to client status (UK authorities are too small to be regional governments) and, since 1979, has denied the need for local industrial policies or public–private partnerships to provide collective services. Business has also concentrated massively, through mergers and acquisitions turning local firms into subsidiaries of remote headquarters and severing regional cross-linkages between firms. The UK will thus lose out most in any move towards the regional regulation of economic activity – it will suffer both from the competitive pressures of the single market and from those competitive pressures which stem from the enhanced efficiency available to foreign firms through their use of regional economic cooperation and collective services.

In other states, regional governments have compensated for ineffective national policies. Italy is the obvious example, with the more successful industrial districts and regions in the north and the 'Third Italy' providing effective economic regulation. One should note that the very weakness and paralysis of the Italian state aided this process in the 1980s. Italy did not fall prey to fashionable monetarist doctrines, and lax government allowed a strongly expansionist (and inflationary) policy (Chapter 3). This benefited the more 'post-Fordist' enterprises and industrial districts at the expense of Italy's large firms, big cities and the south. Italian growth in the 1980s thus benefited those areas and social groups which are in favour of greater autonomy and look on the central state as a liability. The question is if they would fare better under a 'Europe of the regions' in which they would be subject to a federal monetary and macroeconomic policy. As has been noted above, this is likely (if present conceptions were followed), to be 'Euro-monetarist'.

A 'Europe of the regions' has at present no precise shape. Europe's nation states may accept the need to facilitate regional government. France has at least partially decentralized, for example, but most states will not accept their own dissolution – even if they are strongly federal like Germany. The Community cannot create central institutions fast enough and with enough legitimacy to achieve an effective federal–regional split in most economic regulatory functions in the near future. Major nation states will retain the control of nationally distinct military, cultural and legal institutions that, of necessity, give those states extensive economic regulatory powers. The danger is that a 'Europe of the regions' will not emerge because of an equitable balance of power between federal, national and regional levels, but because of the reverse. It will be obvious that there are numerous gaps and lacunae in the economic governance the EC will be able to offer in the next decade and beyond. The Community will lack collective powers in certain areas or, perhaps, gain too much power, as would be the case with a monetarist Euro-Fed. National states will differ in their capacities for economic management, and for effective cooperation with sufficiently autonomous regional governments. The weakest, that is, the most centralized and least socially coordinated states such as the UK, will lose out. But so also will weak regions, especially in weak states. The regions that will benefit most are strong regions in effective national states, such as Baden-Wurttemberg or Rhône-Alpes, or regions in less integrated states that are strong in their own right, such as Catalonia or Lombardy. These regions are linked in the 'Four Motors' consortium across national boundaries. Those are the 'winners' but there will be 'losers' in regional terms and plenty of them – and they will have the electoral power to challenge this result. They may not be able to overturn it, but strife between rich and poor regions, violent divergences over redistribution and the direction of the Community's economic governance, will help to ensure the unsettled character of European institutions and prevent a generous policy towards the East. Europe's future may be decided by continued differences within the Community that prevent it from acting to unite the continent.

Thus, finally, what are the prospects for cooperation and competition in terms of the analytical schemas discussed in Chapter 1? The results from Chapter 2 were optimistic about the evolution of cooperation in the post-Second World War period up to the mid-1980s. The repeat interactions within a range of institutional environments had seen steady progress towards firm modes of cooperation between the European nation states. The suspicions endemic in the Saddam/George-type game theory example discussed in Chapter 1 seemed to have been progressively dissipated. It looked as though 'gain gaps' from cooperation were low enough not to outweigh individual gains in the overall utility functions. There was a definite 'win set' when domestic policy constraints were measured against an evolving European international regime that provided 'reputation' gains from mutual cooperation.

However, the subsequent chapters began to unpick a good deal of the features that had led to this optimistic conclusion. The investigations in Chapter 3 showed the continuing differentiation of the management regimes within the EC, and the contradictory nature of the attempts to marry these around a common European framework. Chapter 4 went on to show the difficulty of justifying the forms of European integration involving the real economy and the way the Commission had misunderstood the contemporary changes in the structure of the European real economies. In terms of macroeconomic policy, the results from Chapter 5 pointed to the deflationary impact of the Maastricht convergence criteria, the difficulties associated with EMU, and the inadequacies of much of the analysis of money for understanding problems of economic union. The lack of a sensible policy towards industrial restructuring and the future needs of a competitive manufacturing sector were pointed to in Chapter 6. The pressures being put on the Community by the transformations in the East and the inability of the EC to provide an adequate response to these were highlighted in Chapter 7.

All these inadequacies of analysis and shortcomings of policy imply that the centrifugal forces undermining the level of cooperation so far achieved were stronger than had been anticipated. Much of this collaboration seems to be on the verge of crumbling in the post-Maastricht period. The general reasons for this have been outlined in this conclusion. The 'win set' of cooperation for European integration seems to be turning into a 'lose set', as the European international regime fails to deliver enough domestic reputation benefits to offset a deteriorating domestic popularity profile, itself based upon economic recession and antagonistic domestic political differentiation.

However, though the signs that the EC will make rapid progress in economic and political union are not encouraging, this does not mean that the nation states of Europe will retreat into open competition. The degree of embedded trust and cooperation established between the key players should be enough to rule out this option. In addition, the 'rationalistic' forms of analysis deployed above overstate the mutual opposition of cooperation and competition. The challenge in the European arena is to provide an analysis, and a set of policy proposals based upon it, that encourages further realistic integrative activity, while at the same time meeting the requirements of a balanced *cooperative competition.*

Bibliography

Abelshauser, W. (1982), 'West German Economic Recovery, 1945–51: A Reassessment', *Three Banks Review*, no. 135, September, 34–53.

Akerlof, George A. *et al.* (1991), 'East Germany in from the Cold: The Economic Aftermath of Currency Union', *Brookings Papers on Economic Activity*, 1, 1–88.

Allen, C.S. (1989), 'The Underdevelopment of Keynesianism in the Federal Republic of Germany'. In Hall, P. (ed.), *The Political Power of Economic Ideas*, New Jersey: Princeton University Press.

Alvstam, Claes and Ellegard, Kajsa (1990), 'Volvo'. In Smidt, Marc de and Wever, Egbert (eds), *The Corporate Firm in a Changing World Economy*, London: Routledge.

Arestis, Philip, Hadjimatheou, George and Zis, George (1992), 'The Impact of Financial Innovations on the Demand for Money in the UK and Canada', *Applied Financial Economics*, **2**, 115–23.

Artis, M. (1989), 'The United Kingdom and the EMS', *Centre for Economic Policy Research, Discussion Paper No. 353*, November, London .

Artis, M. (1991), 'Monetary Policy and the Exchange Rate', *Oxford Review of Economic Policy*, **7**, (3), 128–38.

Artis, Michael (1992), 'Monetary Policy in Stage Two of EMU: What Can We Learn From the 1980s?', *Centre for Economic Policy Research, Discussion Paper No. 629*, January, London.

Artis, M. and Ostry, S. (1986), *International Policy Coordination*, Chatham House Papers no. 30, London: Royal Institute for International Affairs.

Association for the Monetary Union of Europe (1990), A *Strategy for the ECU*, London: Kogan Page (also published in French, Italian, German and Swedish).

Aujean, Michael (1988), 'Evaluation des Economies d'Echelle Pouvant Résulter de l'Achèvement du Marche Intérieur'. In Commission of the European Communities, *Research on the 'Costs of Non-Europe' Basic Findings, Vol. 2*. Luxembourg: Office for Official Publications of the European Communities.

Axelrod, Robert (1990), *The Evolution of Co-operation*, London: Penguin Books.

Baldwin, Richard E. (1989), 'The Growth Effect of 1992', *Economic Policy*, no. 9, October, 248–81.

Baldwin, Richard E. and Lyons, Richard (1991), 'External Economies and European Integration: The Potential for Self-Fulfilling Expectations'. In *The Economics of EMU*, 'European Economy' Special Edition No. 1, Commission for the European Communities.

Begg, D. (1990), 'Britain and Europe: The European Financial Area', *Oxford Economic Papers*, **42**, 659–71.

Berggren, C. (1989), 'New Production Concepts in Final Assembly: The Swedish Experience'. In Wood, S. (ed.), *The Transformation of Work?*, London: Unwin Hyman.

Boltho, A. (1990), 'Why Has Europe Not Co-Ordinated Its Fiscal Policies?', *International Review of Applied Economics*, **4**, (2), 166–81.

Borjas, George J. (1990), *Friends or Strangers: The Impact of Immigrants on the US Economy*, New York: Basic Books.

Borjas, George J. (1991), 'Immigrants in the US Labour Market: 1940–80', *American Economic Review Papers and Proceedings*, **81**, (2), May, 287–91.

Boycko, Maxim (1991), 'Price Decontrol: The Microeconomic Case for the "Big Bang" Approach', *Oxford Review of Economic Policy*, **7**, (4), Winter, 35–45.

Brada, Josef C. (1991), 'The Economic Transition of Czechoslovakia from Plan to Market', *The Journal of Economic Perspectives*, **5**, (4), Fall, 171–8.

Bressand, Albert (1990), 'Beyond Interdependence: 1992 As A Global Challenge', *International Affairs*, **66**, (1), 47–65.

Brunner, K. and Meltzer, A.H. (1971), 'The Uses of Money: Money in the Theory of an Exchange Economy', *American Economic Review*, **61**, (5), December, 784–805.

Buchanan, James M. (1979), *The Economics of Politics*, London: Institute of Economic Affairs.

Butcher, Kristin F. and Card, David (1991), 'Immigration and Wages: Evidence from the 1980s', *American Economic Review Papers and Proceedings*, **81**, (2), May, 292–6.

Caballero, R.J. and Lyons, R.K. (1990), 'Internal Versus External Economies in European Industry', *European Economic Review*, **34**, June, 805–30.

Caballero, Riccardo J. and Lyons, Richard K. (1991), 'External Effects and Europe's Integration'. In Winters, Alan and Venables, Anthony (eds), *European Integration: Trade and Industry*, Cambridge: Cambridge University Press.

Calmfors, L. and Driffill, J. (1988), 'Bargaining Structure, Corporatism and Macroeconomic Performance', *Economic Policy*, no. 6, April, 14–61.

Calvo, Guillermo A. and Frenkel, Jacob A. (1991), 'Credit Markets, Credibility, and Economic Transformation', *The Journal of Economic Perspectives*, **5**, (4), Fall, 139–48.

Carlin, Wendy and Soskice, David (1990), *Macroeconomics and the Wage Bargain*, Oxford: Oxford University Press.

Cecchini, P. (1988), *The European Challenge: 1992*, Aldershot: Wildwood House.

Centre for Business Strategy (1990), *Continental Mergers are Different*, London: London Business School.

Chase-Dunn, Christopher (1989), *Global Formation: Structures of the World Economy*, Oxford: Blackwell.

Codere, H. (1968), 'Money-Exchange Systems and a Theory of Money', *Man*, **3**, (4), December, 557–77.

Cohen, S. S. and Zysman, J. (1987), *Manufacturing Matters: The Myth of the Post Industrial Economy*, New York: Basic Books.

Collier, Irwin L. (1991), 'On the First Year of German Monetary, Economic and Social Union', *The Journal of Economic Perspectives*, **5**, (4), Fall, 179–86.

Colman, Andrew (1982), *Game Theory and Experimental Games: The Study of Strategic Interaction*, Oxford: Pergamon Press.

Commission of the European Communities (1985), *Completing the Internal Market*, White Paper from the Commission to the European Council, Brussels.

Commission of the European Communities (1991), 'Annual Economic Report 1991–92', *European Economy No. 50*, December.

Committee for the Study of Economic and Monetary Union (1989), *Report on Economic and Monetary Union in the European Community*, Luxembourg: Office for Official Publications of the European Communities.

Cooper, R. and Kaplan, R.S. (1987), 'How Cost Accounting Systematically Distorts Product Cost'. In Burns, W.J. and Kaplan, R.S. (eds), *Accounting and Management: Field Study Perspectives*, Boston: Harvard Business School Press.

Corbett, Jenny and Mayer, Colin (1991), 'Financial Reform in Eastern Europe: Progress With the Wrong Model', *Oxford Review of Economic Policy*, **7**, (4), Winter, 57–75.

Cutler, T., Haslam, C., Williams, J. and Williams, K. (1989), *1992: The Struggle for Europe*, Oxford: Berg.

Davenport, Michael (1992), 'Exchange Rate Policy for Eastern Europe and a Peg to the ECU', *Economic Papers No. 90*, Commission of the European Communities, March.

Dertouzos, M.L., Lester, R.K. and Solow, R.M. (1989), *Made in America: Regaining Our Competitive Edge*, Cambridge: MIT Press.

Drabek, Z. and Greenaway, D. (1984), 'Economic Integration and Intra-Industry Trade: The CMEA and EEC Compared', *Kyklos*, **37**, pt 3, 444–69.

Dumke, R.H. (1990), 'Reassessing the *Wirtschaftswunder:* Reconstruction and Postwar Growth in West Germany in International Context', *Oxford Bulletin of Economics and Statistics*, **52**, (2), 451–91.

Economic Commission for Europe (1990), *Economic Survey of Europe in 1989–1990*, New York: United Nations.

Edwards, J.S.S. and Fischer, Klaus (1991), 'Banks, Finance and Investment in West Germany Since 1970', *Discussion Paper No. 497*, London: Centre for Economic Policy Research.

Eichengreen, Barry (1990), 'One Money for Europe? Lessons from the US Currency Union', *Economic Policy*, no. 10, April, 118–87.

Ellman, Michael (1991), 'Convertibility of the Rouble', *Cambridge Journal of Economics*, **15**, (4), 481–97.

Erhard, L. (1958), *Prosperity Through Competition*, New York: Praeger.

Ericson, Richard E. (1991), 'The Classical Soviet-Type Economy: Nature of the System and Implications for Reform', *The Journal of Economic Perspectives*, **5**, (4), Fall, 11–28.

Estrin, S. and Holmes, P. (1983), *French Planning in Theory and Practice*, London: George Allen & Unwin.

European Commission (1988), 'The Economics of 1992', *European Economy*, No. 35, March.

European Commission (1990a), 'One Market, One Money', *European Economy*, No. 44, October.

European Commission (1990b) Annual Economic Report, 1990–91, *European Economy*, No. 46, December.

European Commission (1991) 'The Economics of EMU', *European Economy, Special Edition No. 1*.

Fischer, Stanley (1991), 'Economic Reform in the USS and the Role of Aid', *Brookings Papers on Economic Activity*, 2, 289–301.

Fischer, Stanley and Gelb, Alan (1991), 'The Process of Socialist Economic Transformation', *The Journal of Economic Perspectives*, **5**, (7), Fall, 91–106.

Forrester, David A.R. (1977), *Schmalenbach and After*, Glasgow: Strathclyde Convergences.

Foster, G. and Horngren, C.T. (1987), 'Cost Accounting and Cost Management in a Just-in-time Environment', *Research Paper No. 945 (rev.)*, September, Stanford Graduate School of Business.

Franks, Julian and Mayer, Colin (1990), 'Capital Markets and Corporate Control: A Study of France, Germany and the UK', *Economic Policy*, no. 10, April, 191–231.

Funabashi, Y. (1988), *Managing the Dollar: From the Plaza to Louvre*, Washington DC: Institute for International Economics.

Gallizo, J.L. and McLeay, S. (1988), 'Some Observations on Value Added Accounting in the Annual Reports of Companies and Banks', *Institute of European Banking Discussion Paper*, Bangor: University of Wales.

Geroski, P.A. (1989a), 'The Choice Between Diversity and Scale'. In Davis, E. *et al.* (eds), Chapter 2, *1992: Myths and Realities*, Centre for Business Strategy: London Business School.

Geroski, P.A. (1989b), 'European Industrial Policy and Industrial Policy in Europe', *Oxford Review of Economic Policy*, **5**, (2), 20–36.

Gill, Stephen and Law, David (1986), *The Global Political Economy*, Brighton: Wheatsheaf.

Gilpin, Robert (1987), *The Political Economy of International Relations*, Princeton, N.J.: Princeton University Press.

Gordon, D.M. (1988), 'The Global Economy: New Edifice or Crumbling Foundation?', *New Left Review*, no. 168, 24–64.

Grahl, J. and Teague, P. (1989), 'The Costs of Neo-Liberal Europe', *New Left Review*, 174, March–April, 33–50.

Grahl, J. and Thompson, G.F. (1992) 'European Integration and Development Models', mimeographed, London: Queen Mary and Westfield College.

Grieco, Joseph M. (1990), *Cooperation Among Nations*, Ithaca, N.Y.: Cornell University Press.

Guerrieri, Paolo and Padoan, Pier Carlo (1989), 'Integration, Co-operation and Adjustment Policies'. In Guerrieri, Paolo and Padoan, Pier Carlo (eds), *The Political Economy of European Integration*, Hemel Hempstead: Harvester Wheatsheaf.

Guglielmotto, E. and Passatore, G. (1987), 'The Private ECU Market: A Case of International Financial Innovation'. In De Cecco, M. (ed.), *Changing Money*, Oxford: Basil Blackwell.

Hall, P. (1986), *Governing the Economy*, Cambridge: Polity Press.

Hall, P. (ed.) (1989), *The Political Power of Economic Ideas: Keynesianism Across Nations*, New Jersey: Princeton University Press.

Hammarstrom, Olle and Landsbury, Russell D. (1991), 'The Art of Building a Car: The Swedish Experience Re-Examined', *New Technology, Work and Employment*, **6**, (2), Autumn, 85–90.

Hare, Paul G. (1991), 'Hungary: In Transition to a Market Economy', *The Journal of Economic Perspectives*, **5**, (4), Fall, 195–202.

Harris, R.G. (1984), 'Applied General Equilibrium Analysis of Small Open Economies with Scale Economies and Imperfect Competition', *American Economic Review*, **74**, (5), December, 1016–32.

Hayes, R.H. and Wheelwright, S.C. (1984), *Restoring Our Competitive Edge: Competing Through Manufacturing*, New York: Wiley.

Hayes, R.H., Wheelwright, S.C. and Clark, K.B. (1988), *Dynamic Manufacturing: Creating The Learning Organization*, New York: Free Press.

Heisbourg, Francois (1991), 'Population Movements in Post-Cold War Europe', *Survival*, **XXXIII**, (1), January/February, 31–43.

Helg, R. and Ranci, P. (1988), 'Economies of Scale and the Integration of the European Economy: The case of Italy', *Commission of the European Communities Economic Papers*, no. 68, October.

Henley, Andrew and Tsakalotos, Euclid (1991), 'Corporatism, Profit Squeeze and Investment', *Cambridge Journal of Economics*, **15**, 425–50.

Hirst, Paul Q. and Thompson, Grahame F. (1992), 'The Problem of "Globalisation": International Economic Relations, National Economic Management and the Formation of Trading Blocs', *Economy and Society*, **21**, (4), November, 357–96.

Hirst, P. and Zeitlin, J. (eds) (1989), *Reversing Industrial Decline?*, Oxford: Berg.

HMSO (1992), *Treaty on European Union*, Cmnd 1934, May, London: HMSO.

Hogan, M.J. (1989), *The Marshall Plan*, Cambridge: CUP.

Hogan, William W. (1991), 'Economic Reforms in the Soviet States of the Former Soviet Union', *Brookings Papers on Economic Activity*, 2, 303–19.

Holland, M. (1989), *When The Machine Stopped: A Cautionary Tale From Industrial America*, Boston: Harvard Business School Press.

Holtfrerich, Carl-L. (1989), 'The Monetary Unification Process in 19th-Century Germany: Relevance and Lessons for Europe Today'. In De Cecco, M. and Giovannini, A. (eds), *A European Central Bank?*, Cambridge: CUP.

Hughes, Alan (1991), 'Competition Policy and the Competitive Process: Europe in the 1990s', *Working paper No. 12*, October, Small Business Research Programme, University of Cambridge.

Irving, R.E. and Paterson, W.E. (1991), 'The 1990 German General Election', *Parliamentary Affairs*, 353–72.

Italianer, A. (1990), '1992, Hype or Hope: A Review', *Commission of the European Communities Economic Papers*, no. 27, February.

Jackson, Marvin (1991), 'Constraints on Systemic Transformation and Their Policy Implications', *Oxford Review of Economic Policy*, **7**, (4), Winter, 16–25.

Johnson, R.B. (1984), 'The Demand for Non Interest Bearing Money in the United Kingdom', *Government Economic Service Working Paper*, no. 66, London: HM Treasury.

Johnson, R. and Lawrence, P.R. (1989), 'Beyond Vertical Integration – The Rise of the Value-Adding Partnership, *Harvard Business Review*, July–August, 94–101.

Jones, R.A. (1976), 'The Origin and Development of Media of Exchange', *Journal of Political Economy*, **84**, 757–75.

Jonsson, Sten and Gronlund, Anders (1988), 'Life with a Sub-Contractor: New Technology and Management Accounting', *Accounting, Organisations and Society*, **13**, (5), 512–32.

Kaplan, R.S. (1988), 'One Cost System Isn't Enough', *Harvard Business Review*, January–February, 61–6.

Kaplan, R.S. and Johnson, H.T. (1987), *Relevance Lost: The Rise and Fall of Management Accounting*, Boston: Harvard Business School Press.

Kay, Neil (1991), 'Industrial Collaborative Activity and the Completion of the Internal Market', *Journal of Common Market Studies*, **XXIX**, (4), 346–62.

Keohane, Robert O. (1984), *After Hegemony: Cooperation and Discord in the World Political Economy*, Princeton, N.J.: Princeton University Press.

Kern, Werner (1975), 'The Accounting Concept in German Labor-Oriented Business Management', *The International Journal of Accounting*, **10**, Spring, 23–35.

Kornai, Janos (1990), *The Road to a Free Economy*, New York: W.W. Norton.

LaLonde, Robert J. and Topel, Robert H. (1991), 'Immigrants in the American Labor Market: Quality, Assimilation, and Distributional Effects', *American Economic Review Papers and Proceedings*, **81**, (2), May, 297–302.

Lane, C. (1989), *Management and Labour in Europe: The Industrial Enterprise in Germany, Britain and France*, Aldershot: Edward Elgar.

Layard, Richard, Nickell, Stephen and Jackman, Richard (1991), *Unemployment: Macroeconomic Performance and the Labour Market*, Oxford: Oxford University Press.

Lipton, David and Sachs, Jeffrey (1990), 'Creating a Market Economy in Eastern Europe: The Case of Poland', *Brookings Papers on Economic Activity*, 1, 74–147.

Litwack, John M. (1991), 'Legality and Market Reform in Soviet-Type Economies', *Journal of Economic Perspectives*, **5**, (4), Fall, 7–90.

Locke, R.R. (1984), *The End of Practical Man: Entrepreneurship and Higher Education in Germany, France and Great Britain 1880 to 1940*, Greenwich, Conn.: JAI Press.

Locke, R.R. (1985), 'Business Education in Germany: Past Systems and Current Practice', *Business History Review*, **59**, Summer, 232–53.

Locke, R.R. (1989), *Management and Higher Education Since 1940: The Influence of America and Japan on West Germany*, New York: CUP.

Luria, D. (1990), 'Automation, Markets and Scale: Can "Flexible Niching" Modernize American Manufacturing?', *International Review of Applied Economics*, **4**, (2), June, 127–65.

Majone, G. (1989), *Deregulation or Reregulation in Europe?*, London: Pinter.

Marsh, Paul (1990), *Short-Termism on Trial*, London: Institutional Fund Managers' Association.

Matthews, R.C.O. (1968), 'Why has Britain had Full Employment since the War?', *Economic Journal*, **78**, 556–69.

Mayer, Colin and Alexander, Ian (1990), 'Banks and Securities Markets: Corporate Financing in Germany and the UK', *Discussion Paper No. 433*, London: Centre for Economic Policy Research.

Mayne, Richard (1972), 'The Role of Jean Monnet'. In Ionescu, G. (ed.), *The New Politics of European Integration*, London: Macmillan.

McAuley, Alistair (1991), 'The Economic Transition in Eastern Europe: Employment, Income Distribution and the Social Security Net', *Oxford Review of Economic Policy*, **7**, (4), Winter, 93–105 .

McKinnon, Ronald I. (1991), 'Financial Control in the Transition from Classical Socialism to a Market Economy', *Journal of Economic Perspectives*, **5**, (4), Fall, 107–22.

Meade, J.E. (1991), 'The EMU and the Control of Inflation', *Oxford Review of Economic Policy*, **6**, (4), 100–107.

Miller, M. and Spencer, J.E. (1977), 'The Static Economic Effects of the UK Joining the EEC: A General Equilibrium Approach', *Review of Economic Studies*, **44**, (1), February, 71–93.

Milward, A.S. (1984), *The Reconstruction of Western Europe 1945–1950*, London: Methuen.

Minford, P. (1992), 'Why We Should Leave the ERM', *LBS Economic Outlook 1991–1995*, **16**, (5), February, 31–4.

Montagnon, P. (ed.) (1990), *European Competition Policy*, London: Pinter/ RIIA .

Muelbauer, John (1991), 'Productivity and Competitiveness', *Oxford Review of Economic Policy*, **7**, (3), 99–117.

Murrell, Peter (1991), 'Can Neoclassical Economics Underpin the Reform of Centrally Planned Economies?', *Journal of Economic Perspectives*, **5**, (4), Fall, 59–76.

Myers, S.C. (1984), 'Finance Theory and Financial Strategy', *Interfaces*, **14**, (1), January–February, 126–37.

Narkhoz (1987), *Narodnoe khoziaistvo SSSR v 1996g*, Moscow: Statistika.

Neven, D.J. and Roller, L.-H. (1990), 'European Integration and Trade Flows',

Centre for Economic Policy Research Discussion Paper, no. 367, February, London.

Nicolaides, P. and Thomsen, S. (1991), 'The Impact of 1992 on Direct Investment in Europe', *European Business Journal*, **3**, (2).

Nicoll, W. and Salmon, T.C. (1990), *Understanding the European Communities*, London: Phillip Allen.

Nordhaus, William D, Peck, Merton J. and Richardson, Thomas J. (1991), 'Do Borders Matter? Soviet Economic Reform After The Coup', *Brookings Papers on Economic Activity*, 2, 321–40.

Nuti, D. Mario and Pisani-Ferry, Jean (1992), 'Post-Soviet Issues: Stabilization, Trade and Money', *Economic Papers*, CEC, no. 93, May.

OECD (1991a), *Industrial Policy in OECD Countries, Annual Review 1991*, Paris: OECD.

OECD (1991b), *Economic Outlook*, No. 50, December, Paris: OECD.

Owen, N. (1983), *Economies of Scale, Competitiveness and Trade Patterns Within the European Community*, Oxford: Clarendon Press.

Parker, Stephen (1991), 'Securities: Will London Become the Single Market?', *European Trends No. 3*, 55–65, London: Economist Intelligence Unit, London.

Patell, J.M. (1987), 'Adapting a Cost Accounting System to Just-In-Time Manufacturing: The Hewlett-Packard Personal Office Computing Division'. In Burns, W.J. and Kaplan, R.S. (eds), *Accounting and Management: Field Study Perspectives*, Boston: Harvard Business School Press.

Peacock, A. and Willgerodt, H. (eds) (1989a), *Germany's Social Market Economy: Origins and Evolution*, Basingstoke: Macmillan.

Peacock, A. and Willgerodt, H. (eds) (1989b), *German Neo-Liberals and the Social Market Economy*, Basingstoke: Macmillan.

Peck, Merton J. (1989), 'Industrial Organisation and the Gains from Europe 1992', *Brookings Papers on Economic Activity*, 2, 277–99.

Piore, M.J. and Sabel, C. (1984), *The Second Industrial Divide*, New York: Basic Books.

Pitt-Watson, David (1991), 'Economic Short Termism: A Cure for the British Disease', *Fabian Pamphlet No. 547*, London: The Fabian Society.

Pratten, C. (1988), 'A Survey of Economies of Scale', *Commission of the European Communities Economic Papers*, no. 67, October.

Pridham, G. (1977), *Christian Democracy in Western Germany*, London: Croom Helm.

Rao, S. (1988), 'US–Canada Productivity Gap, Scale Economies and the Gains from Free Trade', *Economic Council of Canada Discussion Paper*, no. 357, September.

Reati, Angelo (1991), 'Are We at the Beginning of a New Long-Term Expansion Induced by Technological Change?, *Economic Papers No. 85*, August, Commission of the European Communities.

Riboud, J. (1991), *A Stable External Currency for Europe*, Basingstoke: Macmillan.

Rollo, J. M. C. (1992), 'Reform of the CAP: The Beginning of the End or the End of the Beginning?', *The World Today*, January, 4–7.

Rosanvallon, P. (1989), 'The Development of Keynesianism in France'. In Hall, P. (ed.), *The Political Power of Economic Ideas*, New Jersey: Princeton University Press.

Rybczynski, Tad (1991), 'The Sequencing of Reform', *Oxford Review of Economic Policy*, **7**, (4), Winter, 26–34.

Sabel, C. (1989), 'Flexible Specialization and the Re-Emergence of Regional Economies'. In Hirst, P.Q. and Zeitlin, J. (eds), *Reversing Industrial Decline?*, Oxford: Berg.

Sabel, C.F., Herrigel, G. and Kern, H. (1990), 'Collaborative Manufacturing: New Supplier Relations in the Automobile Industry and the Redefinition of the Industrial Corporation'. In Mendius, H.G. and Wendeling-Schroder, U. (eds), *Zulieferer in Netz-Zwischen Abhangigkeit und Partnerschaft*, Köln: Bund Verlag.

Sadowski, Zdzislaw (1991), 'Privatisation in Eastern Europe: Goals, Problems, Implications', *Oxford Review of Economic Policy*, **7**, (4), Winter, 46–56.

Salais, R. (1988), 'Les Stratégies de Modernization de 1983 à 1986: Le Marche, l'Organization, le Financement', *Economie et Statistique*, 213, Septembre.

Sannucci, V. (1989), 'The Establishment of a Central Bank: Italy in the 19th Century'. In De Cecco, M. and Giovannini, A. (eds), A *European Central Bank*, Cambridge: CUP.

Scharpf, F.W. (1991), *Crisis and Choice in European Social Democracy*, Ithaca, New York: Cornell University Press.

Schoenfeld, Hanns-Martin (1972), 'Development and Present State of Cost Theory in Germany', *International Journal of Accounting*, **7**, Fall, 43–65.

Schwalbach, J. (1988), 'Economies of Scale and Intra-Community Trade', *Commission of the European Communities Economic Paper*, No. 68, October.

Scott, A.J. (1988), *New Industrial Spaces: Flexible Production Organization and Regional Development in North America and Western Europe*, London: Pion.

Scruton, R. (1984), *The Meaning of Conservatism*, Basingstoke: Macmillan.

Shleifer, Andrei and Vishny, Robert W. (1991), 'Reversing the Soviet Economic Collapse', *Brookings Papers on Economic Activity*, 2, 341–60.

Siebert, Horst (1991), 'German Unification: The Economics of Transition', *Economic Policy*, no. 13, Oct., 289–340.

Smith, Alasdair (1991), 'Discussion'. In Winters, Alan and Venables, Anthony (eds), *European Integration: Trade and Industry*, Cambridge: Cambridge University Press, 51–3.

Smith, A, and Venables, A. (1988), 'The Costs of Non-Europe: An Assessment Based on Formal Model of Imperfect Competition and Economies of Scale', *Commission of the European Communities Economic Paper*, no. 70, October.

Soskice, D. (1991), 'Wage Determination: The Changing Role of Institutions in Advanced Industrialized Countries', *Oxford Review of Economic Policy*, **6**, (4), 36–61.

Storper, M. (1991), 'Regional "Worlds of Production"', mimeographed, UCLA: Graduate School of Urban Planning.

Storper, M. and Salais, R. (1992), 'The Division of Labour and Industrial Diversity', *International Journal of Applied Economics*, **6**, 1–37.

Suhr, D. (1989), *The Capitalistic Cost–Benefit Structure of Money*, Berlin: Springer-Verlag.

Svejnar, Jan (1991), 'Microeconomic Issues in the Transition to a Market Economy', *The Journal of Economic Perspectives*, **5**, (4), Fall, 123–38.

Thompson, G.F. (1986), *Economic Calculation and Policy Formation*, London: Routledge.

Thompson, G.F. (1987a), 'Inflation Accounting in a Theory of Calculation', *Accounting, Organizations and Society*, **12**, (5), 523–43 .

Thompson, G.F. (1987b), 'The American Industrial Policy Debate: Any Lessons for the UK?', *Economy and Society*, **16**, (1), 1–74 (reprinted in Thompson, 1989a).

Thompson, G.F. (1987c), 'The "New Institutionalism" and Political Analysis', *Economy and Society*, **16**, (2), 252–73.

Thompson, G.F. (ed.) (1989a), *Industrial Policy: USA and UK Debates*, London: Routledge.

Thompson, G.F. (1989b), 'Flexible Specialization, Industrial Districts, Regional Economies', *Economy and Society*, **18**, (4), November, 545–72.

Thompson, G.F. (1990), *The Political Economy of the New Right*, London: Pinter.

Thompson, G.F. (1991a), 'The Role of Economies of Scale in Justifying Free Trade: The US–Canada Free Trade Agreement and Europe 1992 Compared', *International Review of Applied Economics*, **5**, (1), 47–76.

Thompson, G.F. (1991b), 'European Integration and Growth Models', *EAEPE Newsletter* no. 7, December.

Thompson, G.F. *et al.* (eds) (1992a), *Markets, Hierarchies and Networks: The Coordination of Social Life*, London: Sage.

Thompson, G.F. (1992b), 'Network Governance, Citizenship and "Consumerism"', Paper to the Employment Research Unit Annual Conference, Cardiff University, September.

Thompson, G.F. (1993), 'Network Coordination'. In Thompson, G.F. and Maidment, R. (eds), *Managing the UK: An Introduction to Its Political Economy and Public Policy*, London: Sage.

Tinbergen, J. (1954), *International Economic Integration*, Amsterdam: North Holland.

Tolliday, S. and Zeitlin, J. (1991), *The Power of Manage? Employers and Industrial Relations in Comparative Historical Perspective*, London: Routledge.

Tomlinson, J. (1981), 'Why Was There Never a "Keynesian Revolution" in Economic Policy?', *Economy and Society*, **10**, (1), 72–87.

Tomlinson, J. (1991), 'Why Wasn't There a "Keynesian Revolution" in Economic Policy Everywhere?', *Economy and Society*, **16**, (2), 103–19.

Tribe, Keith (1992), 'Enterprise Formation and Market Structure in the Five New Bundeslander', mimeographed, University of Keele.

Tsoukalis, Loukas (1991), *The New European Economy: The Politics and Economics of Integration*, Oxford: Oxford University Press.

Van De Wee, H. (1986), *Prosperity and Upheaval: The World Economy 1945–1980*, Harmondsworth: Pelican Books.

Vaubel, R. (1974), 'Plans for a European Parallel Currency and SDR Reform: The Choice of Value-Maintenance Provisions and "Gresham's Law"', *Weltwirtschaftliches Archiv*, Band 110, 194–227.

Vaubel, R. (1977), 'Free Currency Competition', *Weltwirtschaftliches Archiv*, Band 113, 435–59.

Vibert, Frank (1990), 'The Powers of the European Parliament: The Westminster Deficit'. In Buchanan, James M. *et al.*, *Europe's Constitutional Future*, London: Institute of Economic Affairs.

Wallace, W. (1990), *The Transformation of Western Europe*, London: Pinter and the Royal Institute for International Affairs.

Walters, A. (1986), *Britain's Economic Renaissance: Margaret Thatcher's Reforms 1979–1984*, London: OUP.

Walters, A. (1990), *Sterling in Danger: The Economic Consequences of Pegged Exchange Rates*, London: Fontana.

Weimer, S. (1990), 'Federal Republic of Germany'. In Sengenberger, W., Loveman, G.W. and Piore, M.J. (eds), *The Re-Emergence of Small Enterprises: Industrial Restructuring in Industrial Countries*, Geneva: International Institute for Labour Studies.

Wheelwright, S.C. (1985), 'Restoring the Competitive Edge in US Manufacturing', *California Management Review*, **xxvii**, (3), 26–41.

Widgren, Jonas (1990), 'International Migration and Regional Stability', *International Affairs*, **66**, (4), 749–66.

Wilcox, J.B. (1989), 'The Long-Run Determination of the UK Monetary Aggregates', *Bank of England Discussion Papers* no. 41, August, London.

Wilke, Marc and Wallace, Helen (1990), 'Subsidiarity: Approaches to Power-Sharing in the European Community', *RIIA Discussion Papers No. 27*, London.

Williams, K. *et al.* (1989a), 'Do Labour Costs Really Matter?', *Work, Employment and Society*, **3**, (3), September, 281–305.

Williams, K. *et al.* (1989b), 'Why Take the Stocks Out? Britain vs Japan', *International Journal of Operations Production and Management*, **9**, (8), 91–105.

Williams, K. *et al.* (1990), 'The Hollowing Out of British Manufacturing and its Implications for Policy', *Economy and Society*, **19**, (4), November, 456–90.

Williams, K. *et al.* (1992), 'Against Lean Production', *Economy and Society*, **21**, (3), August, 321–54.

Wolf, Thomas A. (1991), 'The Lessons of Limited Market-Orientated Reform', *The Journal of Economic Perspectives*, **5**, (7), Fall, 45–58.

Womack, J., Jones, D. and Roos, D. (1990), *The Machine That Changed The World*, New York: Rawson and Associates.

Wood, E.G. (1978), *Added Value – The Key to Prosperity*, London: Business Books.

Woolcock, S., Hodges, M. and Schreiber, K. (1991), *Britain, Germany and 1992: The Limits of Deregulation*, London: Pinter/RIIA.

Wren-Lewis, S. (1992), 'Why the Pound should be Devalued Inside the ERM', *Economic Outlook 1991–1995*, **16**, (5), February, 35–8.

Yeager, L.B. (1968), 'Essential Properties of the Medium of Exchange', *Kyklos*, **21**, (1), 45–69.

Zeitlin, J. (ed.) (1989), *Local Industrial Strategies* (special issue), *Economy and Society*, **18**, (4), November.

Index